EMPIRE

# Empire

## The History
## of the British Empire

Trevor Lloyd

Hambledon and London
London and New York

Hambledon and London
102 Gloucester Avenue
London, NW1 8HX

838 Broadway
New York
NY 10003–4812

First Published 2001

ISBN 1 85285 259 3

A description of this book is available from the
British Library and from the Library of Congress.

Typeset by Carnegie Publishing,
Lancaster LA1 4SL
Printed on acid-free paper and bound in
Great Britain by Cambridge University Press

# Contents

# *Illustrations*

## *Acknowledgements*

The author and publishers are grateful to the National Portrait Gallery for permission to reproduce the plates.

## Maps

# *Preface*

For almost four hundred years Britain ruled substantial areas of the world outside Europe. In the first 150 years, from 1600 to 1750, expansion was a matter of setting up small but prosperous trading posts and settlements very close to the sea, supported by naval strength and close contact with friends in England. After 1750 imperial rule began to move inland and for the next 170 years, up to the end of the First World War, a steadily increasing part of the earth's surface was ruled from London. The naval and industrial power which made this possible also meant that Britain could exert a great deal of influence in the world outside the empire, but this was a matter of diplomacy rather than direct rule.

Up to the beginning of the nineteenth century British expansion can be seen as an important but secondary part of the overseas expansion of Europe which began with Columbus's discovery of the route to the Americas in 1492. Spain took the lead, closely followed by Portugal; France, England and the Netherlands became involved about a hundred years later. Until 1800 these five European countries all ruled overseas empires. Between 1790 and 1830 all of the other European empires were seriously weakened so that by middle of the nineteenth century the British Empire was not only the largest empire the world had ever seen, it was the only flourishing and functioning empire in existence

This expansion was not a matter of mobilising resources in Britain and sending great armies overseas. Naval strength and eventual naval supremacy were obviously worth having, but British taxpayers were very rarely asked to spend their money on anything outside Europe, and showed no signs of liking it when the occasion arose. Expansion was a matter of handling resources available on the spot, and of prudent negotiation rather than thoughtless aggression. In most of the areas of British involvement countries were ruled by monarchs who depended on the personal loyalty of their subjects rather than on more abstract feelings of patriotic duty; some of

them were overthrown by force of arms and directly replaced as a focus
of loyalty by the British monarch, but many of them were persuaded to
accept the overlordship of the British monarch without any violent dis-
placement of the existing order of things. Sometimes the British authorities
wanted to destroy local institutions, like slavery, but usually they were
content to set up a higher level of law and order than before, so that
British trade and taxation for local government could go ahead peacefully.
And almost everywhere this was accepted by the local population, who
felt that the advantages of peace and quiet outweighed the problems of
rule by men who often did not understand the local way of doing things.

In the late nineteenth century and the first decades of the twentieth
century there was a new outburst of general European expansion, but it
brought with it ideas that destroyed empire. Democracy and nationalism,
mixed in varying proportions, built up the determination of people ruled
from Europe to run their own affairs, and undermined the willingness
of the imperial powers to hang on to their possession. Within fifty years of
the peak of imperial expansion in 1920 the overseas empires had almost
completely disappeared.

The fifty year period of decolonisation saw plenty of attempts to wield
history as a weapon, with advocates of empire pointing to the tranquillity
it had brought and enemies of empire pointing to the wars of conquest it
involved. The son of a British imperial administrator once complained
about 'the enormous condescension of posterity'; and the arguments, for
and against, unavoidably contained a good deal of condescension. All the
arguments were hard to apply sensibly because the British Empire existed
for such a long time and moral values changed so much during its long
existence. In 1600 wars of conquest to gain new territory were the major
way for a ruler to win glory, and slavery was an institution supported by
the Bible, Aristotle and almost every known authority. By the end of empire
slavery and wars of conquest had no open supporters. Indicting people of
the seventeenth century for not living up to the ideals of the twenty-first
century would be a perverse way for a historian to express his views, but
it was a very natural form of propaganda to use during the struggle for
decolonisation. Now that the British Empire is gone, it is possible to
examine what it was and what it did. It is too late to change it; the
important thing is to explain it.

# 1

# *Settling by the Seashore*

In the last four hundred years the political power of European countries over the rest of the world has increased, risen to a peak and then dwindled away, though the after-effects of that dominance remain immense. The British Empire was an important part of the process, and in the nineteenth century it came closer to being a universal empire – ruling a quarter of the population of the world – than has ever been seen before or since. But in the seventeenth century and well into the eighteenth century the British had just a scattering of settlements along the coast in North America, the West Indies, India and West Africa, and in the sixteenth century they had shown little interest in territorial acquisition while Spain and Portugal began the European expansion which transformed the world.

The Portuguese had been working their way down the west coast of Africa for some years before that, and in 1455 the pope (acting as the only authority all European rulers could respect) gave them a monopoly over any trade route leading from Cape Bojador in the west of Africa to the trading world of the Indian Ocean, or Indies. The Muslim Turks had captured the great trading centre of Constantinople, now Istanbul, two years earlier and new routes to the Indies were needed. But before the Portuguese could open up a route round Africa, Christopher Columbus had persuaded the king and queen of Spain to support his attempt to find a way to the Indies by sailing west. When he reached land on the far side of the Atlantic in 1492 he was convinced that he was somewhere near Japan, and that this meant he could say he had reached the Indies. Alexander VI, the devoted father of Caesar and Lucrezia Borgia, was not an exemplary pope but he could see the implications of what Columbus had found, and in 1494 he got Spain and Portugal to accept a dividing line a few hundred miles west of the Azores – about 45 degrees west of Greenwich, to use terms unknown for another couple of hundred years. This was intended to keep the Spanish to the west side of the Atlantic and the Portuguese to the east side. Three years later Vasco da Gama sailed round the Cape of Good Hope into the Indian Ocean, and reached India by the African route; and half a dozen years later Amerigo Vespucci worked out that, on any accurate assessment of the earth's circumference, the land that Columbus had reached could not be part of the Indies and must be a new continent, which he modestly allowed to be named after himself.

In 1490 an educated minority knew that the world was round, but nobody had any idea how the great continents were located, and no useful maps of the globe could be produced. By 1510 the first voyages of transoceanic discovery had produced a dim sketch of what was to come, and provided plenty of encouragement to go forward. In 1522 the few lucky survivors of Magellan's expedition round the world struggled back to Spain: the world really was a globe, and they had sailed round it. The pope had to draw a new line to keep the Spanish and Portuguese from fighting over islands in the western Pacific. The new maps that followed were far from accurate. Nobody could measure longitude accurately and whole continents were placed too far to the east or to the west, but these gross errors did not alter the fact that explorers had established an outline of the world.

Between 1500 and 1580 the Spanish and the Portuguese developed two very different sorts of empire. The Spanish conquered two existing empires, the Aztec in Mexico and the Inca in Peru, and used them as bases for further expansion. Their weapons were better, they were dealing with relatively weak and unsophisticated rulers, and they were able to resist the local diseases far better than the South Americans could resist diseases brought from Europe. They extracted quantities of gold and silver from mines in their new territories, which seemed to promise unlimited prosperity for the rulers of Spain. The Portuguese had very few advantages of this sort. The cannon on their ships were better than anyone else's, so they had to be accepted as a naval power in the Indian Ocean, but the Ming emperors in China and the Mughals rising to power in India would have been very surprised at any idea that European newcomers had to be treated seriously on land. The Portuguese did what they could with their resources and built up a string of bases in Brazil (which was east of the pope's 1494 line), in Angola and Mozambique for the long voyage from Lisbon to the Spice Islands (now Indonesia) and Macao, but they had no hope or intention of setting up a territorial empire.

Philip II of Spain, who also ruled Belgium and the Netherlands and most of South America, had briefly been married to Mary, queen of England.

When she died in 1558 and her Protestant half-sister Elizabeth succeeded to the English throne, Philip was ready to marry her in turn, though she politely declined. In 1580 he succeeded to the crown of Portugal and united the lands outside Europe that had been divided between the two countries, though he had too many troubles elsewhere to pay much attention to his Portuguese lands. His Protestant subjects in the Netherlands rebelled against him and began a fierce sea-based resistance when he tried to subdue them and, to compound the problem, the Dutch received help from England. Philip was becoming accustomed to trouble from the English: in the 1560s they had tried trading with his South American colonies where he claimed a commercial monopoly, and between 1577 and 1580 Francis Drake had sailed round the world on what was more a plundering expedition for South American gold and silver than a voyage of exploration. Drake presented himself as a fiercely Protestant opponent of Catholic Spain but Philip saw him as a pirate. Elizabeth was ready to agree that Drake's behaviour was disgraceful; though, as she then knighted him and collected 4700 per cent on the money she had invested in his voyage, Philip could be forgiven for thinking she was not taking Spanish complaints entirely seriously. He had a claim of his own to the English throne, and when Elizabeth executed Mary Queen of Scots, who had the best claim to the throne of any Roman Catholic, he decided to organise a fleet or Armada to invade England. In 1588 his attack was held off and the Spanish Armada suffered heavy losses as it tried to get back to Spain by going round the north of Scotland, though this naval success still left the English with a difficult and expensive war which made it harder for them to think about settling overseas.

There had been English voyages of exploration in the North Atlantic around 1500, inspired by a hope of finding a route to the Indian Ocean round the north of America and also by the attractions of cod-fishing near New-foundland. By 1550 English merchants had set out to the north east and had found a trading route round the North Cape which led them to Russia and on to Persia, now Iran. A little later, explorers set out north west from the Newfoundland fishing grounds to see if they could reach the Indian Ocean by an Arctic route. Nothing came of it, and the government did from time to time make it clear that Newfoundland ought to be used for fishing rather than for settlement.

The idea of planting a settlement of new people in a new country was already being considered. English monarchs had for centuries had claims

## Francis Drake

After 1688 the English government could run its navy from its own resources. A hundred years earlier, at the time of the Spanish Armada, it needed help from maritime entrepreneurs – calling them pirates may sound more morally unright but makes it harder to understand what they were doing. This was just the situation for the talents of Francis Drake (1540–1596), a Devon man at a time when Devon, with its port at Plymouth, was one of the leading centres in England for ocean-going navigation. His distant cousin, John Hawkins, hoped English merchants could develop a trade in slaves to be brought from Africa to the Spanish colonies in South America. Hawkins's attempt to break into the Spanish slave-trading monopoly was one of the reasons why relations between England and Spain deteriorated in the 1560s. Drake's career started when he sailed on the third of these voyages in 1568. He was lucky to be among the few to escape when the Spanish captured English traders at San Juan de Ulloa. He emerged with strong anti-Spanish and anti-Roman Catholic feelings, which he expressed by organising a form of private warfare with Spain in the early 1570s.

His success in capturing the city of Nombre de Dios near Panama and intercepting bullion going to Spain as royal revenue led to his being made commander of a small squadron that set out in 1577 to plunder Spanish shipping on the Pacific coast of South America. His own ship, the *Golden Hind*, went north up the Pacific coast to a point not far from the present-day Canadian frontier, and then completed a voyage round the world by way of the Moluccas and the Cape of Good Hope. Queen Elizabeth had helped finance the operation, and greatly appreciated the immense return she made on her investment, but this was not the whole story. By providing support she encouraged private individuals to spend their own money building up little navies. These forces could work with the royal navy to provide a larger force than the government could provide from its own revenues. This would only work if the private investors could see a good chance of getting their money back. Drake's example suggested that it was perfectly possible to fight the Spaniards and make a profit. Not many other people were able to do so well, but in 1585–86 Drake was able to assemble a squadron of about thirty ships, attack north-west Spain, plunder the Caribbean cities of San Domingo and Cartagena, and then go north to bring home to England the Virginia colonists whom Raleigh had enlisted without a proper supply of provisions to keep them going. By 1587 Philip of Spain was assembling his Armada for the invasion of England.

Drake's privately organised forces were becoming more fully committed to the royal navy by this stage. He led them in a raid on Cadiz which immobilised the main body of the Armada for a year, and his squadron patrolled the Spanish coast for some months, successfully attacking local commerce. When the Armada eventually came within sight of England in 1588 Drake was not in command, for so important a post could only be given to a nobleman. But his influence was all in favour of the risky strategy of letting it sail up the Channel, merely harassing it from the rear; Drake's enemies suggested that he did this because he needed to plunder the Armada's stragglers to cover his costs. If the Armada had achieved its preliminary objective, and had linked up with Parma's troops in the Netherlands, the English would then have been forced to stand and fight to prevent them from being brought across the Channel. When, however, the Armada took shelter in Calais, well to the west of Parma's army, the English were in command of the situation: they used fireships to force the Spanish to leave the port and fight along the Belgian coast. By the time this battle was over the Armada had sailed well to the north of Parma's troops and had no prospect of working its way back to join them. It had to get back to Spain as best it could. Philip never came as close to launching a successful invasion as he had in 1588 and the English made other profitable raids on Spanish ports, but he was able to protect the flow of South American bullion to Spain effectively. In 1595 Drake and Hawkins sailed out to South America together at the head of a few ships from the royal navy and a larger number provided by private investors. Hawkins died early on; Drake found the defences so impenetrable that there was no prospect of making money out of the attack. With his expedition facing failure, he died at sea.

to rule Ireland, though they rarely got further than controlling territory on the eastern side of the island, and during their marriage Philip of Spain and Mary had set up settlements of emigrants from England in King's County and Queen's County, now Offaly and Leix, in Ireland. New developments like this soon came to be known as 'plantations' (it was not until the early eighteenth century that estates cultivated to produce cash crops came to be seen as plantations).[1] Elizabeth had put Sir Walter Raleigh in charge of plantations in south-western Ireland in case the Spanish attempted to invade the region, and in the 1580s he tried establishing a plantation or colony in what is now North Carolina. It was cut off from its home base during the crisis of the Spanish attempt at invasion in 1588. By the time relief ships reached it in 1590 all of the colonists had disappeared.

No new colonies were launched until after Elizabeth's death, when she was succeeded on the English throne by James VI, the king of Scotland, who became James I of England. The two countries kept their distinct governments and legal systems, but James wanted a peaceful foreign policy and in 1604 the war with Spain was brought to an end. In Elizabeth's last years merchants who wanted to trade in the Indian Ocean had formed the East India Company, which in 1600 received from her a charter giving it a monopoly of the right to bring imports into England from east of the Cape of Good Hope. Sailing ships had so little cargo space that traders could only make a profit on compact and costly goods. The company would have liked to trade with the Spice Islands, or East Indies, which grew cloves, cinnamon and mace, the really expensive spices with the most satisfactory profit margins. But the Dutch had gone on from fighting Spain for independence to organise a powerful naval and commercial empire. While Philip II concentrated on his other problems, they took over most of the Indian Ocean trade the Portuguese had developed earlier in the century, and they were able to exclude the English East India Company almost entirely from trade in the Spice Islands.

The English fell back on trading in pepper from their base at Surat in north-west India, and kept going reasonably well on this, with a substantial re-export trade to northern Europe. The company sent Sir Thomas Roe, a courtier and diplomat, to India to report on political prospects at the Mughal court. Sir Thomas clearly enjoyed his time with the Mughals, and his report shaped company policy for over a century to come. He said that 'the Great Mogul' – the name Europeans gave to the ruler of India in Delhi or in Agra (who, as the descendant of conquerors from Persia, called himself Shahinshah Padishah) – was far too strongly placed for the company to try to organise an army in India. The Mughals were rising towards the peak of artistic creation that built the Red Forts at Agra and at Delhi and the Taj Mahal. They could maintain a perfectly adequate level of law and order, and were not going to be impressed by anything the company could do on land, but Roe added that powerful and well-equipped ships would be immensely useful. The company had very little to sell in India. The woollen cloth and textiles which were England's main export in Europe were to warm to appeal in India. The company shipped out some silver bullion, but it relied on its carrying trade in the Indian Ocean for a good deal of the money it needed to buy pepper and other imports. The company's oak ships were slow by comparison with the teak-built boats of the region, but they were so heavily armed that no sensible pirate would attack them and they earned their freight charges by delivering goods reliably.

The English hoped that trade in the Indian Ocean would give them a chance to build an empire like the Portuguese by acquiring a comparable network of bases to supply their ships. They also began to establish settlements in North America which might lead to an empire of the Spanish type. James gave the Virginia Company a royal charter to launch a colony and in 1607 it set one up on Chesapeake Bay at Jamestown in present-day Virginia, and very uncomfortable its beginnings were. The settlers had very little idea of what they were going to do in Virginia or how to make the best of their situation. They reached reasonably friendly relations with the local Indians, and the marriage of Pocohontas to John Rolfe served as a visible symbol of peaceful alliance. The colony got just enough supplies from England to survive the unusually bad weather of its first years, but it took the settlers some time to get over the idea that, like the Spaniards in South America, they were going to find gold and silver. Once they realised that there was no gold in Virginia, they turned to growing tobacco for the English market and their prospects improved. James detested to-bacco: in 1604 he had published a pamphlet saying smoking was 'loathsome to the eyes, hateful to the nose, harmful to the brain and dangerous to the lungs', and he had also increased the import duty on it forty-fold.[2] But neither the tract nor the tax had much effect; people only smuggled it in and evaded the duty. A little before the Virginia settlers entered the market, the government had brought the tax down to a level where it produced a healthy revenue, whatever it did to the brains and lungs. In a way the import duty was a great help to the Virginia Company, because the government became committed to stopping anyone growing tobacco in England. Collecting customs duties on imports was not always easy, but collecting an excise from hundreds of farmers growing a rough and stringy crop in England would have been far harder. By the 1620s Virginia was doing well enough out of tobacco to make the idea of setting up other new colonies look attractive.

Other colonies were already developing further north. Some Protestants in England, who felt that James's government had become too friendly to Catholics after making peace with Spain, emigrated to the Netherlands. But however sound the religious climate might be there, they found to their regret that their children were drifting into speaking Dutch. A few of them decided they would have to go even further from home. In 1620 they organised a voyage to Plymouth in Massachusetts Bay on the *Mayflower* and launched a settlement which had no official connection with their native land. The region was less unlike England than the tobacco-growing lands of Virginia, and the settlers called it New England. Other settlements followed in the next few years, but they also had no official basis for their activities.

The king was willing to grant charters to companies that operated outside Europe and wanted some indication of royal approval. Some were trading companies like the East India Company or the Muscovy Company (for Russian trade). Some wanted to settle in new land, like the Virginia Company, or the Canada Company which organised a successful attack on the early French settlements along the St Lawrence river in 1628, though a diplomatic desire for good relations with France meant that it had to return its conquests. A large Protestant group from East Anglia and nearby counties, who felt the same dissatisfaction with religious attitudes in England as the original Pilgrim Fathers of the *Mayflower*, got a charter to settle in Massachusetts Bay which gave their company a legal framework for its activities. The charter they obtained in 1629 was unusual because it allowed the company to set up its headquarters in North America without any requirement that it should maintain a connection with England.[3]

Determined Protestants who found the Church of England unsatisfactory were unlikely to agree among themselves about religion, but their leaders were strong and forceful people who – whatever their disagreements on points of doctrine – could all agree with the general principle that, once heretics had been found, they should be burned. The most prominent

The Early Colonies

supporter of religious tolerance in Boston, Roger Smith, had to flee for
his life, but by 1636 he had managed to set up a colony on his own lines
in Rhode Island. Other colonies grew up along the Connecticut coastline,
though this involved advancing in the direction of the Dutch port of New
Amsterdam at the mouth of the Hudson River.

The Massachusetts Protestants were not the only people in England to
feel dissatisfied with the Church of England. Roman Catholics left England
to go to a colony of their own. The head of the Calvert family, Lord
Baltimore, who took his title from a town in Ireland, obtained a grant of
land just north of the Virginia settlements without any company involvement. He used the grant to found the colony of Maryland for Roman
Catholics, and passed his title on to its capital. The tobacco growers of
Virginia and Maryland found that Chesapeake Bay, which is almost an
inland sea with indented coastlines, suited them very well because so much
land was in easy reach of the shore and kept their transport costs down.
Maryland offered good enough prospects to attract a considerable number
of Protestants hoping to earn a living there. It was only while the Calvert
family kept direct control of the government that Catholics enjoyed the
religious freedom that had been the colony's original objective.

By the 1630s English colonies were scattered along five hundred miles of
North American coastline. The tobacco colonies of Chesapeake Bay and
the New England colonies inspired by religious discontent were set up for
different reasons, but it did not follow that they were fundamentally
dissimilar. Settlers around Boston hoped to do well economically in addition
to getting their own way about religion, and the tobacco growers were
quite as concerned about religion as ordinary people in England. All of
the colonies ran their political affairs as if they were establishing countries
very much like England. They had governors who ran the administration
and decided policy with the help of counsellors, but they also had elected
assemblies to vote taxes and pass new laws if any were needed. The governor
would not pay much more attention to advice about policy from the
assembly than the king in England would pay to advice from his parliament,
but it was an ambitious step to set up an elected assembly at all. Other
European countries had stronger central governments which wanted firmer
control over their colonies. Many of the English settlers came from rural
counties, and they might have run their affairs in the same way. The
governor of a colony held a position like that of the lord lieutenant at
the head of the county, below whom authority was in the hands of justices

of the peace appointed from among local landowners without any question of elected county councils. But the colonies never had eminent local landowners for this, and the companies that went overseas were run by commercial men accustomed to elected councils in the cities. People may have felt that nothing less than an elected assembly would command the respect needed to impose taxes and write new laws. Assemblies elected by men with a certain amount of property, who made up a greater minority of the whole population than in England, became a normal part of life in the colonies. Their royal charters usually recognised this.

Every colony had uncomfortable early years. Francis Bacon, who invested in Virginia, Newfoundland and the East India Company, insisted that people had to take a long view and disapproved of the readiness to look for quick profits that had made Virginia attractive: 'you must make account to lose almost twenty years' profit, and expect your recompense in the end; for the principal thing that has been the destruction of most plantations hath been the base and hasty drawing of profit in the first years'.[4] Not many of the investors who simply put down their money and stayed in England did well out of it, even after waiting twenty years. Settlers who went overseas, and merchants who were ready to bring new products into the English market, did rather better.

The strongly Protestant groups in New England had emigrated as families and, after difficult years at the beginning, increased in numbers and prosperity. Virginia and Maryland took longer to settle down because the climate and the local diseases were different from those of England, so the death rate among recent arrivals was high. Relatively few women went there, so there were not many children for the next generation, and settled household life in New England was healthier than frontier life on Chesapeake Bay, but the economic prospects open to tobacco growers looked the more promising, and the religious enthusiasm of New England may have repelled more people than it attracted. The population of the two sets of colonies grew at about the same rate, though New England attracted far fewer settlers and depended on natural increase for its expansion. Landowners in the tobacco colonies were always looking for new workers, and would pay the passages of workers who signed indentures promising to work for them for the first four to seven years after arrival. After they had paid for their passage in this way, indentured labourers were free to work for themselves and could clear a piece of land and become landowners in their turn. The high death rate of newcomers meant that anyone bringing in indentured labourers ran a considerable risk of not getting back the money invested, but enough people crossed the Atlantic for the population to rise steadily.

While a significant minority left England for religious reasons thinking it would never become the God-fearing country in which they would like to live, most emigrants hoped to become better off by going overseas and probably dreamt like many people in later generations of making a fortune and coming home rich. At the lowest level, they might escape from the fears of overpopulation and of insoluble problems of unemployment that troubled early seventeenth-century England. A prosperous and established English landlord could not possibly hope to live so well in the American colonies, because there were no tenant farmers to provide him with an income from rent. Because a relatively large proportion of the population had some small amount of property America always needed lawyers, a need that was met very adequately, but it was not as possible to make a really large legal fortune as in London, Trading and banking opportunities were also not as good as in London. There were no bishoprics in America until the very end of the eighteenth century, and very few really attractive church appointments, though the settlers looked after their clergy gener- ously. They liked to bring some of them over from Britain, and colleges like Harvard opened in the first generation of settlement to train 'the English and Indian youth of this country in knowledge and godliness'. This certainly included training them for the Christian ministry.[5] Below the upper ranks of wealth and power, North America by mid-century was a reasonably comfortable place where ordinary people could be at least as well off as they could hope to be anywhere else in the world.

Whatever the early discomforts of life on the North American sea coast from 1607 to the 1640s, they were far worse for people who went to the small islands in the eastern Caribbean. Success with tobacco in Virginia made planters hope to do equally well further south; but, instead of advancing into what became the Carolinas (with a very slight risk of collision with the Spanish in Florida), they acquired land grants to West Indian islands that were too hot to grow good tobacco, and perhaps too hot for anyone to work hard, short of the cruellest compulsion. Some of the settlers in the half a dozen little islands from Barbados to Antigua in the Leeward and Windward islands of the Lesser Antilles, which had been acquired between 1627 and 1632, simply did not know what they were getting into. Many of them were drawn from Ireland, where they had much less opportunity than in England to find out about the new world. But clearly some people went to the West Indies because they hoped to be close to the legendary land of El Dorado in the jungles of Guiana, or for the possibilities of part-time piracy against the Spanish ships of the region. Enthusiasm for growing tobacco did not last long. People moved on to the east side of the central American mainland to cut logwood for dyeing textiles on the Moskito Coast and in Belize, and in the late 1630s some attempt was made to grow cotton. Even in the West Indian islands elected assemblies became the standard way of running the government during the first generation of settlement. Landlords with substantial estates could be found easily enough, but the islands were so small that it was not easy for men who had come out as indentured labourers to find empty land to work after they had served the required length of time, so either they became landless workers who depended on getting employment from the landowners or they moved on to North America.

James I and his son Charles I would have been very surprised if it had ever been suggested to them that they should provide financial or military support for these overseas activities. If people left the country because they disliked its religious policy, or because they hoped to become richer elsewhere, it was hard to see why their objectives deserved assistance from the royal purse. Giving them charters to provide their operations with a legal basis did not cost the king anything, and the government had no money to spare for anything more. The king of Spain got substantial revenues in gold and silver from South America, and the king of France had enough money to support his colonies on the St Lawrence, but the king of England had to live on a small income, unless his parliament was unusually generous.

In the 1640s financial difficulties and religious discontent led to civil war between king and parliament, in which Charles was defeated in 1645 and subsequently executed. While fighting was going on, the colonies were freer than ever from English control. In North America the strongly Protestant colonies in New England hoped that parliament would win, while the tobacco-growing colonies of Chesapeake Bay hoped the king would, but they were too far away to take part in any fighting and the war did not affect the way they went about their everyday business. Further south, the war led to a change in the economic life of the English West Indies which affected it for centuries to come. For some years the Dutch had been growing sugar in Portuguese Brazil to send to the Amsterdam market. When Portugal rebelled in 1640 and became independent of Spain, it was able to get back to the old system of managing its colonies as commercial monopolies, so the Dutch had to look for new places to obtain sugar. With no effective English government in the 1640s to hold the West Indian colonies in check, the Dutch were able to persuade English landowners, led by those of Barbados, to move on from tobacco to growing sugar.

This required an immense increase in labour and investment. Tobacco was a lazy man's plant, which could be left to grow itself and could be picked at leisure. The soil eventually became exhausted and had to be left to rest; hard work would improve the crop but was not essential. Producing sugar was much more unpleasant: because the juice in the sugar cane solidified within a few hours of being cut, the cane had to be crushed very soon after cutting; and, before it was allowed to cool, the syrup squeezed out of it had to be boiled and then skimmed and strained to produce a liquid that would crystallise into reasonably pure sugar. Mills and vats for crushing and boiling could only be made to pay by cutting a lot of cane at once. So sugar needed a large labour force, mobilised for an operation that demanded a substantial amount of capital, and involved hard work in great heat. It was possible to get men to come from England and Ireland to grow tobacco, but the Dutch knew very well that it would be impossible to get voluntary emigrants to do the back-breaking work needed to produce sugar, and they knew the answer: slaves.[6]

Freedom in the North American colonies was a relative matter. Indentured labourers had to work with political prisoners, who had been transported overseas because of the Civil War of the 1640s and 1650s or Monmouth's rebellion of 1685, and with criminals who, offered a choice between being executed and going to forced labour in the colonies, had unsurprisingly chosen the colonies. None of these workers was free, but they were not as badly off as slaves. All of the people sent out from England could expect that eventually they would be free, or at least that any children they might have would be free. A few African slaves had been brought to the tobacco colonies in the early seventeenth century, but they were not essential for keeping their economies going in the way that slaves were essential for growing sugar.

The Spanish had depended for some decades on slaves from Africa to keep their gold and silver mines in South America going. These workers knew that they would never be free, and that their children would remain part of the labour force. Slaves in the sugar islands, vital for driving the new industry forward, were in the same position. Free men without much money had been able to make something of a living in the West Indies by growing tobacco, but they had no chance of competing in a society based on sugar, which became more and more sharply polarised between slaves and their owners, with a small community of white men serving as a garrison. The few freed slaves were seen as a disturbing force. The tobacco colonies of the American mainland employed more and more slaves, as time went, on but they were never as indispensable as in the sugar colonies or on nineteenth-century cotton plantations.

The Dutch had introduced an economic revolution, but they were not able to enjoy the results for long. Once parliament and its army had defeated the king and established a republic it reconquered Ireland, dispossessing Catholic landlords to give their estates to Protestants, and it gained political control of Scotland. It also set about asserting its authority over the English colonies. It had a large enough navy to do this, and it felt powerful enough to control them and protect them. Its Navigation Act of 1651 laid down that trade between England and her colonies should be either in English ships or those of the colonies. This appeared to be aimed directly at displacing Dutch ships, the great commercial intermediaries of the day, and it was not surprising that England and the Netherlands were soon at war, although trade was not the only point at issue. When the republican parliament was overthrown by Cromwell, its leading general, he made peace with the Netherlands, which he saw as an ally on religious grounds, and turned to fight against Spain instead. This might look like a return to the policy of pirate raids on Spain of fifty years earlier, but Cromwell had more imperial ambitions. In 1655 he sent an expedition to the West Indies to attack the Spanish island of Hispaniola (now divided between Haiti and the Dominican Republic), and was annoyed when his commanders Penn and Venables could do no more than capture Jamaica and drive out its Spanish population. Over the years to come plenty of commanders were to learn how hard it was for forces to capture a strongly-held position at a great distance from their home base, and how much easier it was to find places that were not strongly defended. Jamaica was not nearly as large or as good a commercial prospect as Hispaniola but it was larger than all the islands the English had settled in the eastern Caribbean. It was also the first piece of territory to change hands because European powers were at war over their overseas empires.

Cromwell died in 1658 before he could do much more. The republic did not survive him for long. The return to monarchy in the form of the

Restoration of Charles II in 1660 led to a well-defined policy of Anglican supremacy in religion, and a few attempts to get back to the past in domestic affairs, but the restored monarchy carried on the imperial policy of the 1650s as if there had been no change of government. The Navigation Act was maintained, and its effect was strengthened by drawing up lists of 'enumerated articles', or goods that colonies or trading companies were not allowed to export except by sending them to English ports. In practice the colonies took it for granted that almost all their trade would be with England, and one of their main concerns was to have an assured position in the home market. Colonies usually established themselves by developing a single valuable product which they could export; later on, wheat from Canada and wool from Australia served as staple exports, just as tobacco from Virginia and sugar from Barbados had done in the seventeenth century. If the colony could sell enough of its major export product, the colonists could afford to buy a wide range of imports, mainly manufactured goods, from England. This system sometimes caused friction but survived for about two hundred years, from the mid seventeenth to the mid nineteenth century. By its last years it was being called, not always respectfully, 'the Old Colonial System', but it fitted the needs of the seventeenth century very well. 'Free Trade' – which at that time meant trading with other countries and their colonies, and had little to do with abolishing customs duties – appealed to very few people. All European countries took it for granted that they should monopolise the trade of their colonies, and their colonies took it for granted that their home country should give them a monopoly to supply it with the products that they could export. Spain denied that the English had any right to have colonies in the Caribbean at all, and one important change in the 1650s and 1660s was that the London government was willing to help defend the West Indian islands in a way that it had never tried to do in the first half of the century.

Nobody in the seventeenth century thought very much about whether English colonies should trade with each other. It seemed unlikely that the situation would arise: countries always reckoned that they had to be self-sufficient in food; only a few great cities like ancient Rome had expected to depend on food imports. But sugar was such a valuable product that the landowners of Barbados devoted more and more of their land to growing it and, despite the high transport costs, they relied on importing food to keep the island going. Soon after his restoration to the throne, Charles II transferred to some of his courtiers a large land grant of territory south of Virginia that his father had made in the 1630s, for a region he called Carolina. While no use had been made of the original grant, the new proprietors were more active. They founded a capital which they were grateful enough to call Charles Town, now Charleston, and encouraged settlement round it. Opposition from the Spanish in Florida made it unsafe to go any further south, but those who took up farming around Charleston found a market for their crops by growing rice and other food to export to the West Indies. Tobacco growers moved down from Virginia into the north of the new colony, and another centre of population developed around towns like Raleigh and Durham. As the tobacco-exporting and the food-exporting areas were very distinct regions, Carolina was divided into two separate colonies early in the eighteenth century.

In the mid 1660s England did badly in a war with the Dutch, yet the treaty at the end of the war now looks like an English triumph: England lost the small and insecure Georgetown settlement, in a little bit of what is now Guyana, but kept the Dutch colony of New Amsterdam which had been captured early in the war. This was the first transfer of territory which put other Europeans under English rule, raising questions that came up frequently in the next 150 years. The difference of language was obvious enough and, although they were Protestants, the Dutch were uneasy about the Anglicanism of the new authorities. It took about thirty years to bridge the gap between Dutch and English, even though they had a common enemy to the north in New France on the St Lawrence, and a Dutchman was king of England for part of the time.

The Dutch had expanded north up the Hudson river and Charles gave this new territory to his brother the duke of York, for whom New Amsterdam was renamed New York. This region was ruled with much less reliance on an elected assembly than was normal in English colonies. As constitution-makers in London came to see more clearly the different types of colonies under English rule, they worked out lines of division: law-abiding Englishmen overseas could always expect to have elected assemblies; other Europeans who had come under English rule after a war would get elected assemblies once it was clear that they had accepted the new situation; and non-Europeans who had come under English rule would have to wait a very long time before they were allowed anything of the sort. The land just west of New York was given to royal supporters from the Channel Island of Jersey, who renamed it New Jersey. Still further west a large grant of land was given to a son of Cromwell's commander, Admiral Penn –

the royal family owed money to the younger Penn. As he had become a Quaker and wanted to set up a colony on a basis of religious tolerance, the land grant settled the debt satisfactorily. Pennsylvania became the first (and for a hundred years to come the only) colony to be named after a non-royal Englishman. The policy of religious tolerance, and an advantageous position a little way up the Delaware river, made its capital Philadelphia into one of the most prosperous cities in North America, and its Quaker leadership worked out a system of good relations with the local Indians.

For the Netherlands to give up territory with all these prospects, while keeping Georgetown, looks surprising, but at the time it was not so hard to understand. The Dutch colonists of New Amsterdam, like the English settlers of New England, enjoyed a secure and comfortable way of life that they might not have been able to achieve at home, but they produced very little for export. They could grow more than enough food for themselves, but this was unlikely to do much for the economy of the Netherlands. Sugar, on the other hand, was emerging as one of the first raw materials that could be carried long distances for processing by industries in Europe, and plantations for growing it were spreading all over the West Indies. As the area round Demerara could provide sugar for the distillers and food processors of Amsterdam, it was more obviously valuable than New Amsterdam in North America.

The Caribbean region was not yet peaceful enough for activity to be confined to growing sugar. While the English government sent out troops and ships in the 1660s to provide support for the colonies in a way that they had not done before, the islanders still had to help fight to defend themselves against Spanish assertions that they had no right to be there. They obtained official letters to show that the government had approved of their organising ships to fight for their country as private individuals (or privateers). These letters were not likely to convince the Spanish that they were anything other than pirates, and privateers sometimes behaved exactly like pirates. In 1670 the Spanish government acknowledged in the treaty of Madrid that the English had rights in the Caribbean. The news did not cross the Atlantic quickly enough. Captain Morgan, the most formidable of the island privateers, had assembled a small force which landed on the mainland, stormed the great city of Panama and plundered it mercilessly before he or his opponents heard about the treaty. Over the next few years Morgan was treated as a low-grade version of Drake, imprisoned for his close association with pirates but then released and knighted as the indispensable defender of the English position in the West Indies.

Food, whether imported or grown locally on a commercial basis or on the slaves' own little plots (which were sometimes the only thing that saved them from malnutrition), was essential for the sugar islands; but assembling the labour force of slaves from Africa was just as important. Early in the 1660s the king granted the Royal Adventurers into Africa a charter to trade with the Guinea coast in West Africa. At first the company brought back 'elephant's teeth' (ivory) and gold, which was of such high quality that the pound coins made from it contained gold worth more than a pound. They were melted down for their gold until eventually they were renamed guineas and declared to be worth one pound and one shilling. In the course of the 1660s the company was reorganised and renamed as it moved on to a new line of activity. In the end it settled down as the Royal Africa Company, primarily committed to trading in slaves, with forts at Accra and Cape Coast Castle as its main bases for buying captives from African rulers to transport across the Atlantic and sell to the West Indian sugar-growers. Unfortunately for the company, the sugar-growers expected to buy slaves on credit, a facility not provided by the African vendors, and the costs of financing the planters and keeping up the forts proved too much for it in the long run.[7]

The company was displaced by dealers operating on a smaller scale, and the sugar-growers had to look for other sources of credit. Spending money to build the forts had been unnecessary because buying slaves was a matter of negotiating with local rulers on the coast, who were perfectly ready to guard the people they were selling until it was time to pack them aboard ships for the Atlantic crossing. There was some truth behind the legend that an African ruler had told a slave trader: 'You have three things we want: powder, musket and shot. And we have three things you want: men, women and children.' Many other things such as metal products and textiles were used for buying slaves, but it was true that slave trading rulers could arm and equip their people to fight more effectively because they were in touch with European suppliers, and often enough this enabled them to provide more captives for sale. The traders did not really want to buy women and children, as men commanded a much better price in the West Indies.[8] This helped cause a demographic problem that the sugar growers never solved. The slave population in the sugar islands did not have enough children to replace those who died, so landowners or their managers constantly had to buy new slaves to keep up the numbers in their work force. This was the natural result of the harsh conditions of life, and also of bringing in relatively few female slaves. Potential mothers were so small a part of the slave population that they could have raised enough children to maintain the working population only if they had been treated with care and even kindness. The slave-owning way of life had no time for such things, because owners were concerned to get a quick return on all of the money they had invested in buying slaves. They saw no need to wait until the population stabilised, because they could drive their workers on and buy new slaves to fill the gaps in the labour force. If the sugar growers were going to follow this policy there would always be room for small-scale individual dealers who sailed from England to West Africa with trade goods, bought slaves and took them across to the West Indies, and returned to England carrying sugar. This kept the triangular trade going steadily, but at a much less complex level of organisation than the Royal Africa Company had intended.

The Hudson's Bay Company, which got a charter from Charles II in 1670, enjoyed a much longer history than the Royal Africa Company, but it went through awkward moments in its first forty years. French farmers were becoming well-established along the St Lawrence river. Some of them raised a little capital to start a farm by travelling into the North American interior to buy beaver skins to produce the hats, made out of a shaped piece of felted material, that were fashionable in the seventeenth and eighteenth centuries. Two Frenchmen, sure that the best way into the interior was to establish bases on Hudson Bay but unable to find supporters in New France, offered their idea to the English, who welcomed it. Charles did not want to quarrel with France. The company's charter therefore declared that it was to trade in the basin of the rivers flowing into Hudson Bay, simply to stop it trying to go beyond the watershed into the St Lawrence valley. Although nobody had any idea when it opened trading posts in the bay, that the river basin of Hudson Bay covers about a fifth of North America, the company found its metal goods, thick woollen blankets and firearms attracted Indian traders who paddled their canoes from regions far to the west to see what they could buy for their beaver skins. The company operated like all the other English overseas, sticking firmly to the coastline in the seventeenth and early eighteenth century, and it did not send its employees inland to trade. Its business depended on getting ships through difficult northern seas into Hudson Bay, and maintaining trading posts there all through the year. The staff at these posts was small and not intended to provide a military garrison. When war broke out between England and France, any force that was prepared to undertake the long march from New France could easily capture the trading posts. The company then had to rely on diplomacy to get them back.

The East India Company was reorganised at the beginning of the 1660s and, from the point of view of the shareholders, the next twenty-five or thirty years were the happiest in its history. It moved on from its pepper trade in north-western India to exporting cotton textiles to England and to much of Europe. The seventeenth century introduced people in England and Europe to a variety of new things to cheer and soothe them. Tobacco, for smoking or for snuff, became increasingly popular. Distilled spirits had certainly been used in Scotland from the late fifteenth century, but sugar from the West Indies opened up great prospects for rum. The Levant Company brought in opium from the Ottoman Empire. While the East India Company played its part in this trade, providing tea from China and coffee from Arabia, its imports of cotton textiles made up over two-thirds of the goods it brought to England.[9]

Charles II acquired Bombay as part of the dowry when he married a Portuguese princess, and he gave it to the company, but most of the cotton trade was with the eastern side of India, based at first on Madras in the south. A little later the company's main activity moved north to Bengal and it launched a new base at Calcutta in 1690. Previously it had operated from its ports on the coast, Surat, Bombay and Madras. The decision to turn the little village of Calcutta into a trading centre showed it had become slightly more willing to move inland, but it had no intention of cutting itself off from the sea. The new port was less than sixty miles up the Hooghly in the delta of the Ganges, about as far upriver as sailing ships could prudently travel, but it did have the advantage of cutting down the distance that the textile producers had to carry their goods overland.

While the company did not go inland to trade, it began to modify the policy Roe had recommended at the beginning of the century. Sir Josiah Childs was less concerned than his predecessors about good relations with the Great Mogul and under his direction the company began to fortify its bases in India and to raise small armies to defend them. Aurangzeb had established himself as Great Mogul by 1648, by killing all of his brothers and other potential rivals, and until his death in 1707 he drove Mughal expansionism forward to its furthest limits. The East India Company could not challenge his power with any hope of success, but there were occasional disputes in which the company was able to show that at sea it could be an inconvenient opponent. Aurangzeb was far more concerned with extending his power on land down to the southern tip of India, and also with making sure that he was obeyed throughout his territories. The best he could do was to arrange a type of feudal system by installing people he could trust as rulers of large subdivisions of his empire. This worked well enough in his time because his subordinates were men who had worked with him and had helped lead his army to success. They also knew that he was apt to have disobedient officials trampled to death by elephants. This left the question of what would happen when power passed to a less commanding Great Mogul or to less loyal subordinates.

For twenty years after his Restoration Charles II accepted the tacit balance of power, between himself and his subjects, that had put him on the throne. Around 1680 he found his position challenged by powerful subjects who wanted to use anti-Catholic feeling to reduce royal power and increase that of parliament. Helped by Louis XIV of France, he was able to fight back, managing financially without parliament, and challenging his opponents by investigating the charters of the strongly Protestant cities that had given them some of their power. The aggressive Protestants in Massachusetts found their charter was declared forfeit because they had gone beyond the powers it allowed them.

While Charles was perfectly willing to do without parliament, and was secretly inclined to Roman Catholicism, he reckoned that he had to keep the Church of England on his side if he was to stay on the throne. His brother, the duke of York, who succeeded to the throne when Charles died in 1685, was an open Roman Catholic. As James II, he followed a pro-Catholic policy which threatened to deprive the Protestant majority of its comfortable position in Britain and to destroy its position in Ireland altogether. A much wider coalition than had previously opposed Charles II arranged for William of Orange, the ruler of the Netherlands, to invade England and drive James out.

William was able to do this in 1688 with virtually no fighting. While he had a good claim to the throne, his wife Mary had a better, and they took the crown jointly. The old idea of unrestricted monarchical control of policy could not survive this revolutionary change. After 1688 the monarch

SETTLING BY THE SEASHORE

had to be a Protestant and had to have the active support of parliament. The monarch could still take the initiative in choosing who should hold the main ministerial offices, and had considerable influence over who should be in the government, but the House of Commons was turning its power over taxation into a right of veto over the monarch's choice. The monarch had a great deal of freedom of action in negotiating with political leaders and deciding which groups should form the government for a hundred years to come, because no clear-cut political parties existed to give a single leader a parliamentary majority, but after 1688 royal power had to be shared with parliament in a way that had not previously been necessary.

Governments in the colonies returned to the position before Charles and James had tried to increase royal power in the 1680s. James's attempt to set up a Dominion of New England, with a governor who ruled the north-eastern colonies without any elected assembly, collapsed at once, and Charles's attack on the charters of the colonies was reversed, but governors paid no more attention to the elected colonial assemblies on policy questions than they had done previously. This was understandable enough. Governors could not allow assemblies in North America to make decisions which could cause trouble with New France or let West Indian assemblies push the empire into war with France or with Spain or with the Netherlands; and, once war had broken out, governors had to follow instructions from the London government on military questions because it provided well-trained troops and paid for them. The colonies could see that they needed English protection against other European powers, so they had to follow English direction which included accepting London's coordination of trade policy. The vital importance of questions of defence for seventy years after 1688 meant that the position of the governors was secure, but they did not have the influence over their local assemblies that the monarch or the ministry exercised at Westminster. Politics at Westminster depended to a considerable extent on using patronage to build alliances, but government jobs were relatively few in the colonies; and, in any case, politicians in London frequently used them to help their own friends in England rather than let the governors use them to build up solid support based on patronage within their colonies. In later decades assemblies sometimes used their control of finance to push governors into accepting legislation that was not welcome in London. This did not involved anything very serious – several colonies wanted to have marriage laws that made divorce possible, and the London government wanted to make sure that English rather than Scottish law should prevail in this case – but governors felt no more menaced by their assemblies than the monarch felt dominated by parliament.

# 2

# War with France

William had not undertaken the 1688 invasion just for the sake of parliamentary government or even of Protestantism. He believed that the king of France, Louis XIV, was becoming too powerful, and his main concern was to make England into part of a great coalition against France. England had stayed out of most European wars in the seventeenth century, partly because warfare had become much more expensive and the country's financial system would not stand full-scale involvement. All this changed when William came to the English throne. The country was at war for sixty-one of the 125 years from 1690 to 1815, large amounts of money were spent on the navy, and the financial system was changed to enable the government to raise short-term loans to finance wars, while fighting went on, and then issue long-term loans to fund the debt after peace had been made. Governments needed institutions that would take up the loans, preferably charging below-market rates of interest, and trading companies concerned with the colonies were one of the places where they would look for loans.[1] The bulk of the fighting was against France, and in some ways it looked very dangerous for the English. In almost every one of the wars they felt they were in danger of invasion or of civil war. This was partly because the struggle had begun with the overthrow of the existing monarch. James II had not been pushed out of Scotland as easily as he had been pushed out of England, and the French supported him and his son and grandson in their efforts to regain the throne. There were Jacobite rebellions in Scotland to support their cause in 1715 and 1745, although they had very little support in the Presbyterian Lowlands. In Ireland the Jacobites could not call on family ties or clan loyalties, and James II lost his best chance to hold William back when he was decisively defeated at the battle of the Boyne in 1690, but some Catholic support could at times be roused against English rule and the dominance of the Anglo-Irish Protestant minority.

These internal divisions were unimportant compared with the underlying facts that France had a much larger population and a political system which gave its ruler money to pay for a powerful army. The English could hardly have survived if they had had to fight the French without any allies, but the French never concentrated on England, or on imperial problems, because they also wanted to dominate the kingdoms and principalities that were later to be unified as Germany. The French threat to states in Germany, to Austria under the Habsburgs and to the Netherlands meant that the English could find continental allies easily. Taxpayers were ready to pay for a navy to keep the country safe from invasion, and this led to a command of the sea which was an essential step towards imperial expansion. while France could always muster a much larger army than Britain for operations in Europe, their armies in the world beyond the oceans were far smaller and the British could very often bring larger forces to bear. So the 'Second Hundred Years War', which began as a war over problems in Europe, spread to become a world war. Even though the French overseas empire melted away during the last decades of fighting, Britain kept up the policy of expansion which had begun during the struggle. The most rapid territorial growth took place in the later stages of the long wars; though so much of it took place in areas like India, where France had never been deeply involved, that it could not be said to have been directly caused by war with France.

Once England and France were at war in the 1690s conflict in the West Indies and in North America was bound to follow. Almost all the islands in the West Indies were vulnerable to raids by small military forces. These forces did not wait to be counter-attacked after they had captured an island but set out to do as much damage as they could in a short time. Because Barbados was some way to the east and was hard to reach against the prevailing winds, it was never attacked. All the other English islands were invaded at least once, with the losses that naturally followed when slaves were taken away as plunder, sugar canes were burnt down and sugar stocks destroyed. No doubt it was a consolation to the sugar growers that equally destructive attacks were carried out on French, Dutch and Spanish islands. The English suffered one heavy blow which had nothing to do with war; in 1692 Port Royal in Jamaica was swallowed up by an earthquake. Pirates or irregular privateer sailors or anyone else who had a lot of money to spend could reckon that Port Royal was the place to spend it as quickly and enjoyably as possible, and it earned such a reputation as a den of vice and iniquity that its destruction was attributed to the direct intervention of the Almighty. Pirate influence in Jamaica faded away soon after this, and the sugar-growing interest rose to the monopoly of power that it had already gained in Barbados and some of the smaller Leeward Islands. Privateering and its inevitable accompaniment of piracy flourished during the wars from 1690 to 1713 and, once the war was over, pirates based in the Bahamas enjoyed a short period of slaughter and plunder. When they were driven out of these last bases by the campaign against piracy launched by Woodes Rogers in 1718, the Atlantic became safer for shipping than it had been at any time since Columbus's first voyage.[2]

In North America conflict developed as the English and French settlements expanded and the space between them shrank. English farmers in upstate New York or western Massachusetts were never so close to the French of the St Lawrence valley that they turned their ploughshares into swords to fight their next-door neighbours. The struggle was much more a matter of alliances and wars with the Indians in the region that lay between the European settlements. Whenever Europeans wanted to take more land for cultivation the Indians who had previously been using the land had to decide what to do next. Sometimes they fought back against expansion and sometimes they settled down inside the area the English or the French were going to cultivate; but usually they simply withdrew to the west. As the rate of expansion was never very fast until the nineteenth century, withdrawal was almost always easy enough, but Indians in upstate Massachusetts, New York and Pennsylvania were in an unusual position. Because they were sandwiched between the English and French settlements in this region, withdrawal was difficult, but they could always try to maintain their position by diplomacy because there was very little sense that white men should stand together against the Indians. War almost always took the form of fighting between the English and their group of Indian allies against the French and their set of Indian allies. Christianised Indians might be thought slightly more reliable allies than their pagan cousins, but this had very little effect on negotiations along the border.

Treaties in the seventeenth century were not necessarily between parties of equal standing. The first concern of the English in their treaties with their main Indian allies, the Iroquois, was to control their foreign policy, and this principle could be seen in a long series of treaties with many other local allies over the next couple of centuries. Usually this could be achieved simply by including a clause saying that the Iroquois (or whatever other group made a treaty) would not make a treaty with anyone else without English consent, while the English never conceded a parallel control over their own policy.[3] In this way they put their allies in a position where no one else would discuss diplomatic arrangements with them, because of the English veto over any firm or permanent relationship, and these treaties often enough became the first step to absorption in the British Empire. While the Spanish had made very few such treaties in South America, both the English and the French made local alliances in North America and then in India, and treaties with African rulers were to be the foundation of European expansion in Africa in the late nineteenth century.

Immediately after the first in the long series of wars between England and France had come to an end in 1697, the Scots undertook an imperial venture that was entirely distinct from English activities. William was king of England and king of Scotland, but there was no legal connection between the governments of the two countries and, unless there was firm royal direction, they could follow different policies. A wave of enthusiasm swept over Scotland for the proposal that a colony should be set up at Darien on the Panama isthmus, where it could carry on trade between the Atlantic and the Pacific sea routes, and the Edinburgh government encouraged it to go ahead and set up its colony late in 1698. The site chosen was far too close to the Spanish provincial capital at Panama for the Spanish to let it prosper without intervening, but the settlement was able to defend itself against direct attack. The Panama government watched events at Darien with great care, but was able to capture the settlement in 1700 only when the whole undertaking collapsed as fever devastated the colony and no revenue-producing trade came to it. The English government was horrified at the idea of setting up a colony which would complicate relations with Spain at a moment when they were of immense international importance, but the Scots blamed English lack of support for a failure that swallowed up much of their country's disposable capital.[4] The disaster was one of the forces that made Scots and English realise that, short of returning to being two separate states as they had been before 1603, they must arrange a basis for working together. In its way Darien helped provide some of the impetus towards the 1707 Act of Union, after which it was possible to speak of a British state with a British policy. Within the Union the Scots kept their own church, and their own legal system, but in the empire overseas it was English law, not Scots law, that was applied: and, when there was to be an established church as a focus for religious activity, it was the Church of England, not Scots Presbyterianism, that fulfilled this role. Scots went into the army; the navy, whose command of the sea underlay many of the ways in which the British Empire differed from other empires, remained much more of an English institution.

War in the 1690s meant that William established himself as ruler of the whole of the British Isles, but otherwise the fighting in Europe, in North America and in the West Indies was inconclusive. At the time it was seen as something like a rehearsal for the struggle over the Spanish Empire that was bound to come when Charles II of Spain, the last descendant of Philip II, died without any male heirs. Rulers in Europe were not deeply concerned about the Spanish overseas empire in South America and the Philippines, but present-day Belgium and various territories in Italy, as well as Spain itself, would all go to the successor. The men with the best claim to succeed were too close to the Habsburg Emperor in Austria (reuniting possessions that had been divided over a hundred years earlier because they were too large for one monarch to manage), or to the Bourbon King of France (already alarmingly powerful), for monarchs or politicians to feel comfortable about the situation, and they tried to find a successor who was less dangerously well-connected. These were the negotiations that made it so worrying that the Darien Project was going to complicate relations with Spain, though in the event an entirely different issue made it impossible for the diplomats to reach a compromise. When the dying king of Spain said that the whole of his empire should go to the French royal family, England and the Netherlands joined the emperor to try to stop this. They were unsuccessful and, after ten years of fighting, a grandson of the king of France did become king of Spain, but France and Spain were forced to give compensation to their opponents in the treaty of Utrecht which ended the War of the Spanish Succession in 1713.

From the British point of view, the war ended with some useful gains in the colonies, but the French saw these concessions simply as a necessary part of the price of establishing Bourbon rule in Spain. France had captured the Hudson's Bay Company's bases and had to return them, and also had to give up its territorial claims on Newfoundland, though its fishermen retained the right to come ashore on the western side of the island to dry and salt their fish for the long voyage back to France. The treaty also transferred to Britain the French colony of Acadia, which included what is now the Canadian province of New Brunswick and also the mainland area of what is now Nova Scotia, though the substantial Cape Breton Island, the north-eastern part of present day Nova Scotia, remained French. Transferring these colonists under a peace treaty was harder than the earlier changes in New York had been. The treaty gave the Acadians unusual guarantees of religious freedom, but they did not like British rule. With New France just across the border, and Catholic priests whose message to their flocks was sometimes more concerned with politics than religion, they were unlikely to settle down as loyal subjects of Protestant monarchs. Forty years later, when war between Britain and France looked likely, they were asked to take oaths of allegiance to George II. The British government, alarmed to find how many of them refused to do so, deported some of them to Louisiana.

During the land fighting in Europe the English had captured Gibraltar and the Mediterranean island of Minorca from Spain, and kept them as part of the compensation for letting the Bourbon candidate retain the Spanish throne. Britain also gained two trade concessions in Spanish South America: merchants could send one ship laden with British products to the Spanish colonies every year, and could sell 4800 slaves a year there. As the government was not going to go into business on its own account, it had to find some organisation to use these concessions. The South Sea Company, which had just been formed to trade with South America and other places in the Pacific, naturally thought it could make the best use of them.

Companies were becoming a more important part of the national economy, but there was no obvious way to tax them for the national exchequer. There was no income tax on individuals and certainly no corporation tax, and most of the taxes imposed on rich people came from the land tax on fixed property, which would not raise very much from a trading company. In practice companies knew they had to pay something and, when it was doing very well in the 1670s and 1680s, the East India Company acknowledged this by making gifts and loans to the king and his government. The chairman of the company, Sir Josiah Childs, was outspoken enough to make it all too clear that he was committed to supporting James II, and after 1688 Childs's enemies were able to argue that a new company, committed to the new monarch, was needed. The old company would no doubt have settled down to making payments to whatever government was in power, just as it paid taxes or tribute in India and would have paid its taxes in England if the government had had a system of corporate taxation, but creating the new company gave the government a chance to push the

East India Company into increasing its contribution to national revenue. Eventually, after a number of MPs had been very adequately rewarded for their political services, the new company and the old company united in 1709, but the united company had to lend the government £3,000,000 on concessional terms to retain its charter. At a time when the government was working out a new system for financing warfare by long-term borrowing, it was useful to have economically strong institutions to lend the money, but linking corporate finance and national finance together in this way could lead to overbidding for financial favours and so to disaster.

The new East India Company went about business as usual, but the political situation in India was changing in a way that led to dramatic changes in the next generation. Up to the death of Aurangzeb in 1707 there were no visible signs that the central power of the Mughal Empire was weakening, although it was suggested later on that Aurangzeb had overstretched its resources in his efforts to win control of the whole sub-continent. In the early decades of the eighteenth century power moved away from Delhi to the great feudal vassals, like the nizam of Hyderabad and the nawab of Bengal, whom the Mughals had used to control their empire, and also to less controllable forces, like the Marathas, outside the system. When a Persian plundering raid captured Delhi in 1741 and took the emeralds of the Peacock Throne back to Isfahan, the breakdown of central power was too clear for anyone to ignore. The fortifications in India that had been begun in Childs's time turned out to be useful when local rulers began to use their armies to demand financial favours, but East India Company diplomatic policy, which had rested on maintaining good relations with the central government, was less well suited to the new situation. The profits of the new company stagnated because of the burden of government debt that it had undertaken to carry at a below-market rate of interest, but also because it did not keep up with the shift in the Indian political scene.

In its eagerness to win the right to use the Spanish trading concessions which the government had gained at Utrecht, the South Sea Company offered in late 1719 to manage the whole National Debt from the wars against France at a reduced rate of interest. In ordinary economic terms this was absurd; the East India Company, with its well-established trade, was managing only one-tenth of the debt under the 1709 arrangements. The South Sea Company's proposals could be financed only by issuing wild overestimates of the profits it expected from the trade concessions, in order to push the price of its shares up to a premium at which they could be used to buy government bonds very cheaply. When, some months later, people asked how this share price could be justified, the whole 'South Sea Bubble' collapsed. The South Sea Company had to lay aside its stock market ambitions and get back to using its trade concessions to do normal business with South America. Sir Robert Walpole became head of the government to reorganise the National Debt and reassure people that there would be no more fiscal misadventures.[5] He remained in office for twenty years because he could deal with the two centres of power in the political system: the Hanoverian kings George I and George II trusted him as their chief minister and he was able to win the support of the House of Commons to carry on financial business. His years of tranquillity in Britain were accompanied by withdrawal from European diplomatic involvements and an inactivity in imperial affairs which in later years of bitter trouble in North America was looked back on as 'wise and salutary neglect'.[6]

In the 1720s and 1730s this peace and prosperity were enough to keep people happy in Britain and America. Individual colonies still consisted of a capital where the governor lived and where courts of justice were established and occasional meetings of the assembly were held, and a hinterland which normally saw the capital as its main port for transatlantic trade as well as a political centre. The Atlantic seacoast was not yet densely enough populated for settlers to cut down the forests that lay between one colony and the next. Travel by water continued to be much easier than travel by land, and for the American colonies this very often meant travel by sea to England. While the rivers that ran a short distance inland from the Atlantic allowed British settlers to get to the sea easily, they did nothing to help them go further inland or get into contact with other colonies. The lack of contact made it hard for the colonies to think of themselves as a single country, and there was very little reason why they should do. They had been launched at different times for a variety of reasons, and the tendency was for colonies to break up rather than come closer together: Rhode Island had been launched by people who wanted to escape from the religious dogmatism of Massachusetts; the three counties that made up Delaware had felt geographically separated from the rest of Pennsylvania and had become recognised as an additional colony; and North Carolina and South Carolina had different economic systems serving different markets.

The inhabitants of the colonies in the first half of the eighteenth century seem to have thought of themselves as Americans only in the geographical

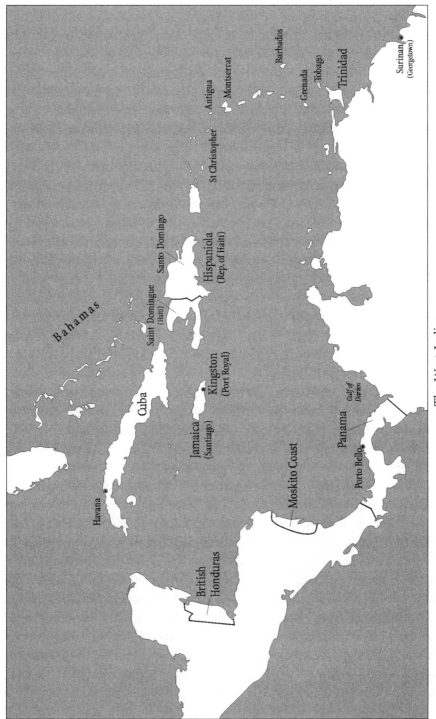

The West Indies

sense that they all lived in America. In political terms they felt that they were British,[7] though people in Britain did not see things in quite the same way and irritated the inhabitants of the colonies by thinking of them as provincials. While the richest Americans had nothing like the wealth of English or European nobility, and the most successful bankers and lawyers still did better in England than in the colonies, settled members of the next rank of American society had a higher standard of living than they could enjoy anywhere else in the world, and immigrants had a good chance of reaching this status. But immigration from England dwindled in a way that suggests seventeenth-century emigration had been at least partly the result of desperation about life in a country that was divided on religion, unsure that it could feed all its population and in danger of civil war on more than one occasion. By 1714 these problems were under control and people in England could feel comfortable about their prospects. They might do even better if they crossed the Atlantic, but that was a large step to take for what would be only a marginal gain. In Scotland there were far fewer reasons to stay at home. The Scots were not at all sure that the 1707 Union with England had brought any benefits and they were still divided over the claims of the exiled Stuarts; and it was not until later in the century that prosperity, some of it based on imperial trade, and a reconciliation of Highlanders and Lowlanders gave them a more settled country. Ireland was equally and more irreconcilably divided, and its economic prospects were less good. Emigrants from Scotland and Ireland, joined by people from other parts of Protestant Europe, moved to America in such numbers that by the 1770s it had a population of over 2,000,000.

When John Wesley came to America in 1735 to preach the restrained and decorous Anglicanism of the day, he met a group of Moravians (Protestants from what is now the Czech Republic) who put him on the road to a belief in the need for enthusiasm and a more active religious involvement than anything he had known previously. The colonies were on the verge of 'the Great Awakening', a religious revival that spread more easily than Wesley's Methodism did in England because there was so much less of an established church and upper class to hold it back. It helped give the colonies a greater sense than before of having something in common. Wesley went back to England and carried on his work of evangelism there, but the other great Methodist preacher, George Whitefield, travelled back and forth between England and America frequently, and it was in America that he died thirty years later.[8]

The New England colonies were developing ship-building, with all the advantages of unlimited stocks of timber. Some industries were becoming well enough established for a small amount of intercolonial trade to take place. Several colonies had large enough surpluses of food to export it to the West Indies and import sugar to use directly and to turn into rum. The people in London who passed the Navigation Acts and the other legislation to control trade had never imagined colonies could develop in this way. In the seventeenth century they had been distant settlements that carried on bilateral trade with the mother country, exporting one or two staple products and importing a wide range of metropolitan products. By the eighteenth century even the West Indian islands did too much trade with the American mainland colonies to claim that they observed the Navigation Acts to the letter, but they came much closer to it than the mainland colonies, with their complicated patterns of trade and their steps towards setting up industries of their own. All of the colonies, West Indian and mainland, were very good customers for British products and in the second quarter of the eighteenth century the British government felt that, while people in the American colonies were not observing either the letter or the spirit of the Navigation Acts, the whole economic process was working so well that there was no need to interfere with it. Interest groups sometimes lobbied the Westminster parliament, obtaining legislation directed against American trade in hats or in iron or in woollen goods, but getting the legislation enforced on the other side of the Atlantic was quite another matter. The British authorities in North America were mainly concerned with the prosperity of the territory they were ruling; the British government expected colonies to cover their own costs and was not going to pay the expenses of supervising legislation so far from home. Smuggling was so widespread in Britain that politicians were hardly going to worry if trade legislation was regarded in America as a matter of guidelines to be treated with respect rather than laws to be obeyed.

The population of the American colonies grew very quickly. Once men and women were roughly equal in numbers, large families flourished, with more children surviving infancy than was usual elsewhere. Immigration brought in large numbers of free men and women in the north, and even larger number of slaves in the Carolinas, Virginia and Maryland. Slaves were not going to increase in numbers without fresh imports, but they did not dwindle away as expensively as they did in the sugar plantations. Free immigrants to the southern colonies were discouraged by the difficulties of competing with a slave population, but if they went a little way inland they could find frontier land without much difficulty, although transport costs were still high enough to mean that commercial agriculture for export could not be carried on very far from the sea. People had moved inland some way from New York up the Hudson river and its tributary the Mohawk, but further north they had not got into the Green Mountains and to the south only a few settlers in Virginia had gone past the Blue Ridge mountains and the Shenandoah and begun to get to grips with the Alleghenies. By later standards they were confined to a small and very prosperous area, where they carried on intensive farming in regions dominated by the difficulty of land transport and the need to keep in touch with seaborne commerce.

In 1732 a new colony was launched, Georgia, which could easily be seen as the thirteenth colony by those who reckoned that Nova Scotia was too far away to be counted as one of them. Dozens of miles of uncut woodland divided one colony of English settlement from another along the coastline from New Hampshire to Georgia, but Nova Scotia was separated from the other colonies by hundreds of miles of forest. Georgia was at first intended to give poor and even bankrupt emigrants from Britain a new chance in life, with plenty of free land which they could cultivate for themselves. The philanthropists who launched the colony were so far ahead of their time that their original grant ruled out slavery, but the settlers saw no reason why they should be deprived of a right to own property enjoyed by all the other white people in the American colonies and, after twenty years, they succeeded in changing the terms of the grant to let them own slaves. Georgia was not closely linked to its northern neighbours in the Carolinas; its real concern was to remain free from attack by its Spanish neighbours in Florida.

Although the Spanish authorities resented the establishment of Georgia in an area they had claimed as their own, they knew they could not do anything about it. They also suspected, accurately enough, that the South Sea Company had no intention of confining itself to the limits on its trade laid down in the treaty of Utrecht. Once it was accepted that the British could sell some slaves, it was very hard to count individual sales to keep the total down to the official maximum of 4800. When the annual trading ship reached a South American port it took a very long time to unload, because extra goods were rowed to it at night from ships standing over the horizon. The South Americans were glad to have suppliers eager to sell more slaves and they welcomed the choice of British goods, but the Spanish government wanted to maintain as much of the pre-1713 monopoly of trade as possible. Any British ships in South American waters were going to be suspected of smuggling, and perhaps of a little piracy as well. It was against this background that Captain Jenkins claimed to have had one of his ears cut off, when he was unfortunate enough to have been captured by the Spanish coastguards. In 1738 a House of Commons committee, examining the country's relations with Spain, asked him how he had responded to this, to which he replied that he had committed his soul to his God and his cause to his country. Whatever actually happened to Jenkins's ear, a phrase like this was just the thing to rouse public fury over difficulties about trade with South America. The government realised that, because MPs and merchants felt its previous policy had been too pacific, it had to go to war with Spain.[9] The mood of the period was symbolised in the two patriotic songs, 'Rule Britannia', published in 1740 and 'God Save the King', published in 1742, which became the anthem of loyalty when Jacobite invaders came alarmingly close to London in 1745.

The naval war with Spain which began in 1739 spilled over into a war with France which meant rather less to people and politicians in Britain. The Habsburg Emperor Charles VI had worked hard to get the rulers of Europe to accept his daughter Maria Theresa as his successor, but he was barely dead before Frederick II, the king of Prussia, seized the Austrian province of Silesia and Louis XV of France started trying to install a different emperor. George II was a straightforward man; he was descended from German princes and had a little German kingdom of his own in Hanover, and he felt Maria Theresa ought to be supported against France and Prussia. Politicians knew that a war against France would never be totally without supporters, but they also felt that they were getting further into German politics than was really prudent. Too pacific a policy would be unpopular, but a policy that concentrated too much on German issues would also be unpopular. Walpole resigned because the Commons turned against him, but nobody else in the 1740s could find a policy that reconciled these currents of opinion: successes in the naval war with Spain like Vernon's capture of Porto Bello and the voyage round the world of Anson's squadron did not lead to anything decisive, and in Germany the king and his army fought honourably and played some part in helping Maria Theresa and the Habsburgs to keep their lands and the imperial title, although Silesia was never returned.

Some developments in the war pointed to the future. Although the historian Macaulay was weaving the separate threads of war together rather too neatly when he wrote that 'in order that [Frederick] might rob a neighbour [Maria Theresa] whom he had promised to defend, black men fought on the coast of Coromandel, and red men scalped each other by the Great Lakes of North America', it was true that this was a war spread over three continents in a way that had never been seen before.[10] French and British settlements far from Europe took an active role in fighting; the Massachusetts colony organised its militia to march 500 miles to the north east to help capture the French stronghold of Louisbourg on Cape Breton Island, and on the Coromandel coast the French seized the East India Company's southern Indian base at Madras. The two acquisitions were returned when the war came to an indecisive end in 1748, but Americans had shown that they were ready to move long distances rather than stay close to home as they had done ever since 1607, and India was clearly a less peaceful place for European traders than it had been in the seventeenth century. The British Empire had been until this point a relatively tranquil collection of small colonies, none of them very far from the sea. All of this was to change.

# 3

# First Moves Inland

In the 1740s the East India Company was drawn into the politics of the Indian interior by the activity of the French East India Company. The French governor of Pondicherry, Joseph Dupleix, felt sure he could strengthen his company's position by establishing alliances with the rulers in south India who were becoming more and more independent of the Great Mogul in Delhi. He pressed on with this policy after peace in 1748 and the British company's recovery of Madras. The British company saw Dupleix's alliances as a threat to its position. When war broke out among the Indian states near Madras, Robert Clive, the second-in-command of the company's little army, seized Arcot, the capital city of one of the members of Dupleix's alliance, and held on to it for seven weeks until the besieging force was broken up.

Clive succeeded because he was the first general to turn an Indian army from an ill-organised and infrequently-paid crowd of men expected to win by weight of numbers into a modern military force. Some Indian rulers set off on the same path, but were never quite able to catch up with the lead the East India Company had gained. Loyalty to an alliance in difficulties was as unusual in eighteenth-century India as in Renaissance Italy, and Dupleix's diplomatic arrangements collapsed when his Indian allies realised that the French could not protect them from the military power the East India Company was beginning to assemble. Clive went back to England briefly in the mid 1750s to try to get into British politics, but the fortune he had made in the south India wars was too small for this. By the time of the larger conflicts of the late 1750s he was back in India.

The peace made in 1748 never looked very durable. Maria Theresa and the Austrians were ready to change all their old alliances in order to get Silesia back from Prussia. Frederick's contempt for women, which gave the king of France's close friend Madame de Pompadour and the Russian Tsarina Elizabeth plenty of personal reasons for wishing him ill, greatly helped them in carrying out this diplomatic revolution. The British were at the same time drifting towards war with France in North America. The water system of North America allowed people in the French colonies to go up the St Lawrence, through the Great Lakes and then on to the Mississippi system with only a short break (or portage) in which they had to carry their canoes from one waterway to another, after which they could travel south down the river to New Orleans.

This gave the French a splendid skeleton for growth, but it remained no more than a skeleton because the French colonies were very sparsely populated by comparison with the British. The St Lawrence valley was so cold in winter and New Orleans was so hot in summer that the French were understandably unwilling to settle in either place; the result was that at the middle of the century these colonies found it hard to survive even in time of peace without help from France. The French Mississippi Company had never been able to do much to help because it had overreached itself in stock exchange dealings very like the South Sea Company's bubble, but the French government continued to support its colonies generously. The contrast is pointed in two novels about two women sent to the colonies in the hope that this would improve the moral tone of their native lands and increase the birth rate overseas: Prévost's Manon Lescaut dies miserably a few miles from New Orleans, but Defoe's Moll Flanders flourishes like a green bay tree after settling at the North Carolina end of Chesapeake Bay.[1] The British colonies were prosperous enough to offer people, no matter how disreputable, a chance to become better off. They never received assistance on the same scale as the French colonies but by 1750 they already had a large enough population to launch a rich and independent country if the question arose, though they were too far from being united, and were perhaps too English in their beliefs and loyalties for such a step to be at all likely.

The immediate objective for those Americans who were beginning to move beyond their old-established settlements on the Atlantic coast was the rich lands of the Ohio valley, which lay within the French river system of the Mississippi. The career of George Washington, one of the early leaders in this movement inland, shows how little expansion inland had taken place up to this point. His family home, Mount Vernon, named after the hero of Porto Bello, was almost on the shores of Chesapeake Bay and yet, 150 years after the first English settlements there, it was still easy for him to ride to the frontier and become a leading land surveyor (and also land speculator) along the line that led north west from Virginia to the Ohio. The French took military action to drive the Virginians out of the new territory. The British responded early in 1755 by sending an expedition under Braddock into the area west of the Pennsylvania settlements, but it fell into a French and Indian ambush before it could reach the French base at Fort Duquesne. Washington, who was serving as second-in-command, pulled some of the force together, but the problems of moving troops through American woodlands were made unpleasantly clear.[2]

In 1752 the British authorities, encouraged by Benjamin Franklin, the Philadelphia entrepreneur and polymath, had invited the colonies to send representatives to Albany in upstate New York to consider the problems of defence against the French. Only three or four of the colonies were directly affected by the question, and so few people came to the conference that it showed the colonies had no feeling of common political purpose to make them unite to protect one another. The British found themselves heading for a war in Europe, where they had made no preparations to protect George II's kingdom of Hanover, and a war in North America, where the fact that their colonies had a much larger population than New France would be of little use.

The war began badly enough to leave the government exposed to its opponents' attacks. In Europe the British had to make an alliance with Frederick of Prussia to save Hanover from being defenceless before the French, even though this meant facing Austria and Russia as well. At sea Admiral Byng showed so little willingness to fight the French and help the island of Minorca that he was court-martialled and shot 'to encourage the others', as Voltaire put it in *Candide*.[3] The prime minister, the duke of Newcastle, afraid that it might soon be the turn of politicians to be executed, resigned office late in 1756 rather than stand up to William Pitt's denunciations of the government's failures. Newcastle had such a large band of supporters in the Commons that no stable government could be formed without him, but public opinion could have its effect even in eighteenth-century politics and, led by the corporations of the big cities, it showed that it wanted Pitt to lead the government.[4] After four months when Pitt tried to run a government without a parliamentary majority, and three months with no government at all, Pitt became secretary of state to direct policy and Newcastle undertook to provide him with a solid parliamentary majority. Pitt was able to reconcile support for George's position in Germany with British interests in America; his policy could be summed up in the phrase 'America must be fought for in Europe'.[5] He gave it solid meaning by supporting Prussia with troops to hold back the French in western Germany and with financial subsidies to help Frederick defend himself against Austria and Russia. In 1758 Prussia was able to maintain its position in Europe, and the British attacked the eastern and western outposts of the French position in America, capturing Louisbourg and Fort Duquesne, which was renamed Pittsburgh.

The British had already been encouraged by events in Bengal. When the old nawab, Alivardi, died, his throne passed peacefully to his grandson, Siraj-ud-Daula, who was spared the lethal but educational struggle for the survival of the fittest which usually accompanied succession to a throne in Mughal India. Over the following year or so Siraj-ud-Daula annoyed his Hindu bankers and lost the trust of some of his Muslim generals. He also infuriated the British by storming their trading centre at Calcutta in June 1756, making things far worse by locking up a few dozen prisoners in a tiny punishment cell from which less than half of them emerged alive next day. For decades to come the British recalled the 'Black Hole' as the archetypal Indian atrocity, but at the time their business was to restore their position in Bengal. Clive was sent north from Madras with a small army and Siraj-ud-Daula, who was beginning to realise that he was making too many enemies, allowed the British back into Calcutta. Clive could see the weakness of the nawab's position and began conspiring with Siraj-ud-Daula's enemies, who were ready to abandon him if the British challenged him. Clive marched the company's little army north from Calcutta and in June 1757 it confronted the Bengal army at Plassey. Clive had about 3000 men, the nawab had an army of the old, ill-organised sort of perhaps 50,000 men, some of whom were led by members of the conspiracy. The two sides stood and fired at each other for an hour or two, and then the Bengal army began to slip away and break up while the company army held its ground. The nawab, seeing his followers were about to desert, fled but was pursued and killed by supporters of Mir Jafar, the leading Muslim in the conspiracy.

In a military sense Plassey was trivial, a simple matter of disciplined soldiers standing firm while their opponents disintegrated, but in a political sense no event in British imperial history was more important. After Plassey, any nawab of Bengal would clearly owe his position to the support of the British; but, after eight years of trying with successive nawabs to find one who would be subservient to the company yet able at the same time to command the respect of his subjects, the company gave up trying to square the circle and took the place of the nawab. It ruled more people than the king of England, and it had taken over more foreigners and made them into subjects than anyone had done since the Spanish conquest of South America. It now had to work out relationships with its new subjects and with the British government.

Clive argued that the government in London should take responsibility for Bengal, partly because he felt that political power would be bad for the company. Certainly it did far less for shareholders' dividends than they might have hoped, because the company employees in India used their newly-acquired political power to make fortunes for themselves. Years later the chairman of a parliamentary committee, John Burgoyne, asked Clive about the wealth he had acquired. He replied that, after Plassey, 'An opulent city lay at my mercy. Its richest bankers bid against each other for my smiles. I walked through vaults which were thrown open to me alone, piled on either side with gold and jewels. By God, Mr Chairman, at this moment I stand amazed at my own moderation'.[6] Some of his subordinates had even less reason to feel that they had restrained themselves.

While Clive did not advance inland beyond Bengal and the Madras region and insisted that the company should expand no further, a policy that was followed for nearly forty years, it makes good sense that he is known as 'Clive of India'. Before Plassey, the East India Company had been one of several dozen minor powers in a subcontinent in which effective control was drifting from the central government into the hands of six or eight major political powers. After Plassey, the company was among the richest of the major powers and could mount a formidable challenge to the central government whenever it chose. In 1765 the Great Mogul and his allies came down the Ganges to attack the British, but the company had turned the army of Bengal into a modern force in good time, and the forces from Delhi were defeated at Buxar. They fought with more determination than Siraj-ud-Daula's army had done, but the battle simply confirmed the earlier victory. The Great Mogul accepted the company as the ruler of Bengal, with some confidence that taxes would be sent to him on time, and his ally the nawab of Oudh was forced to sign a treaty with the company which recognised its control over his relations with other states.

By then the war in Europe and America had ended in British triumph.

Pitt's system succeeded: in Europe, Frederick survived and Hanover was saved from the French, who were tied down so effectively that they could do nothing to help their American colonies. In 1759 the French were defeated at Minden, which secured the position of Hanover. In North America Wolfe brought an expedition up the St Lawrence to Quebec, the best-defended point in New France. After some weeks of manoeuvring on the river, he found a way to bring his troops up the cliffs to attack the city. A short battle, in which both commanding officers were killed, left the British masters of the city and the supply route to western New France open. Later in the year Hawke's naval success in Quiberon Bay gave the British command of the sea, which virtually guaranteed their position in America. Celebrating the victory, the great actor, David Garrick wrote a patriotic song, 'Heart of Oak', 'to bring fresh pride to this wonderful year' and also to indicate that the main maritime skill of the French consisted of running away. In 1760 the rest of New France had to surrender, and the British gained sugar-rich islands in the West Indies. In 1761, when the Spanish prepared to come to the assistance of France, Pitt laid plans for successful attacks on Havana and Manila. But by then George II had died and had been succeeded by his grandson George III who was much less concerned about his German kingdom and much more concerned about the financial impact of Pitt's ambitious planning. Pitt resigned and George found new ministers, who began negotiations for peace so quickly that Frederick was left feeling betrayed, making him unlikely to help Britain if assistance on the Continent of Europe were to be needed in the future.

In the peace of Paris Britain took all of New France east of the Mississippi and a few of the smaller Windward Islands from France, and took Florida from Spain. The French kept their large sugar islands. The English sugar processors would have been happy to have more islands from which to import their raw material, but the sugar growers wanted as little competition from new islands brought inside the British trading system as possible. The government also had to work out a new system of government for its French-speaking Roman Catholic subjects in New France. Merchants who came to Montreal and Quebec City from New England and from Scotland were eager to have a government run by Protestants for Protestants but, while the government could see that this would not work, it did not have a policy of its own to propose. Canada's governor, Sir Guy Carleton, had his own ideas for recognition of the position of Roman Catholics and the creation of a nominated assembly in which the French-speaking majority

## James Wolfe

James Wolfe (1727–1759) came from a military family and began his active career young: he fought at Dettingen in 1743 and at Culloden in 1746, and took part in the brutal suppression of the Highlands that followed, though he did refuse to carry out one of the duke of Cumberland's harsher orders. In 1758 Wolfe led the landing on the seashore when the British were setting out to attack Louisbourg, the heavily fortified town and port from which France expected to dominate entry to the St Lawrence river. Louisbourg was captured, but several senior generals were killed or discredited during the campaign, opening the way for Wolfe to be given command of the force that set out to capture Quebec the following year. Wolfe was tall, thin, a little gawky and, according to one of the king's helpful advisers, mad as well. George II, who knew a good deal about military matters and had led his troops on the battlefield (the last king of England to do so), replied 'Mad, is he? Then I wish he'd bite some of my other generals'. Naval support on the St Lawrence gave the British forces a commanding strategic advantage, but Wolfe was not able to set up an effective seige of the city. Only when he heard of a path up the cliffs west of Quebec was he able to assemble his troops in a position that divided the French forces and left them to fight in the open field or else let the British set up batteries of naval guns which would have soon destroyed the city. The battle was short; the British troops were trained to hold their fire until the range was close enough for muskets to be effective, and a couple of massed volleys was enough to destroy the cohesion of their opponents. Both Wolfe and the opposing general, Montcalm, were killed on the field of battle. The city surrendered and Wolfe's successors took the rest of New France easily enough.

Benjamin West's painting of *The Death of Wolfe*, departing from the older conventions of classical dress and laurel for the victors, was seen as a new and realistic departure, and it added to the glamour of death on the battlefield. Wolfe was buried at Quebec, with the inscription on his tomb 'Here lies Wolfe victorious'. Over the years English-Canadians too often referred to Wolfe's victory as a reason why the views of French-Canadians could be ignored. The inscription on the tomb now simply says 'Here lies Wolfe'.

would hold a large number of seats, but the government did not take up these ideas until a moment, some years later, when they caused more trouble than they would have done if brought forward at a quieter time.

People in the American colonies now saw that French opposition to expansion into the territories beyond the Alleghenies had been eliminated. The British government thought an advance into this area would alarm the Indian population and might cause a war in which the British taxpayer would have to rescue American frontiersmen from the effect of rash expansion. The British felt confirmed in their view by the hostile alliance put together by the great Indian leader Pontiac in 1762, but the Americans felt that the defeat of Pontiac's conspiracy showed that the dangers had been exaggerated. The British government responded in late 1763 by drawing its Proclamation Line a little west of the area of settlement to stop the advance and laying down rules about acquiring land from Indians in the area between the line and the Mississippi. Americans, confident that they could solve their own Indian problems, thought the British decision to place a small army in the area of the Proclamation Line was an unnecessary expense, and one that showed British mistrust of them.

Only a minority of Americans had any idea of moving into the area west of the Proclamation Line, but a great many Americans were stirred to an unprecedented degree of unity by hostility to British proposals for taxation. In 1764 George Grenville set out to deal with the rearrangement of national finances and the refinancing of war debts that always accompanied peace. He believed the American colonies ought to pay something to the government in London, if only because so much wartime expenditure had been undertaken to defend them and to drive the French out of North America. He also wanted to obtain revenue which was at the disposal of the governors in North America rather than of the colonial assemblies – the taxes he imposed would have provided the governors with funds under their own control which reduced the danger of assemblies gaining fiscal power over them.

The Sugar Act of 1764 regulated the trade between the West Indies and the American mainland more effectively than before, and also provided some revenue. The Stamp Act of 1765 was a very mild piece of legislation by European standards: legal transactions including buying land would have to be completed on paper stamped by the government to show that a fee had been paid, and some luxury goods like playing cards would be wrapped in paper stamped to show that a type of purchase tax had been paid. Americans were infuriated by the Act; their own assemblies taxed them very lightly, and they believed the Westminster parliament had no legal right to impose taxes on them directly. At this stage no question was being raised about the authority of the monarch. Colonies owed their legal existence to royal charters and were ruled by royal governors, and they acknowledged that the king was better placed to decide on foreign policy than they could be. But parliament had never imposed taxes on them directly, and the Americans could argue that the only time it legislated for them was when it exercised its right to lay down a trading policy for the empire as a whole. While the colonies might not like restrictions on their right to trade in their own manufactured goods, or limitations on their trade with the islands of the West Indies, they had accepted them reasonably willingly as part of a wider policy. The stamped paper raised entirely different issues and representatives of twelve of the colonies met in the Stamp Act Congress to launch a united protest that parliament had exceeded its powers. Something had happened that could be seen as a threat to all Americans, awakening a national feeling that inspired a con-trolled rebellion against any sort of acceptance of the Stamp Act.

Grenville left office, and his ministry was replaced by a government that hoped to get back to the world of the 1740s. It repealed the Stamp Act, though it passed a Declaratory Act to say that parliament had the right to impose taxes on the colonies even if it did not choose to do so. The king was not pleased by what seemed to him an excessively conciliatory approach, and a few months later he was able to persuade Pitt, now ennobled as earl of Chatham, to form a government. Chatham enjoyed great prestige, but at this stage was not mentally stable enough to control the ministers in his government and coordinate policy. Grenville had been serious about financial problems; Chatham's chancellor of the exchequer, Townshend, was far more light-hearted. He said that he would take the Americans at their word about taxation and that, if they would not pay direct taxes but were ready to pay taxes that regulated trade, he would impose taxes on glass, paper, paint, lead and tea in order to regulate trade. Townshend's speech made it clear that, whatever he said about regulating trade, he was imposing these taxes to obtain revenue in just the same way as Grenville had done three years earlier. The Americans responded by saying that they would boycott goods that paid the Townshend duties. Although they were not as totally united about it as they had been about resistance to the Stamp Act, they were able, partly by abstaining from dutiable articles and partly by smuggling, to keep up the boycott effectively enough to leave British exporters feeling that they had become the main losers. When Chatham was finally driven from office by mental collapse, the more diplomatic Lord North became chancellor of the exchequer and removed most of the duties that had caused the trouble, though he retained the tax on tea to avoid giving the impression that he had surrendered to American opposition.

During Chatham's administration the East India Company was doing so well that the government, which still had not worked out a way to tax corporate profits, pushed it into agreeing to pay the treasury £400,000 a year. This arrangement took it for granted that the company was going to make profits, but from 1768 to 1770 a serious famine raged in Bengal. Famine was nothing new, but it made people in Britain afraid that the rapid rise to wealth of company employees was destroying the Indian economy. It also left the company with no money to pay the government. By 1773 North wanted to find some way to help the company realise its assets. Its main asset was a large quantity of tea which sat unsold because the high British tariff meant that it could not meet the competition from smugglers. If the duty were removed the tea could be sold and, more specifically, if the British duty were removed from tea re-exported to America, it could be sold cheaply enough to mean that the Americans would be offered a bargain so irresistible that they would no longer boycott it, the company could meet its payments to the government, and the British government would have a revenue raised in the colonies for its own purposes.

The most idealistic and the most sordid Bostonians, the smugglers and those who felt they were American citizens rather than British subjects, were afraid that the reduction in taxes would work precisely as North intended. In December 1773 they stormed three tea-ships which had entered the harbour, and threw the tea overboard. This was seen in Britain and in America as unjustified violence, but the retaliatory legislation that parliament passed in response to the Boston Tea Party convinced Americans that they had to stand behind the Bostonians. The collective punishment imposed on the port of Boston and the transfer to new locations of trials involving the death penalty might have been accepted, but the Americans saw the amendment of the Massachusetts charter by Act of parliament as an un-precedented assertion of parliamentary supremacy over the constitutional basis of colonial government. Judicial decisions had led to the cancellation

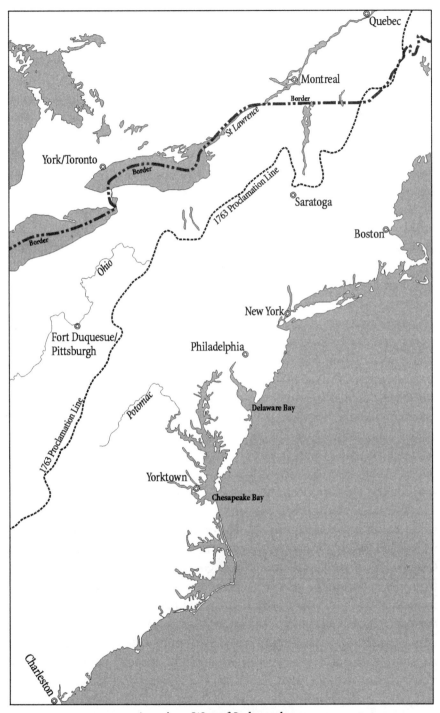

Quebec

Montreal

Border

York/Toronto

Border

St Lawrence

1763 Proclamation Line

Saratoga

Boston

Border

Ohio

New York

Fort Duquesue/
Pittsburgh

Philadelphia

1763 Proclamation Line

Potomac

Delaware Bay

Yorktown

Chesapeake Bay

Charleston

American War of Independence

of charters in the seventeenth century, but only for specific abuses by the governments of the colonies. Parliament was now claiming that (by extension) it could cancel all the political and civil rights of people in the colonies.

By an awkward quirk of parliamentary timing the Quebec Act was passed at just the same moment. It fulfilled the commitment in the 1763 peace treaty that the Catholics of New France should have religious toleration, and it set up a nominated assembly in which they had more seats than the representatives of the Protestant minority, though the governor and his officials had enough seats of their own to hold the balance of power between the two groups. It also brought the boundaries of what was now called Quebec south to the triangle of land between the Mississippi and the Ohio. There were probably more French-speaking than English-speaking people in the triangle at the time, but the Virginians and Pennsylvanians who had been looking forward to moving into the Ohio valley were not pleased to find that the north-west side of it was going to be ruled by a legislature in Quebec City which used the French legal system. Americans would never have liked this Act, and in the circumstances of 1774 they saw it as part of a plan for giving the British government arbitrary power in North America. Some people were afraid that the Catholics were being conciliated so that they should provide an army to coerce American Protestants. When the Massachusetts constitution was changed to have members of the council (or upper house) nominated instead of being elected, the intention in London was to create something more like the House of Lords, but in America it was seen as a step away from elected representatives towards the creation of a nominated assembly similar to that in Quebec.

A Continental Congress met in 1774 to consider how to respond to what it called the 'Intolerable Acts', supported by a deep popular feeling which had taken control of the assemblies of the thirteen colonies from Georgia to New Hampshire. When governors dissolved the assemblies, they met again on an extra-legal basis and served as local centres for the resistance that was developing. The Continental Congress had not yet decided what to do, and it spent 1775 debating whether there were arrangements short of independence which would satisfy it, but fighting had already broken out in several regions of the thirteen colonies and men under arms naturally wanted a clear-cut objective. The British saw no reason to make concessions to the Americans. They would in any case have had difficulty in doing so without reconstructing the form of their own constitution. The king was expected to run the executive side of government activity without much interference from parliament, and his governors had much the same role in the colonies. In practice the king's ministers acted as a link between king and parliament. People accepted this as a convenient way to handle some problems rather than acknowledging it as the central feature of the constitution, so it was not easy to think of ministers in the colonies shaping policy. There was also a practical problem: while the king was at the centre of the system it was natural for the whole empire to have a unified foreign and defence policy, but devolving power to the colonies raised the possibility that each colony would pursue a foreign policy of its own.

The Americans were developing small armies which could march some distance from their bases. In 1775 they launched an attack on Canada which, though unsuccessful (and hard to explain in terms of their comments on the Quebec Act), showed they could move troops through difficult countryside. Early in 1776 opinion in the Continental Congress shifted away from the idea of negotiation and, on 4 July 1776, the United States declared itself independent. By then the British had assembled a strong army at New York and the following year it moved by sea to launch a successful attack on the Americans at Philadelphia from the south west. At the same time Burgoyne, who had moved from Bengal politics to American military affairs, led an army south down the Hudson valley from Montreal towards New York, which would have cut the lines of communication between Washington's army in Pennsylvania and its determined supporters in New England. As the New York army was committed to its Philadelphia campaign it could give no support to the Montreal force, which was caught in the woodlands at the north end of the Hudson valley and had to surrender at Saratoga in October 1777.[7] In military terms this did not damage the British much, because the immediate question was whether Washington could hold his Pennsylvania army together at all. The important effect of the surrender was to encourage the French to feel that a small involvement in America might cause the British considerable embarrassment. The French government was uncomfortably aware that it had acute financial problems and had no desire to commit itself to a full-scale war, but Britain had in 1763 risen to such a level of dominance that most countries in Europe hoped that its power would be reduced. Europeans, while certainly not revolutionaries, felt a good deal of sympathy for the Americans who got some direct help from enthusiastic friends. They also benefited because

## John Locke

The political philosopher John Locke (1632–1704) was directly involved in imperial affairs in the 1670s and the 1690s. His political theories were affected by the experience and later on had a considerable impact on imperial affairs. As secretary to Lord Ashley (usually known by his later title of earl of Shaftesbury), the most energetic of the Carolina proprietors at the end of the 1660s, he helped draw up the colony's constitution, an interesting blend of feudalism and modernity, with the secret ballot, titles of nobility for landowners, religious toleration and quit-rents for the proprietors all mixed together. Because most colonial activity was a matter of private ventures like those of the Carolina proprietors, Charles II's government had no minister for the colonies, but Shaftesbury persuaded him to set up a council for plantations to give the privy council well-informed advice and Locke was secretary to the council in 1673–74. Shaftesbury then went into opposition, and Locke had to give up his government job and help him in domestic politics. When Shaftesbury's attempts to impose strict limits on royal power were defeated early in the 1680s Shaftesbury and Locke had to flee for their lives to the Netherlands, as Charles prepared to destroy his opponents. Shaftesbury died in exile before William of Orange's successful invasion in 1688, but Locke came back to England and from 1696 to 1700 was one of the most influential members of the board of trade, which was designed to give the government advice on imperial policy in much the same way as the council for plantations had done.

Locke's ideas were based on a good deal of political experience but his political theories, mainly expressed in his *Second Treatise on Civil Government* (published in 1690, though fairly certainly written some years earlier), turned out to be even more relevant to the eighteenth-century American colonies than to seventeenth-century England. Locke approved of the Revolution which put William on the English throne and realised that hostility to James's pro-Catholic activities was the main driving force behind it, but he saw very little need to put religion into politics. In the colonies religious diversity was already so well developed that the highest level of agreement that could be reached was a general conviction that Roman Catholics were dangerous, whether they were French and might attack the northern colonies or Spanish and might attack the southern colonies. Locke's relatively detached attitude to religion meant that he had never joined in any arguments about claims that the Church of England ought to have a special position in the state. When problems developed in the Thirteen Colonies after 1763, it was hard to argue that George III was an enemy of religion or of Protestantism, but Americans were convinced that he was an unsatisfactory ruler and should be removed. Locke had said enough in favour of a 'right of resistance' (or revolution) to put a good case for dissatisfied subjects to change their ruler if their natural right to life, liberty and property was not being respected. This was not to be done frivolously, but there had been enough friction in the dozen years before the Declaration of Independence to convince Americans that there was something about George III which made it impossible to reach agreement with him.

Locke's arguments about property were even more helpful to Americans worried about their right to own the land in North America that they occupied. He spoke of a right to property based on the proprietor going out and making the soil fit for cultivation by his labour. Things had not been done in England in that way for hundreds of years, but all the American colonies had large enough minorities of men who had shouldered their axes to attack the forest and to open it up for growing crops to make Locke's account look convincing. The original population seemed to have left the forest untouched, so the settlers had a right to the land, and also had a right to bring over servants (or employees) who, if they were lucky, could go on to open up land of their own. Locke's theory of government was intended to apply to all possible situations, and certainly did not make specific references to North America (it would have been surprising if he had included anything of the sort, because he never went there), but it suited Americans so well that they embraced it almost without reservation. Thomas Jefferson felt that Locke's moral tone could be more elevated and, when he was writing the Declaration of Independence, changed Locke's idea of natural rights into an assertion of a natural right to life, liberty and the pursuit of happiness, but the rest of the Declaration left it clear enough that property was an important part of happiness.

activity in other theatres of war served to distract the British from the struggle in America. The British tried to negotiate with the Americans. They passed legislation to ensure that parliament would not impose taxes on colonies in future, and offered other concessions which might have solved all the immediate problems if they had been brought forward a few years earlier, but none of this made any impression in the new situation created by the Declaration of Independence.

In 1779 the British opened up a new area of activity in the southern colonies, and over the next two years marched steadily north through Georgia and the Carolinas. This brought the war to its decisive moment. Cornwallis advanced through Virginia and took up a position on the shores of Chesapeake Bay which depended on command of the sea, but at this point the French fleet held the mouth of the bay and the British fleet lost touch with its army. Washington moved his army south from Pennsylvania faster than anyone had thought possible. Late in 1781 Cornwallis was forced to surrender at Yorktown, a few miles from Jamestown, where British permanent settlement in America had begun. The British had become steadily less enthusiastic about the war as it became clear that the Americans were serious adversaries who believed that important principles were at stake. Cornwallis's surrender made it clear that the war in America was unwinnable. Fighting a war against France and its ally Spain was difficult enough to mean that Britain could not expect a favourable settlement from them. In the event, Spain regained Minorca and Florida, though France got very little out of its involvement in the war.

The government was immensely relieved that the British position in India had survived unscathed, despite heavy pressure during the American War of Independence. The arrangements to remit the tea duty which led to the Boston Tea Party and on to the War of Independence had been part of an agreement between the government and the East India Company which gave political control over the Calcutta, Madras and Bombay settlements to a governor-general who had a council of four other members, three of whom were appointed by the government. The first governor-general, Warren Hastings, was a company employee, or 'servant' in the language of the time, and a civil servant rather than a military servant. The government nominees almost inevitably regarded him with some suspicion. Ideas of proper behaviour in government were changing: ever since governments had existed people had made fortunes out of holding high political office, and things had been no different in the early eighteenth century Britain of Sir Robert Walpole. By the 1750s new ideas were coming forward in Britain, but East India Company men of the generation of Clive (born in 1725) or Hastings (born in 1732), who had been brought up under the old system, had not seen how things were changing while they were in India. The government-appointed members of council spent a couple of years trying to stop Hastings doing anything at all; he was very lucky that one of the three government nominees died before real difficulties faced the company, and he was then able to run the council because he had one supporter and also the right to a casting vote. As the War of American Independence absorbed more and more of Britain's attention, the French prepared to challenge Britain's position in India and gain command of the sea in the Indian Ocean, company officials in Bombay provoked a dispute with the Maratha confederacy, the dominant power in north India controlling territory in the area south of Delhi which stretched from around Bombay almost to Calcutta. At the same time, the sultan of Mysore attacked the company's south India base in Madras. Hastings had to mobilise forces in his Bengal base and compel rulers like the nawab of Oudh to fulfil their treaty obligations to help sustain the company's position against a general attack. In Europe the War of American Independence could be seen as a combined assault on Britain's rising strength by a number of powers threatened by it, assisted by the hostile neutrality of others less deeply involved. The East India Company found itself faced by much the same problem. Hastings was able to hold the company position together and, while he saw no need to depart from Clive's policy of refraining from expansion, the company's ability to survive such a variety of challenges showed that it might well be able to displace the Great Moguls and dominate all India if that policy were to change.

When Hastings retired and returned to Britain he was at first warmly welcomed for his success, but later on he was strictly investigated on the details of his activities. The House of Commons voted to prosecute him before the House of Lords, by the process of impeachment, on the grounds that he had enriched himself unlawfully and had not treated the Indians with whom he had political dealings properly. The leader of the prosecution, Edmund Burke, had at first laid down the principle that India must be governed according to Indian methods of government, but it was soon clear that this was exactly what Hastings had done and that he had certainly behaved no worse than other players in the Indian political game. Burke shifted his position to say that it was intolerable for people from Britain to behave in India in a way that would be unacceptable in Britain. Hastings was much more vulnerable to this line of attack. Financially he had behaved like a British politician of the early eighteenth century, and in diplomacy his conduct sometimes showed signs of the influence of Frederick the Great and of Macchiavelli. After a trial lasting seven years he was acquitted, but the point of principle been made: British rulers in India would have to act in accordance with the new ideals gaining ground in Britain, which meant they would have to pay some attention to the wellbeing of their subjects. While they could do well from satisfactory salaries and pensions, they should give up hoping to make fortunes quickly out of bribes or plunder.[8]

British politicians had already tried to work out a new structure for governing the company's possessions in India, but their efforts were not quite as high-minded as their comments on Hastings might suggest. Even if jobs in India were no longer going to provide fortunes, opportunities to earn good salaries and pensions were not so common in Britain that the right to make appointments to Indian jobs could be waved aside as unimportant. Members of the government that had made peace with America went on to try to deal with the problem in 1783 by legislation to give a committee of its own nominees the right to make appointments. The king saw this as a plot to deprive him of authority in British politics, while the East India Company saw it as an attempt to strip it of the power to run its own staff and deprive its officials and shareholders of the right to look after their friends and relations by helping them get jobs in India. The king and the company were able to persuade William Pitt, the younger son of the earl of Chatham, to become prime minister and resist this approach to patronage in India. Pitt realised that the problem had to be settled and, once he was established as prime minister, his 1784 Act gave the government the power to supervise the company's political policy and to fill the half-dozen important positions which directed it. He left the company the right to make all the other appointments in India, so it could still run its own commercial policy, but the government in London was not going to let it have its own foreign policy, which might lead to war at a time which did not suit national policy. The 1784 Act, and a new charter issued in 1793, also tried to make sure that the company would not follow an expansionist policy.

Despite his defeat at Yorktown, Cornwallis went to India as the first government-appointed governor-general, to secure greater stability for the government and higher profits for the shareholders by establishing a policy of peace, frugality and an end to corruption. Perhaps a little complacently, the company and the government believed that corruption had been brought under control in Britain and deplored the prominent role it still played in Indian life. The natural conclusion was that a civil service had to be set up in which the important posts were held by British administrators trained for ruling India, with a large subordinate staff of Indians employed under careful supervision. This civil service was designed for Bengal and the few other territories the company controlled in the 1780s, but it was organised efficiently enough to mean that it could be expanded quickly when the need arose.

While Cornwallis and the company were perfectly serious about wanting peace and higher commercial dividends, they had to work in a competitive political system in which other Indian states were reorganising themselves. This was no immediate danger to Bengal, but in southern India Sultan Tipu of Mysore had taken the process of modernisation far enough in his thirty years of power to become a threat to Madras, so Cornwallis departed from his pacific policy to hold Tipu back. His main concern was still with internal reorganisation. Indians who had been collecting land taxes from the peasants were turned into landowners by fixing their payments to the company treasury in perpetuity, becoming something like a quit-rent. Eventually the Permanent Settlement, as this system was known, left the new landowners paying rather a small fraction of their income to the treasury but at first it was not at all a bad bargain for the government. Under the Mughals taxation had been much more a matter of negotiation than the company realised. The original assessments were taken as starting points for discussion rather than a simple demand for payment. This was one reason why the Indian system of government looked so corrupt by the standards of late eighteenth-century Britain, and under Cornwallis and his successors the company expected its tax demands to be met. The effect was to increase the level of taxation, which strengthened the company's financial position and made it easy to move from the policy of peace and frugality to one of war and expansion.

The government that made peace with the United States in 1783 was determined to get back on to good terms with the Americans and was ready to give up all its territory south of the Great Lakes. It had, however, to do something for its United Empire Loyalist supporters in the thirteen colonies, who wanted to leave or were being driven out by fervid American patriotism, so it stipulated that it could retain land south of the Lakes until their debts and legal claims had been settled. The Loyalists were a minority but not unimportant. Some remained in the United States but regretted the move to independence and others migrated to Britain or the West Indies and settled down in the general population, but those who went north to Canada had a more significant effect.

Those who fled from New England arrived at the thinly populated south-west corner of Nova Scotia. The colony was divided in two in 1786, to let the new arrivals run their own affairs without disturbing the existing arrangements on the peninsula around Halifax, and a new colony was created, called New Brunswick after the family name of the British monarchs as a pledge of its Loyalist beliefs. The new colony also included the Acadian settlements that had caused tension in the 1750s and, although the anticlerical views of the United States soon led French-speaking Roman Catholics to see the advantages of British rule, the line of division between Loyalists and Acadians did not disappear.

It was harder to make political arrangements for those who moved north west from New York and Pennsylvania and reached British territory at Niagara Falls at the west end of Lake Ontario, where they came under the 1774 Quebec Act. They naturally wanted to have an elected assembly and to live under a legal system based on the common law as they had done in the colonies they had left. They were a long way from the capital at Quebec and the commercial centre at Montreal, but giving them a separate colony raised more questions than carving New Brunswick out of Nova Scotia had done. Drawing a boundary along the Ottawa river was easy enough, as the Loyalists and the soldiers who took up land in the new western region on demobilisation would outnumber the few French-speaking settlers there and could establish Protestant schools and an English legal system. The question was whether they could also have an elected assembly as they had done in the colonies they had left. If not, they would feel their loyalty had cost them some of their freedom; but, if they were given an assembly, the much larger population east of the Ottawa river would feel entitled to have one as well, which would probably be dominated by a Catholic majority which would alarm the prosperous English-speaking minority in Montreal and along the northern side of the United States border.

The nominated assembly of the 1774 Act was not really an appropriate body for increasing taxes and, as the British government had promised that it would not impose taxes on colonies from Westminster, it found itself paying out of British revenue for a large garrison to protect Quebec against American expansion. This was a powerful reason for creating elected assemblies. The 1791 Constitution Act divided Quebec into Upper Canada and Lower Canada, each with an assembly. Grenville, the minister in charge of the legislation, said that its purpose was as far as possible 'to assimilate the Constitution of the Province to that of Great Britain',[9] with the implication that an elected assembly was the normal way to run a colony unless there was some obvious reason for doing things differently. Grenville may not have thought about the way to transplant the dynamics of the British constitution to Canada. The 1791 Act made it clear that freedom for colonies to run their own laws and taxation was not to be confined to British Protestants, but governors were still able to run their colonies with far less attention to public opinion or their local assemblies than the king had to pay to parliament. This meant it was possible that the problems that had grown up in the thirteen colonies before 1776 would recur.

The division of Quebec had effects across the continent. Montreal had become the centre of a fur trade which built on the experience of the French before 1763. Traders pressed on further west, until in 1793 Alexander Mackenzie found a route that enabled fur traders to paddle their canoes from the Great Lakes to the Pacific Ocean with only two brief portages. The Hudson's Bay Company was at first unable to resist this active competition but was saved when Lord Selkirk, a Highland chief with a sense of responsibility for his clan, recognised that life in northern Scotland had little to offer his followers and led them to Canada. He invested in the company and it gave him a grant of land on the Red River, around present-day Winnipeg, which dominated the Montreal fur traders' route to the west. A commercial struggle between the Hudson Bay and the Montreal traders broke out, sometimes at the level of giving too much spirits to the Indians from whom they were buying, sometimes at the level of gang warfare. The advantages of the Hudson Bay route were too great for the Montreal traders, who were merged into the Hudson's Bay Company by the 1820s, and for fifty years to come British North America was divided in two by a great empty space north of Lake Superior. The government of the united pre-1791 Canada might have tried to help the Montreal traders, but Lower Canada was too far away from the fur-catching regions to be able to influence the outcome.

Providing elected representatives for the French Canadians may have been seen as something of a gamble by politicians in London, but they could feel completely certain that no question of elected assemblies would arise in the colonies being launched in Australia at the same time. The thirteen colonies had served as a very convenient place for the British government to transport political prisoners and convicted criminals, who were treated rather worse than indentured labourers and rather better than slaves. The Americans had complained about this in the last years before independence, and after 1783 the British government had to decide what to do with its convicts. In the 1760s and 1770s James Cook had gone on from surveying the St Lawrence before Wolfe's capture of Quebec to carry out three very successful voyages of exploration in the Pacific. He had sailed round New Zealand and charted its coasts and also those of the eastern side of Australia and the north-western shores of North America, and had established that Australia was a large island and not a northern projection of a great southern continent. These voyages were triumphs of seamanship in which he lost very few sailors, and the new developments of the chronometer enabled him to chart the longitude of the places he visited with far more accuracy than ever before. The East India Company was eager to develop additional trade with China, and was trying to establish bases on the Malayan peninsula for the purpose and, while Cook never came near the Straits of Malacca or took any interest in company developments in posts like Penang, a base in the southern hemisphere might be useful for a wider range of operations in the Pacific. The convict question reminded the government of the advantages of the new lands Cook had added to the map. It was felt it would be cruel to send prisoners to Canada or to West Africa, but Cook's account of the east coast of Australia suggested that it was an attractive area which looked reassuringly like South Wales and held out some prospects of providing masts, tar and other items necessary for producing ships.[10] While nothing came of this latter idea, the government was convinced that Australia would serve very well as a prison, and that the prisoners should be sent to a location that the Cook expedition had named Botany Bay because so many species of plants and animals had been identified there which were previously unknown.

In 1788 the First Fleet reached Botany Bay. Although its commander very soon decided that Sydney Cove offered a better harbour, the original name stuck. Successive fleets of convicts were always said to be going to 'Botany Bay'. Obviously a convict settlement of this sort was quite different from colonies of people who had emigrated of their own free will and could readily be trusted with political power. New South Wales would have to be ruled by the direct military command of the troops sent out as gaolers to guard the convicts. Even when the convicts had served their sentences and could earn their living as free men (or at least as emancipists) in Australia, they were normally not allowed to go back to Britain and had to stay in a colony which had no more chance of having an elected assembly than territories that had just been taken from foreigners by conquest. The same arrangements were made for convicts in Van Diemen's Land, the attractive island a little way south of Australia.

Pitt wanted a policy of peace and frugality for Britain. Pulling the economy together after the American War of Independence and removing clumsy and ineffective methods of taxation were the main questions for him, but he took an active interest in imperial problems and was young enough to look forward to a long period of office. The East India Company and the surviving colonies in North America had to be reorganised, and Pitt was also deeply concerned about the slave trade. Slavery in the West Indies and the American colonies had been accepted without question in the early eighteenth century, and at first nobody had been worried when sugar or tobacco planters brought slaves with them as domestic servants when they visited England. Doubts began to grow after 1750, and were made much more explicit in 1772 when the lord chief justice decided in Somersett's Case that an owner did not have the right to take an unwilling slave out of England, adding that slavery must be based on 'positive law', by which he meant legislation of the sort to be found in almost all colonies in the Americas, and he went on that 'in a case so odious as the condition of slavery [the law] must be taken strictly'.[11] This comment was not directly relevant to the case, but it gave a lead to other courts and owners soon realised that they had no legal hold on their slaves in England. Ending the practice of bringing slaves to England was a great encouragement for people who felt that taking slaves from Africa to the Americas was wicked, and in the 1780s they began pressing parliament to abolish the slave trade, which had become a substantial part of the British economy. About 3,500,000 slaves were taken from Africa to British colonies in the eighteenth century, of whom about 3,000,000 survived the ocean voyage. Because about twice as many men as women were taken across the Atlantic, the slave labour force did not reproduce itself and the system could be kept going only by importing new slaves or by a dramatic change in the way slaves were treated. Pitt's government sympathised with the abolitionists; in 1787 it gave them the legal backing needed to set up a colony in Sierra Leone to which freed slaves from Britain or the West Indies could go, and it supported legislation to make conditions on slave ships less brutal. Pitt spoke strongly in favour of abolition in the 1792 debates on the issue, but he did not feel secure enough to bring the weight of government support to push doubtful MPs to oppose the trade. He probably thought he had plenty of time to handle the question later.

# 4

## *The Only Empire in the World*

The storming of the Bastille on 14 July 1789 launched France on the road to revolution. Pitt at first felt some sympathy for the spirit of change, and then became convinced that the revolutionary government would collapse because of its foolish economic policy. Political enthusiasts like Burke almost immediately wanted Britain to oppose the revolution; but it was only when the French set out in 1793 to control the mouth of the Scheldt, one of the best places to assemble a fleet to invade England, that Pitt's government went to war.

As the British population was still little more than half the size of the French, the only sensible way for Britain to fight was to find allies on the Continent of Europe by providing them with financial support to mobilise their armies to resist France. But the forces of revolution were able to organise an successful army, though one of the results of its success was the overthrow of republican government in France. Burke had predicted, before war began, that 'some popular general, who understands the art of conciliating the soldiery, and who possesses the true spirit of command, shall draw the eyes of all men upon himself'.[1] By the end of the 1790s Napoleon Bonaparte turned this prediction into reality and had become ruler of France, and a couple of years later he crowned himself emperor. France defeated her continental opponents time and again, and forced them to make peace time and again, but Britain remained steadily at war, with two brief pauses, until 1815, and was always ready to encourage new anti-French coalitions. The French made two attempts to invade Ireland, and the position of the Anglo-Irish Protestant minority was so shaken by this and by rebellion in Ireland that in 1800 the British government arranged for the Dublin parliament to vote itself out of existence and enter a union with Britain on the lines of the earlier union of England and Scotland. British troops had gone to the Continent on expeditions to help successive coalitions against France, but it was not until 1808 that they established a permanent foothold in Portugal, from which to rally Spanish and Portuguese resistance to French invasion. Britain's Peninsular War was never more than a secondary part in the struggle, and the French had no difficulty in maintaining their dominance in Europe until Napoleon's disastrous decision to invade Russia in 1812 and the destruction of the *Grande Armée* in the winter snows. The French never regained their dominance after this, and in 1815 the long wars came to an end when Napoleon proved unable to break the duke of Wellington's defensive line at Waterloo and was crushed by the arrival of a fresh Prussian army.

In 1790 France, Spain, Portugal and the Netherlands had overseas empires which were more or less as large or as prosperous as the colonies which Britain kept after 1783. About thirty years later, all the other empires had been destroyed or at least deeply undermined by events in the revolutionary wars. Other empires were broken by the events of the period, but Britain survived the strain and emerged with an empire expanded in territory and made far more dominant by the disappearance of all its European rivals.

Early in the war Pitt thought Britain should build up her economic strength for the struggle by capturing additional colonies outside Europe, though new industrial developments inside the country were the real source of the financial strength that carried the nation through the struggle. Britain's position at sea, which had always been precarious in the American War of Independence, was much stronger in the 1790s, and rose to complete dominance after Nelson's victory at Trafalgar in 1805. In earlier wars the navy had been powerful and had established a well-defined superiority over the French, but between 1794 and 1805 its attitude became even more aggressive – the objective became the annihilation of the enemy fleet. Superiority in artillery and the confidence that came from imposing a blockade on the French took the Royal Navy a long way toward achieving its objective. Sea power kept Britain safe from invasion and made it easy to launch attacks all over the world outside Europe, although it was not so easy to keep up large enough military forces to bring success. Early in the war the French sugar islands in the West Indies were attacked in the traditional manner, but the results hardly justified the loss of troops from fever. Much the heaviest blow to the French sugar industry was the loss of St Domingo, where a successful slave rebellion led to the creation of the black republic of Haiti and a sharp drop in sugar production.

The successes of its revolutionary armies gave France control of the

Netherlands – known as the Batavian Republic from 1795 until the end of the war – and the Dutch overseas empire became the main target of British activity outside Europe. In 1796 the sugar producing colony of Demerara was captured. The British had already occupied Ceylon and the Cape of Good Hope to cut the lines of communication with the Dutch East Indies, which the British East India Company could capture whenever it had enough leisure to assemble an expedition.

Leisure was the last thing the company could expect. In 1798 the policy of peace and frugality was abandoned. Pitt and his faithful lieutenant Dundas agreed with Lord Wellesley, who was about to go out as governor-general, that the company should make itself the most important power in India – the paramount power, in the language of Indian administration. This decision looked all the more sensible when Napoleon crossed the Mediterranean to Egypt at almost the same time as Wellesley reached India. Alexander the Great had led his army from Egypt to north-western India with no reason to expect to find friends there. Napoleon, if he marched to India, could reckon on finding at least one ally against the British, as Sultan Tipu of Mysore had already expressed support for the French Revolution. In the event Napoleon advanced towards Constantinople and was held up at Acre, but Wellesley had good reasons to want to settle Indian problems sooner rather than later.

He began by securing the company's position in central India by reaching an agreement with the nizam of Hyderabad. The more detailed Hyderabad treaty signed in 1800 can be seen as a major step in building up the system of alliances with princes and their states which was an important part of British rule in India right up to independence. Some earlier treaties had imposed heavy financial burdens on defeated enemies, and Hastings had made subsidiary treaties on less onerous terms, but the Hyderabad treaty came closer to being a model for the future. Wellesley was able to persuade the nizam to let the company control his foreign policy and refrain from making alliances with other princes in return for the company's guarantee that it would protect his position against attacks from anyone else. In this he was successful.

Before that, Wellesley had moved south to make sure that the potential French alliance with Mysore never became effective. He had a high opinion of his family, relying on his brother Henry for diplomatic negotiations and on his brother Arthur for military operations. Arthur, who went on to become duke of Wellington after his victories in the Peninsular War, had to manage problems of moving troops and supplies across distances in India which were immense by the standards of western Europe. Mysore had a more efficient army than any state the company had faced previously, but it was defeated in 1799 and the storming of Tipu's capital at Seringapatam was for years seen as an event almost as important as Plassey. Most of Mysore was placed directly under company rule and only the inner core of the state remained in Indian hands under a treaty which made it clear that the ruler was subordinate to the company. Like the original Oudh treaty which was the beginning of company diplomacy with the Indian princes, it was imposed on a defeated enemy, and Wellesley's subsequent diplomacy revolved round the twin poles of favourable treaties of the Hyderabad type and harsh treaties of the Mysore type.

The company did not think the Great Mogul, whose power had shrunk to a small area around Delhi, could be any use to its diplomatic offensive, although it was at least as polite to him as any of the other effective rulers in India had been. Wellesley began pushing all the princes willing to hand control of their foreign policy to the company into a framework of treaties which left them internal autonomy to rule their states as they thought fit, as long as they paid the subsidies and provided the military support required of them. Eventually about 40 per cent of the land area of India was controlled indirectly by the company through these treaties, although, as they covered a good deal of the desert area of Rajputana and very little of the highly populated Ganges and Indus valleys, the princes ruled only about a third of the population.

The treaties would not have remained effective for long unless the company had showed its allies that it was able to protect them, and between 1802 and 1805 Wellesley confronted the Maratha Confederacy. It was not as united as it had been twenty years earlier and, while there was some fierce fighting in 1803, the company was able after Arthur Wellesley's victory at Assaye to make treaties with different Maratha sections, giving it diplomatic control of the area south of the Ganges. The company rounded off this career of conquest and expansion by advancing up the Ganges and taking over so much of the land ruled directly by the Great Mogul that he was reduced to being its puppet. In half a dozen years Wellesley had turned the company from one major political power among six or eight others into a dominant force that could expect other powers in India to acknowledge its superiority and respect its wishes. The East India Company could never have moved forward against the power of a united Mughal

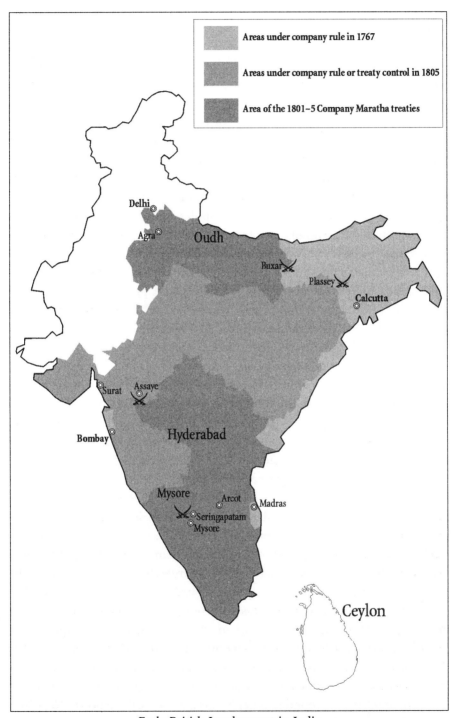

Early British Involvement in India

empire, and probably would not have wanted to do anything of the sort had it been able to count on the level of law and order which had let it build up its trading position so satisfactorily in the late seventeenth century. Once the unity of the Mughal empire had broken down and the company had become one of the leading powers in India, it could use its wealth and resources in Bengal to displace all the other potential contenders for power. A well-trained army, a steady flow of funds to its soldiers and suppliers, and a greater concern for peace and stability than any of its rivals, made the company acceptable as the paramount power to people in India who saw warfare and anarchy as the alternative.

Wellesley's triumphs were far from popular in London. The shareholders much preferred Cornwallis's approach, which had brought increases in dividends, to a policy of expansion which brought deficit and debt. Wellesley had a nobleman's disdain for the instructions from the company directors asking him to keep down expenditure. He could probably have got away with telling the cabinet minister in charge of Indian affairs of his 'utter contempt' for the directors (whom on less official occasions he called 'the cheesemongers') if the government had continued to believe in his policy, but the ministers who had previously supported preemptive expansion grew uneasy about the scope of his ambition. He managed to send his resignation to London in 1805 before the directors could dismiss him, but the company was clearly determined to get back to the earlier policy of peace and frugality.[2] Cornwallis was appointed to a second term as governor-general; although he died very soon afterwards, the government did its best to work with the directors in bringing back his policy.

This was a period of far greater government spending, and far larger debts, than ever before. Wellesley's policy of expansion increased the company's debt by £20,000,000, but this could be seen as a small price for such a large step towards rule over a subcontinent. The British government was increasing its own National Debt by a larger amount every year in the wars with France, which were imposing a great strain on its resources. For a time Napoleon seemed to be a less disturbing force than the revolutionaries of the 1790s, and peace was agreed in 1802 on terms which required the British government to return the colonies taken from France and its allies (and also to abandon the empty claim to be kings of France that British monarchs had maintained for centuries). But the peace of Amiens lasted for only about twenty months. When it was clearly breaking down, Napoleon showed how little he thought of the prospects of France's overseas empire by selling to the United States the old territory of Louisiana, or New France, west of the Mississippi, which had been retained under the 1763 treaty.

When war resumed the British once more captured all the territory taken from the Dutch which had been returned at the peace of Amiens, and later in the war the government of India felt local conditions were stable enough for it to organise an expedition to capture the East Indian island of Java and a number of bases in the other Dutch islands. Spain had originally been allied with France in the years after 1714 because the two countries were ruled by two related branches of the Bourbon family. The alliance had survived even after the French executed their Bourbon monarch, with the result that the Spanish navy suffered along with the French in the culminating British naval triumph at Trafalgar. But when Napoleon turned on Spain and tried to secure the throne for one of his brothers, Spain resisted, and the Spanish colonies began declaring themselves independent. The subsequent fighting in South America went on longer than the American War of Independence; the Spanish Empire was far larger than the thirteen colonies and the Spanish monarchy had much more effective support among the local population than the British had had in North America. The British and American governments were sympathetic to the movement for independence, but never provided the direct assistance that France had given the thirteen colonies. By the 1820s the Spanish had been forced out of all their mainland colonies, though they retained islands like Cuba and the Philippines until the 1890s. Napoleon's attack on the Spanish monarchy had developed into an attack on the Portuguese monarchy as well, and the king of Portugal had had to take shelter in Brazil. When the Brazilians thought of independence, they were much more polite and moderate than the Spanish colonies. In 1822 Brazil became a separate kingdom under the king's brother, who in the fullness of time elevated himself to the rank of emperor.

When the peace settlement was completed in 1815, the British took colonies from the Dutch in the West Indies. They withdrew from the Dutch East Indies but kept the supply points of Cape Colony and Ceylon, which meant that the Dutch would not be able to help their colonies in any future wars. The restored Dutch monarchs got financial compensation for the loss of the Cape, and also became rulers of Belgium until this union fell apart in 1830, but their position outside Europe was weakened more directly by the peace settlement than that of any other country. The Spanish and Portuguese empires in America were ended by internal revolt, in the same way as the British lost the thirteen colonies, but the Dutch lost their imperial position because of British naval supremacy.

Britain was certainly the most successful imperial power of the period. It stood alone as a worldwide empire at the end of the war, though the British expansion in India which was such an important change during the period of the long wars had very little to do with the misfortunes of the other European powers. One of Britain's objectives in the peace negotiations had nothing to do with territorial acquisition: in 1807 the British parliament had made the slave trade illegal, and the government wanted the other European powers to do the same thing as part of the peace settlement. The British gained the diplomatic agreement they wanted: Russia, Austria and Prussia, the continental powers which had done most to defeat France, had no interest in the slave trade and no reason to disagree with a valued ally, while France was in no position to oppose the idea. Spain and Portugal, which could still hope to do well out of slave-grown sugar from their American colonies and in particular from Cuba and Brazil, were unwilling to defy the other European powers openly; but they, and the United States, were unwilling to support serious steps against the slave trade. Slave-grown cotton and sugar continued to depend on a trade that had been made illegal by international agreement. Britain kept up a 'slave squadron' to intercept ships carrying slaves across the Atlantic, but final success in fighting the trade only came after the abolition of slavery in the United States in the 1860s.

Britain had been at war with the United States in the last stages of the long French wars. To put pressure on Napoleon's France, Britain had established a blockade which became increasingly restrictive after the battle of Trafalgar. British sailors working on American ships intercepted by the blockade were likely to be pressed into service in the Royal Navy. The blockade itself and the claim to conscript sailors on American ships caused friction between Britain and the United States, eventually becoming the official cause of the war that broke out in 1812. American enthusiasm for the war was much stronger inland than in coastal districts, which suggests that expansion into Upper Canada, which had good water connections with the outside world for its grain and lumber, was what really roused the American 'war-hawks' of 1812. British forces and the Canadian militia were able to hold the Americans back. When the Americans sent a force across Lake Ontario which burnt down part of York (later Toronto), the

British carried out their own waterborne attack on the new American capital at Washington, though a similar raid on New Orleans was unsuccessful. By then peace terms had been agreed: the existing border was maintained up to the western end of the Great Lakes, and the dangers of future disputes in the region between the Great Lakes and the Rockies were reduced by running the border along the 49th parallel, which anyone could define with a sextant on a sunny day, instead of relying on the previous, potentially controversial line along the watershed between Hudson Bay and the Missouri.

Drawing a line on the map was the way Alexander VI had set about separating the claims of the Spanish and Portuguese in 1494 so that they did not fight each other; but it was not the normal way to establish boundaries, which usually paid some attention to the attitude of the local population. In North America the British and the Americans realised that they would have to work out their own arrangements with the existing inhabitants within the areas allocated to them. The 49th parallel was useful for separating the claims of the British and Americans, but it did nothing to settle the question of relations between the existing inhabitants and the local representatives of the national governments which, so far as the British were concerned, meant the Hudson's Bay Company. As a trading company it was reasonably successful, but it could never develop a political system like that of the East India Company. The best it could do was to make treaties with the Indians of western Canada in the name of the British government to enable it to go on trading, and in the 1820s it had to rely on the British government to negotiate with Russia over the expansion of Siberia into Alaska.

Fighting long wars against France and at the same time conducting more distant wars in India and in North America imposed an immense strain on the British economy. It had shown itself powerful and resilient in earlier wars which had not lasted as long and had not taken up so much of the nation's total resources. The strain of the Napoleonic wars was greater, but in the late eighteenth and early nineteenth centuries the economy went through changes of a type that had never been known before. Coal was being used to fuel a much larger metal-working industry than had existed previously. Lancashire demand for cotton from the southern American states to make into cloth soon drove imports from the United States to levels far higher than had come from the thirteen colonies. It had been hard to make the Australian colonies economically self-supporting until it was realised that they had virtually unlimited stretches of grazing land on which sheep could produce wool in the quantities required to meet the expanding demand of the Yorkshire mills. In the later years of the French wars gas extracted from coal began to be used to illuminate cities and houses which had previously had to depend on candles and flaming torches, and steam engines which had provided stationary sources of energy to pump water and drive looms and spinning wheels were used for the first time to move goods and freight around the country on railways. The long wars stimulated the metal trades, and kept up a high level of demand for some textiles, though other pressures would have driven the economy forward even if the whole world had been at peace throughout the 1780–1820 period of change. The population began to rise in a number of countries around 1750 at a rate which led Robert Malthus to his predictions of disaster, and in the nineteenth century disaster did strike some countries, including China and Ireland, which did not develop new methods of production. Wars from 1792 to 1815 helped particular sectors of the economy but they consumed national resources that could have been just as productive in time of peace. The new industries enabled Britain to keep fighting and at the same time feed its growing population and keep its standards of living from falling, as it did in later wars that made equally intense demands.

Historians enjoy debating whether it is useful to call all these changes an industrial revolution.[3] Napoleon certainly believed the British economy was becoming something different from anything seen before. Scarcity had been the general rule of life in the past, but the British seemed to be developing an economy which produced some things in quantities that were by all previous standards unlimited. It looked as if the way to injure them was to deprive them of markets in which to sell the flood of new goods. The British blockade of Napoleon's Europe was simply a traditional siege carried out on an enormous scale, but Napoleon's attempt to weaken his enemy by keeping British goods out of the Continent of Europe rested on the idea that the British economy was vulnerable in an altogether new way.

After the long wars were over a new route of escape was found from the problems of growing population and economic tension. Between 1815 and 1914 several million people left the British Isles to go to other parts of the English-speaking world. Hundreds of thousands of people left for India and other colonies to rule them as civil servants, or to develop them economically as businessmen, or to defend them as soldiers in colonial garrisons, but they had no intention of staying overseas permanently and usually went out with some contractual arrangement that would bring them back to England if they lived long enough. Much greater numbers went to the United States or to Canada, Australia, New Zealand or South Africa, where they could earn a good living even as members of the working class. Between 1843 and 1900 emigration to the United States ran at an average of about 125,000 a year, and emigration to the four colonies in the temperate zone at a little over 50,000 a year.[4] As in the past many of the emigrants hoped to come back to Britain and even to bring back some sort of fortune when they returned, but in the event most of them settled down and became perfectly happy to stay in their new homes. For generations they went on thinking of themselves as British, and until very late in the century most people in Australia and New Zealand and in some parts of Canada had been born in Britain. The flow of emigrants to the United States reinforced the tendency of Americans in the nineteenth century to see Britain as the only country with which they had much in common. When Bismarck, late in the century, pointed out the importance of the fact that Britain and the United States used a common language, it was still not certain that this would wipe out the effect of the numerous small points of friction that divided them. People who had gone to British colonies and stayed under the British flag sometimes thought they might have been richer in America, but pointed to the moral superiority of living under English laws and to superior prospects of economic growth in the future. For some decades in the late nineteenth century this seemed justified.

Industrial development in Britain led to a great change in the economic connection with India. For over a hundred years after 1660 the main business of the East India Company was bringing Indian textiles to Britain. By the beginning of the nineteenth century British mechanised production could import raw cotton from the United States, spin and weave it in Lancashire, and sell it in India at lower prices than local producers could offer. The company did not try to transform itself into an export agency for British manufacturers and in 1813 its monopoly of Indian trade was ended by parliament. The Indian textile trade became the largest single item in British export trade. The company was left with the China trade, and the growing British appetite for tea, then grown exclusively in China, made this a profitable but difficult line of activity. China did not welcome trade with the outside world, or see much need for it, so tea exporters expected payment in silver, and the company faced the difficulties of earning silver which in earlier years had confronted it in India.

The London directors of the company continued to hope for peace, quiet and a clean balance-sheet, but its representatives in India had taken up the policy of expansion, and this could not be opposed as directly as the corruption of the age of Clive and Hastings had been. The rulers of Rajputana were pushed into signing treaties with the company, which brought its territories up to the line of the Indus and its south-eastern tributary, the Sutlej. Ranjit Singh had established tranquillity in his Sikh kingdom on the other side of this boundary and the frontier in north-western India remained stable for over twenty years. The company was constantly pressed to expand by its army and by ambitious members of its civil service, and there were plenty of places outside the Indus valley where expansion was easy enough. In the 1820s it advanced across the Bay of Bengal and acquired strips of coastal territory to the north and to the south of the Irrawaddy delta, which was the centre of the Burmese kingdom, and it also established a base at Singapore to secure its position in the Malacca Straits, the best route from India to China.

Concern about trade with China led it still further. Almost the only product that could be exported from India and command a market in China was opium, and this trade expanded very quickly. The Levant Company and its successors supplied Britain with about 50,000 kilos a year of opium from the Ottoman Empire as a painkiller, as a soporific or simply for pleasant relaxation. It was seen as something (like alcohol) that could cause trouble if taken to excess, but the British government in the mid nineteenth century would no more have thought of making it illegal than it would have thought of making alcohol illegal. The opium exported from India to China had a much lower morphine content but, even allowing for this, by the 1830s more opium was being sold to China than was being sold to Britain. The Chinese authorities tried to ban the trade, partly on moral grounds and partly because so much opium was being sold that it not only paid for the British tea trade but also led to a drain of silver from China. The unconcealed contempt of the Chinese for people from Europe might have been accepted by British traders in the eighteenth century, when China was regarded as a repository of ancient wisdom, but by the early nineteenth century it was seen only as one more sign that the Chinese were out of touch with the modern world. The idea that the Chinese government had a right to exclude opium if it wanted to was not taken seriously. The company convinced itself and the British government that the Chinese were only pretending to forbid importation in order to be bribed to let the opium in, and in 1840 war broke out. The British were quite right to see China as out of touch with modern industrial development and easily defeated the Chinese forces sent against them. The 1842 Nanking treaty gave the company a small base at Hong Kong and removed the obstacles to selling opium in China.[5]

While the company remained expansionist, it adjusted to the fact that it was likely to be in India for a long time and that its government ought to keep in step with the broad drift of change in Britain. Trying to prevent widow-burning and eradicating the practice of thagi by people whose religious beliefs required them to murder travellers were exotic issues which naturally attracted attention, but probably India was affected more deeply by changes taken for granted by people in Britain. Nobody expected elections and representative assemblies, but newspapers began to appear in English and in Indian languages and the government encouraged English-language education; political development in India would obviously have run in a very different direction if nothing of this sort had been undertaken. Lord William Bentinck, the governor-general from 1827 to 1835, was one of the first people to apply the terminology of 'reform' in India, by which he meant what later on would be called modernisation. He knew that British economic advance had caused dislocation and, while he could see that the provision of machine-made cotton cloth was reducing the cost of living for the great majority of Indians, he could also see that it was destroying the way of life of Indian handloom weavers in much the way that it was affecting the position of men doing a similar job in Britain.

At the same time as they started to export a flood of metal and textile products, the British were able to offer a new range of services. During the long wars with France the City of London had floated loans for the British government and its allies, and after 1815 it began lending to almost all parts of the world which needed large loans. Governments in North and South America soon took the place of European governments, and governments in British colonies were naturally seen as attractive customers who would negotiate in English about loans and could be expected to repay punctually. The City was ready to lend to large operations in Britain like railways, but the family firms which dominated the rest of British industrial activity were never seen as attractive financial prospects.[6]

The long period of resistance to the dynamic force of the French Revolution left the British government in no mood for radical domestic change.
It was ready to give a certain amount of support to independence movements
in South America and in Greece, but it could see little need for reform in
its colonies. The new territories gained in 1815 had brought a number of
Dutch subjects under British rule. While this did not raise religious
prejudices in the way that the Catholicism of the French in Quebec had
done, the government saw no need for elected assemblies which the Dutch
would dominate, just as it did not want to have an assembly in New South
Wales that would be controlled by ex-convicts. It set up a nominated
council of important members of the colony to assist the governor when
legislation had to be passed. Governors of colonies of this sort, which came
to be known as Crown Colonies, were given powers much more like those
held by governors in India or a military base like Gibraltar than those in
the West Indian or the old American colonies. Quebec had been an early
example of a Crown Colony until it had moved on to representation in
an assembly in 1791, but no similar changes followed for several years. New
South Wales flourished as the market for wool grew and a new section
with fewer convicts developed further south around Melbourne. An altogether more respectable colony was launched in South Australia, but all
of them remained as Crown Colonies. People from Australia went further
east to New Zealand and began settling there. The British government took
its time deciding how to respond to this but eventually it asserted a claim
to the two islands, if only to guard against a faint risk of French involvement,
and in 1840 it committed itself to the treaty of Waitangi with some North
Island Maori leaders. They had no claim to speak for all Maoris, but the
principles of the treaty, and its restrictions on the way that land passed
from Maori control into the hands of British settlers, established a framework for relations with the existing population rather like that provided
in British North America by the 1763 proclamation. No such framework
was set up in Australia, where the settlers were more ready to think of the
existing population as wild animals who could be shot as game.

While the creation of elected assemblies was not taken for granted in
the early nineteenth century as it had been fifty years earlier,[7] the authority
of some existing assemblies was also questioned. The assemblies in the
West Indian islands, which naturally were devoted to maintaining slavery,
were regarded with disapproval. Abolition of the slave trade led on to a
willingness to attack the institution of slavery, and to intervene in West

Indian affairs. When the local assemblies were unable to defend themselves against slave revolts without calling on British assistance, anti-slavery opinion in Britain won support by asking why garrisons provided by taxpayers to resist invasion were being used for these operations. In the 1830s a spirit of reform dominated British politics, and the emancipation of slaves throughout the empire was high on the agenda. Owning slaves had been entirely legal in its day, and when slavery was ended in 1834 the owners received compensation of £20,000,000 (the British government's total revenue for about six months), a payment made partly because the plantation owners were so deeply in debt to so many financial interests that emancipation without compensation would have ruined as many people in Britain as in the West Indies.

Parliament barely considered the effect on Cape Colony of the change. The British had originally thought they could secure Cape Town as a very useful naval base and leave the existing Afrikaner population to look after its own affairs inland. But some of the flood of emigration from Britain after 1815 flowed out to the Cape and increased the demand for land; British missionary societies also took an interest in the new colony and its African population. The Afrikaners, who had first come to Africa when religious feeling in Europe was high and embittered by the seventeenth-century wars of religion, saw the Africans as children of Canaan who ought to be slaves in accordance with their reading of the Bible.[8] Missionaries from Britain saw the Africans as souls to be saved. No doubt they agreed with the imperial officials who ruled Cape Colony that the Africans were primitive and uncivilised, but then neither the officials nor the missionaries thought the Afrikaners were much better. Disputes and misunderstandings about the policy to be adopted to the African population had led to tension on a number of occasions, tempered by the fact that there was a great deal of relatively empty, if rather barren, land on the western side of southern Africa into which people could move if they were discontented.

Emancipation of slaves in 1834 made matters much worse. Although the Boers (farmers, in Afrikaans) who owned slaves were entitled to share in the compensation, they had no agents and lawyers to help them collect their money, and they saw the whole process as a piece of robbery, and as neglect of the teaching of the Bible which could only be explained by the malign influence of the missionaries. Some Afrikaners were so angered by the new policy that they decided to leave the British colony and move into the interior to acquire new land there. This Great Trek was a bold step to take. The muskets of the day were barely enough to protect them against African spearmen; when Africans tried to drive them back the best the Afrikaners could do was to link their ox-carts together in *laagers* or defensive formations and stand a siege until the Africans gave up. Southern Africa was much more densely populated on the east side than on the west side and the eastward advance of the Europeans along the coastline from Cape Town was already running into stiff resistance around the River Kei. Afrikaners who trekked east towards the Indian Ocean when they went inland encountered the formidable Zulu warrior kingdom and had great difficulty maintaining a position there. The British authorities were not pleased by the advance inland, with all the disturbance that it might cause among Africans. They were particularly worried by the possibility of an independent Afrikaner state with access to the sea, and officially established a small British settlement at Durban in 1842 to control the coastline. The Afrikaners gave up their move to the east and advanced into less densely populated land north of the Orange river and then of the Vaal river where they could push aside the Africans and take almost unlimited land to set up very large farms for grazing their cattle. After an attempt to extend imperial authority over them, the British made agreements with the Afrikaners between the Vaal and the Orange river (the Orange Free State) in 1848 and with the Afrikaners north of the Vaal (the Transvaal) in 1852. While the agreements required the Afrikaner states to undertake not to reestablish slavery and contained the usual provisions to stop them conducting a foreign policy of their own, they gained complete freedom to run their local affairs.

This was a very different approach from the policy of tight central control of the empire that had been visible around 1815, but it was only a natural parallel to changes that had been taking places in a number of colonies in the 1830s and 1840s. English-speaking Upper Canada and French-speaking Lower Canada broke into revolt in the late 1830s, when some of the discontent was attributed to a problem that could be seen in both colonies. Small groups of the privileged and prosperous gathered round the governor of Lower Canada and the lieutenant governor of Upper Canada and set about persuading these representatives of the London government that people who asked for reform were disloyal revolutionaries who wanted to overthrow British institutions and hand the colonies over to the French or the Americans. The governors, who tended to feel lucky to have such loyal supporters to warn them of danger, went on to give the 'château clique' and the 'family compact' – as their enemies nicknamed them – preferential treatment for government jobs, grants of frontier land and funds for development projects.

This may simply have been the normal process by which governments reward their supporters, but it certainly led to discontent, articulated clearly and passionately in Upper Canada by the politician and journalist, William Lyon Mackenzie. In Lower Canada it was intensified by differences of religion and language which left the majority of the population feeling excluded. In the late 1830s most of the industrialised world was suffering from the depression which encouraged movements like Chartism in Britain. Rebellions broke out in Upper and Lower Canada in 1837. The *patriotes* of Lower Canada may have hoped that troops in Upper Canada would be unable to move east because of Mackenzie's rebellion there, but the British authorities soon saw that Mackenzie was no danger and that the local militia was ready and able to deal with his uprising. The British regular army in Canada was concentrated at Montreal and defeated the rebels, though these rebels had sufficient determination to launch a second rebellion in 1838, which was also suppressed.

The British government was relieved that law and order had been restored but realised that this was not the end of the problem. Lord Durham was sent out to assess the situation in the two Canadas, and given wide-ranging powers as governor. He spent five months in Canada from May to November 1838, and published his report in February 1839. He was disturbed by the great gap between English-speaking and French-speaking Canadians, and by the old-fashioned constitutional arrangements for government in Canada. He put the case for merging the two Canadas with a single parliament, and for giving that parliament effective power. In Britain, he argued, parliament and the monarch had shared power ever since 1688 because the monarch chose ministers acceptable to parliament, but in Canada (and, he could have said, in all other colonies as well) the governors chose their ministers and the local assemblies had no power to do anything about it. Durham said that governors ought to choose ministers who were supported by a majority in the assembly and were responsible to the assembly in the sense that they had to resign if they lost the support of the majority. He added that the French-Canadians should be assimilated by being convinced that British political institutions fitted their needs very well.

In London the government thought there was a lot to be said for Durham's approach but was worried that, if ministers in a colony directed its foreign policy, they might get into a war which involved the whole empire. Britain was powerful enough at sea not to be very worried about diplomatic problems caused by the colonies and – except in Canada – they had no neighbours who could threaten them in the way France and Spain had threatened the West Indian and North American colonies in the seventeenth and eighteenth centuries. While the colonies were not going to be allowed to involve Britain and her military and naval strength in local quarrels, the British government was ready, with this reservation, to unite the assemblies of the two Canadas and to instruct governors to choose ministers who could put together a majority in the assembly. Upper Canada and Lower Canada remained distinct units with separate legal and ecclesiastical arrangements, rather like England and Scotland, but the Act of Union of 1840 gave them a single parliament with equal numbers of MPs from Upper and Lower Canada (now to be known as Canada West and Canada East). In the 1840s the governors of Canada took their instructions to mean that they should act like eighteenth-century monarchs, choosing ministers who suited their views and then deploying the influence of the executive to support them. These governors responded to the feelings of the assembly in the way that British monarchs after 1688 had kept in touch with movements of opinion in parliament, which may have been all that Durham intended or the government in London was ready to provide. Governors were able to keep in office the governments they wanted by active intervention in the elections of 1840 and 1844, though this clearly had dangers for the future.

In Britain parliamentary activity had been changing in the early nineteenth century. Political parties became more united and more firmly organised; and more and more often the monarch had no choice except to appoint the head of the largest party in the House of Commons as prime minister. In the eighteenth century only a leader who could command the Commons by his own power as an orator or debater could be an effective prime minister, but in the nineteenth century party organisation enabled party leaders to control parties in both houses, even if they sat in the Lords. Once party organisation of this sort appeared in the Canadas the governor would lose the power to choose whom to appoint, and might indeed have to appoint someone whom he had actively opposed. The British government may have seen the problem, or may simply have thought that governors in the colonies ought to become impartial umpires who accepted the pre-eminence of party leaders because that was what Queen Victoria was doing in Britain. In 1846 it advised the governor of Nova Scotia to take it for granted that all Canadian politicians were trustworthy men who wanted to do their best for their country and the empire, and to appoint the leader who had the best chance of forming a government with a stable majority. In 1847 it gave the same advice to the new governor of the two Canadas.

This acceptance of everyone's good intentions was put to something of a test in 1849, when the Canadian parliament voted to pay compensation from government funds to everyone whose property had been damaged during the 1837 rebellions. Some Canadians protested vehemently at using government funds to give money to rebels as well as to those who had stood by the government, and in London the British government had to remind parliament that the Canadians were free to run their own affairs and spend their revenue as they thought best.

Durham had been asked to deal with the problem in the two Canadas and it was not his role to suggest that the ideas put forward in his report should be put into effect all over the empire. The British government realised the advantages of the idea that ministers should be responsible to their local assemblies, and at the end of the 1840s it set out to see how easily it could be applied to all colonies with a substantial population of settlers from Britain or other European countries. The other colonies on the North American sea coast – New Brunswick, Prince Edward Island and Newfoundland – were just as able to look after themselves as Nova Scotia and the two Canadas. They might find themselves drifting towards hostilities with the United States over problems like fishing rights, a danger which led Disraeli to say these colonies which 'will all be independent in a few years' were 'millstones round our necks',[9] but the British government could expect to keep this difficulty under control if it went on directing foreign policy. The principle of responsible government was introduced in New Zealand with surprisingly little concern about the local situation there. If the Maoris were dissatisfied about their relations with the settlers, nothing but British military assistance could enable the settlers to survive. The establishment of responsible government in New Zealand made it entirely possible for the settlers to behave in a way that led to war with the Maoris and then rely on the British taxpayer to provide troops to rescue them. The British government decided that in Cape Colony and Natal it would have to retain authority to run its own policy without having

## John Macarthur

In 1789 John Macarthur (1767–1834) sailed to New South Wales in the Second Fleet to serve as a lieutenant in the garrison which guarded the convicts and protected the new colony against attack. He immediately saw the commercial prospects for the new country: he obtained grants of land, did well out of his position as inspector of public works and joined a group of his fellow officers who turned a not-entirely-honest penny out of selling rum to the soldiers and convicts for cash and also instead of wages for work on their private commercial undertakings. In 1801 he was summoned back to London for duelling, but he was simply invited to leave the army and in 1805 he was allowed to return to Australia as a civilian. The following year Governor William Bligh took up office and set about trying to suppress the trade in rum, imprisoning Macarthur in 1808 as part of his campaign of reform. The officers of the garrison, led by their commander William Johnston, arrested Bligh and deposed him, and for some months ran the colony on the basis that sales of rum were more important than military discipline and the safety of the colony. Bligh was not an endearing character – he had already, as Captain Bligh, been the victim of a mutiny on the *Bounty*, in which he and loyal members of the crew had been put into an open boat in the middle of the Pacific and left to their fate. Bligh had saved his crew by a brilliant piece of seamanship but a suspicion remained that the mutiny had not, even by the severe standards of the eighteenth century, been entirely unprovoked, and people clearly thought his personality had not become less abrasive with the passing years. Perhaps nothing else, including even Macarthur's powerful friends in London, led by Lord Camden (after whom he named his Australian estate, which has now become a thriving New South Wales town near Sydney), could explain the leniency with which the mutiny was treated. Johnston was dismissed from the army but not otherwise punished; no legal penalties were imposed on Macarthur, who clearly had encouraged the mutiny and worked with Johnston's military rule after it. The British government recognised that Macarthur was a dangerous man; convicts might be sent to Australia to make life easier for the British government, but Macarthur was kept in Britain and Europe until 1817 to make life easier for the Australian government.

Fortunately for his family his wife Elizabeth was able to take over running the estate during his long absences, and managed it very well. He spent his period of exile learning about agriculture and in particular sheep-farming, preparing himself to go ahead with his idea of making a fortune out of life in Australia, but by now in a way that was a great benefit to his adopted country. The colony devoted its efforts to subsistence farming and almost the only export-oriented activity was whaling. In Britain, industrialisation was leading to a great increase in the production of woollen cloth, which drove up in the demand for wool. Highlanders were driven from their farms and across the Atlantic to make way for sheep, and woollen spinners imported as much as they could from Saxony and from Spain. Merino sheep from Spain were acknowledged to produce the best wool, and merinos had been brought to New South Wales within eight or nine years of the founding of the colony, but other breeds had already been brought in by people thinking about the short-term problems of getting enough to eat. Macarthur devoted himself to building up flocks of sheep in Australia and to making sure that, as far as possible, wool came from pure merinos, though it took a long time to protect the position of the wool-growers and make sure that crossbreeds did not lower the quality of the wool. He did not himself go into the areas beyond the Blue Mountains, but land there offered immense areas on which energetic sheep could find enough grass to grow good fleeces and provide rather tough and muscular mutton. Macarthur was prominent enough in the colony to be selected as a member of the governor's council and forceful enough to become the leader of a group who were sometimes called the 'Exclusives' because they argued that anyone who had come to Australia as a convict should never be given a position of responsibility. Their claim to be free of any taint of convict descent (never easy to prove in a colony to which so few women had gone of their own free will that a large number of people had convict grandmothers) led to their being called 'Pure Merinos' by the 'Emancipists' led by William Wentworth, who argued that convicts who had served their time could perfectly well become useful members of society. Wentworth's view prevailed and Australians grew to be unconcerned about people's origins, but the merino, and the Macarthur family estate, remained as symbols of Australian life until very recently.

to pay too much attention to local opinion, and governors continued to control the armed forces in these colonies.

The Australian colonies were so far from any countries with effective military power that no foreign policy problems were likely to arise, and the local or aboriginal population were so few in numbers and militarily so weak that they could easily be controlled by a local militia. British distrust of the Australian colonies as dens of iniquity dominated by convicts was wearing off, and after 1840 the flow of convicts fell steadily to much lower levels than before. In 1842 a legislative council with some elected members was set up for New South Wales, though the governor kept all the powers that governors in colonies like Canada had had before 1837. Australian workers detested the idea of competing against convict labour, and they were an important enough part of the community to mean that letting Australians run their own local affairs would involve ending transportation. By 1850 hostility was beginning to take organised form in the Anti-Transportation League. It was a stroke of luck for the British and the colonial governments that gold was discovered the following year in inland New South Wales and Victoria. It was found in such quantities that it led to a gold rush that attracted people from all over Australia to give up their jobs and start panning for gold, and then brought a flood of immigrants form the outside world. The additional revenue meant that Australian governments could look after their own financial affairs without needing any more help from Britain. Voluntary immigration meant that there need be no fears of a convict majority in political life. The British government had not wanted to give up transporting convicts in circumstances that showed that pressure from the colonies had affected the decision; now it only needed to say that sentencing people to go overseas and live next door to a gold mine would not be a real deterrent to crime.[10]

The new colony of Victoria had been divided from New South Wales just before the gold rush began and in 1859 Queensland was also split off from the original colony. Representative assemblies of the New South Wales type were set up in the new colonies and South Australia, Western Australia and Van Diemen's Land (which took on the more respectable name of Tasmania). The British authorities continued to be more uneasy about the position in Australia than in the British colonies in North America or in New Zealand, but by 1855 governors in almost all the Australian colonies were getting the same instructions – they were told simply to look for the political leader who could form the most stable government and welcome him as prime minister. Western Australia went on accepting convicts until 1868, and there the governor continued to control things in the old way until public opinion turned against transportation and it was clear that responsible government would not lead to government by ex-convicts. Political parties in Britain and in the Canadas were not as stable in the 1850s and 1860s as they were earlier or later in the century, but Australian political parties were much more fragile and governors often found themselves trying to hold together a set of ministers who had as little in common as some of the more fractious British politicians of the eighteenth century.

The shift to making colonial governments responsible to local assemblies may have happened because it had often been said that people in the colonies ought to have the same political rights as people in Britain, or it may have been an acknowledgement that the system in Britain was changing so much in the 1830s that changes ought to happen elsewhere. It was also true that the years of the shift to responsible government were also years in which the empire's economic system was transformed. For at least two hundred years, from the passage of the 1651 Navigation Act, the empire had been a more or less united commercial system. The original simple idea that colonies could trade only with Britain and could send their products only in their own or in British ships had faded as the years passed, but the colonies still wanted a secure British market in which they could hope for a monopoly, and the British continued to want supplies of the commodities the colonies could provide, which led to grants of monopolies of parts of the market for imports into Britain. By the early nineteenth century production had expanded so much that Britain's main concern was to find worldwide markets, and the more efficient producers in the colonies also wanted to trade with all the world. In the seventeenth century 'Free Trade' had usually meant freedom from absolute prohibitions against trading with other countries, and it was accepted without question that countries normally imposed tariffs on imports. By the early nineteenth century 'Free Trade' was a matter of removing all taxes that favoured one producer rather than another, which meant it would be acceptable to impose a tax on imported brandy as long as a similar tax was imposed on locally produced gin, providing the government with its revenue without penalising foreigners or giving a privileged position to local producers. By 1800 opposition to penalising or privileging was the wave of the future for economic theorists.

The British took a step back from this policy at the end of the long wars with France, introducing the Corn Laws, which imposed heavy duties on imports of grain. In the past it had been very hard to imagine that a whole country could become a regular importer of food, whatever might have happened in a great city like ancient Rome or in small territories with a specialised export product like the West Indian sugar islands. Britain in the early nineteenth century had not reached this point, and its farmers and great landowners hoped the Corn Laws would make sure that it never did. The emphasis on corn, in a country where bread was still the main food of the poor, gave the debate an added depth of bitterness and made tariffs into the policy of the old-established rich, but Free Trade was such a great departure from the way things had always been done that it could never have been established without exciting and disturbing people.

In the decades after 1815 the tariffs on grain were reduced. They were modified to give Canadian grain a preferential position in the British market by letting it in at a lower tariff than imports from foreign countries paid. When a great many duties were removed in the early 1840s, the Corn Laws remained as the great symbol of protective tariffs. Their abolition in 1846 was a sign that all the other taxes and regulations that protected the British market were going to be removed. The duties which had given sugar grown in the British West Indian islands a preference against 'slave-grown' sugar from Cuba and Brazil were removed; economic efficiency prevailed when it was a matter of choosing between opposing slavery and encouraging economic efficiency. In economic (as opposed to social) matters this was the real moment of change in the West Indies, where inegalitarian prosperity gave way to stagnation and poverty. The Navigation Acts, with their restrictions on shipping, were abolished, though this had very few economic consequences because British dominance of world shipping was rising to a level it had never reached during the days of sail.

The British had built up an empire larger and ranging over far more diverse territory than had ever been seen before, most of it acquired between 1760 and 1840, but in the same eighty years they had mobilised an engine of economic development that generated a flow of trade for which the empire was too small. Industrialisation had been so successful that it could flourish most effectively by finding markets all over the world rather than accepting a system restricted by the boundaries of the empire. The British government appreciated the advantages of Free Trade, and it accepted a very full-blooded version of the theories of the Free Trade economists.

Their argument was that Free Trade was twice blest and benefited the suppliers as well as the purchasers of goods, and this meant Britain's move to a Free Trade policy was a kindness to exporters in the colonies. The Free Trade argument depended on the assumption that government economic policy ought to aim at making the income of each individual citizen as large as possible, but this was not always the main objective for politicians in the colonies. They were often concerned about the difficulties of getting things done in small, thinly-populated countries and saw an increase in the density of settlement as a first step towards controlling their economic circumstances enough to be able to do anything else.

Colonies had in the past found the idea of a preferential system quite as attractive as people in Britain had done and, once they had begun to work out their own economic policies, they began to ask for a return to it. This could first be seen in Victoria, where the gold rush of 1851 had drawn in lots of people who had difficulty in finding jobs once the excitement had died down. Syme, the editor of *The Age*, put the case for protective tariffs as a way to secure the position of new immigrants and maintain their numbers, and argued it so successfully that tariffs became the policy of the working class. This approach spread to most Australian colonies, though not to New South Wales. Other self-governing colonies accepted similar arguments, and the issue came to dominate economic discussions between them and Britain for over eighty years to come.

The great difference between the commercial position of Britain and the colonies was that most colonies exported more to Britain than to all their other customers put together, but Britain did more trade with independent countries than with the empire. A preferential system that helped imperial trade would do her no good if it damaged trade with the rest of the world. For over two centuries it had been perfectly natural to think that empire was commercially useful because it provided access to resources and access to markets. Around the middle of the nineteenth century, this argument ceased to apply. The British still felt an attachment of sentiment to the colonies to which emigrants had gone from Britain and to which they would continue to go in large numbers. British opinion was ready to encourage those links and to use the Royal Navy to protect these colonies. In several other parts of the world the British desire for peace and quiet in which to trade – and, as time went on, to invest – gave them a different reason for intervention. The eighteenth-century breakdown of central authority in India had given the British a reason for wanting to expand their power, and also had made it possible for them to do so. Between 1750 and 1850 the British had advanced into a great deal of territory where the only way to bring about peace and quiet seemed to be to take over the role of government; but for a short time in the third quarter of the nineteenth century they were not involved in areas like this. At the same time economic transformation and the new politics of responsible government went with general prosperity. Peace, prosperity and responsible government made it look as if imperial expansion had reached its natural geographical limits. This period of stable frontiers from 1850 to 1875 was also one in which other European powers showed equally little interest in acquiring new territory, but it ended with a new period of expansion.

# 5

## *Pause and Expand*

The frontier in the north west of India had remained stable in the 1820s and 1830s when expansion was taking place elsewhere, but in 1838 the British began to worry that the ruler of Afghanistan, Dost Mohammed, was becoming attracted by the idea of an alliance with Russia. If he made this alliance and it led to the sort of subordination that the British expected of their own princes in India, Russia would have added another useful piece to the collection of disorganised states it was acquiring to the south of its Siberian territories. Dost Mohammed had become ruler of Afghanistan by overthrowing Shah Shuja. Lord Auckland, the governor-general, decided to restore Shah Shuja, so that it would be the British who had a reliable subordinate in Afghanistan. Passage for an army through the Sikh kingdom was negotiated with Ranjit Singh, and Dost Mohammed was deposed. Shah Shuja was put back on the throne, but he had not acquired during his years of exile either the forcefulness or the cunning needed to hold on to power. When a revolt broke out in his capital, Kabul, the British force protecting him did not respond decisively enough to do any good. Shah Shuja was overthrown again and this time killed, some of the British were taken as hostages, and in January 1842 the British force fled from Kabul for the Indian frontier. Dr Brydon was the sole survivor to tell the story of the disaster and, although an expedition marched into Afghanistan to prove that the British could still do so, it was accepted for a generation that the sensible policy was to leave the country alone, intervening only to make sure that its ruler could maintain his independence from the Russians as well. Dost Mohammed, who was perfectly capable of doing this, saw no reason to hold any grudge against the British for deposing him.

The desire for expansion, once reawakened, was not so easy to put back to sleep. Although there was no connection between the two regions, administrators in India and observers in Britain felt that the Afghan disaster

had been avenged in 1843 when Sir Charles Napier stretched his orders
to the very limit and annexed the district of Sind around the mouth of
the Indus. Further up the Indus, Ranjit Singh died in 1839, very soon after
allowing the Shah Shuja expedition to march through his territories, and
left no clear successor. The British, worried when the Sikh kingdom
dissolved into the type of war over the succession that had been normal
in India fifty years earlier, were not surprised when the Sikhs tried to
achieve internal unity by invading British India in 1845. Fighting in the
battles with the Sikhs was as fierce as any that the British had experienced
in the time of the Wellesley brothers, and the British generals fell noticeably
short of Arthur Wellesley's genius, but the campaigns were successful and
by 1849 British rule had been pushed forward to the Afghan border. In
the far north Kashmir was transferred to a Hindu magnate allied with the
British rather than being brought under direct British rule. This border
region was about as peaceful as the border region between England and
Scotland had been in the centuries before 1603, but it was not the first or
the last place where peace and quiet took a little time to catch up with
the spread of British rule. Expansion in this region came to an end at just
about the same time as it had done in several other parts of the empire
and in the third quarter of the century the frontiers of India were almost
as stable as those of other colonies.

In the Sikh kingdom itself, reorganised as the Punjab, British rule was
made effective much more easily than had been expected. The death of
Ranjit Singh, and the subsequent succession struggles, left a vacuum in
which the puritanical administration of the Lawrence brothers was accepted
by the Sikhs, and by their former Hindu and Muslim subjects, as the best
available guarantee for stability. It persuaded them of the advantages of
British rule extremely quickly. Lord Dalhousie, who came to India as
governor-general in 1848, had already been in charge of some economic
improvements as vice-president of the board of trade, regulating the railway
companies in one of their major periods of expansion in Britain. In India,
as in Australia, railways were at an early stage of development, and no
doubt some people felt that Edwin Arnold was lapsing into poetry when
he wrote that 'Railways may do for India what dynasties have never done
– what the genius of Akbar the Magnificent could not effect by government ... they may make India a nation'. While railways did not cover the
whole of India until the 1860s and 1870s, Dalhousie was able to draw up
the basic plans for a complete system and make sure that the railway lines

starting out of Calcutta or Bombay were laid with a uniform gauge for the whole country. Lord Grey, the secretary for the colonies, had done no more than suggest that a uniform gauge might be useful in Australia, but his suggestion was waved aside as yet another case of an Englishman imagining that he knew best which, in this case, he did. Dalhousie was also able to set up a postal service for all of India. Britain in the 1840s had introduced a system of buying a stamp beforehand to stick on the envelope to pay to have letters delivered all over the country at a standard rate of one penny. Wages in India were lower, so its universal system delivered letters anywhere from the Himalayas to the southern tip of India for three quarters of the British price. For people who wanted something faster, cables carrying telegrams by morse code began to link important cities. If India's domestic textile industry was being overwhelmed by the low prices asked for British factory products, growing tea was beginning to provide a cash crop that could challenge the Chinese monopoly.[1]

While Dalhousie was an energetic supporter of economic development, and was ready to see the government intervene much more than would have been thought proper in the *laisser faire* Britain of his day, he was also eager to expand the area of effective British rule. In Burma he united the two existing strips of coastal territory by acquiring the land of the Irrawaddy delta, including the old capital of Pegu. An independent Burma survived inland for another generation, cut off from the sea, but the British had a secure position in the Bay of Bengal. Dalhousie also expanded the area of his control by placing as many of the autonomous Indian states under direct British rule as he could without explicitly denouncing the treaties on which princely power rested. His main instrument for this was the doctrine of 'lapse', which declared that, if a prince died without acknow-ledged male heirs, his state would lose its autonomy. Indian princes often had no acknowledged direct heir and frequently chose a successor by adoption. Dalhousie declared that, while this would be accepted for religious purposes and for the inheritance of the prince's personal property, political power could no longer be passed on by adoption.

In Oudh he went further. The nawab was incompetent and unable to control his subordinates. While Dalhousie wanted to reduce him to the position of well-paid and luxurious inactivity into which the Great Mogul had been pushed in an earlier stage of British expansion, politicians in London wanted him deposed and the nawab himself saw no need for any change at all. He was deposed, a drastic step, taken not because he had broken his treaties or had no heirs but simply because he was not an effective ruler. This left other princes wondering how long they would enjoy the security and stability that were the great attractions of British rule.

Uneasiness about this continued after Dalhousie had returned to Britain, but it might not have had any noticeable effect if Indians in the army had not been worried about a different set of problems at the same time. Serving in the ranks of the army was much more socially acceptable in India than in Britain, and for many Hindus it was the natural way to meet the requirements of their caste. Englishmen in India in the eighteenth century had been so unconcerned about religious questions that difficulties rarely arose, but a large number of nineteenth-century British officers took an evangelical approach to religion and Indian soldiers became afraid that their faith was going to be undermined as a prelude to inducing them to become Christians. The campaigns in Burma had presented problems for Hindus, who had to undertake difficult purification rituals if they crossed salt water. The Lawrences in the Punjab were deeply religious, but they understood how to avoid annoying people of the region over questions of ritual. A disastrous innovation came when new cartridges were introduced which had to be bitten open. As the cartridges had originally been greased with a mixture of beef fat and pork fat, they seemed deliberately devised to cause religious problems for both Hindus and Muslims. Despite assurances that no cartridges had been made in this obnoxious way in the arsenals in India, discontent spread through the army and in May 1857 mutiny broke out near Delhi. The mutineers marched on the old capital and restored the last Great Mogul to his throne.

British and Indian myth-makers have seized on the struggle; even the names applied to it have the inaccuracy that often goes with myths. The rebellion had much wider popular support than an ordinary army mutiny could expect, but it was fought out in a much narrower area than the word 'Indian' implies. In the upper Ganges region, from a little way north of Delhi down the river to Dinapore, the mutiny opened the way to a revolt against the changes of recent decades. To the immense relief of the British this revolt did not spread, even when there were mutinies outside the upper Ganges area. The war against Russia in the Crimea had ended recently, so Britain had an unusually large numbers of troops under arms which could be sent to India, while troops from the rest of India were brought to the Ganges region to defeat the rebellion and crush the

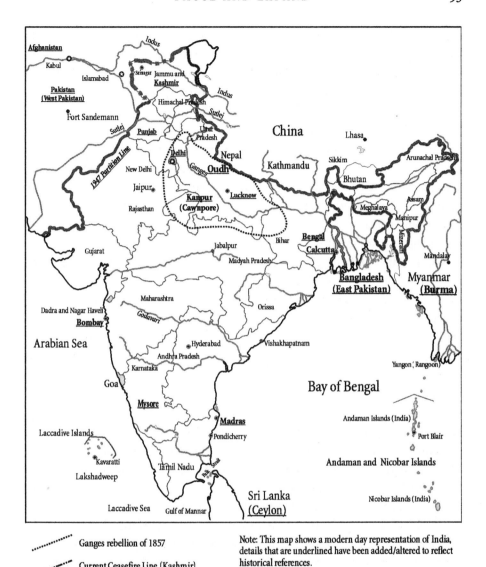

Ganges rebellion of 1857

Current Ceasefire Line (Kashmir)
between Pakistan and India

Note: This map shows a modern day representation of India,
details that are underlined have been added/altered to reflect
historical references.

India: The Mutiny and Partition

mutineers. The rebel army had no effective central command and could not concentrate its forces against the armies advancing upon it from north west, south east and south. The British were particularly pleased to find they could raise troops in the recently conquered Punjab and send them south east to help with the attack on Delhi and the western end of the area of the revolt, but this was not as surprising as it seemed. While religious opinions counted for very little in the fighting, linguistic differences did affect the situation. The rebellion was popular in the area where Hindi was spoken but gained no support in Bengali areas to the east or Punjabi areas to the north west. If British rule had ended in 1857, it might easily have been succeeded by states based upon different languages, as happened when the Habsburg Empire in central Europe broke up in 1918.[2]

The rebellion left Indian nationalists a myth for the future; at the time the British developed their own myth of British courage, with the defence of Lucknow under seige as the great set-piece. They also denounced Indian cruelty and treachery because of the slaughter of women and children in the original mutinies, and the massacre at Cawnpore after it had surrendered to the mutineers. The immediate British response was one of ferocious vengeance on the mutineers or on anyone suspected of being a supporter of the mutineers. Longer-term changes followed in due course, and made better administrative sense than the pretence at rule by the East India Company that had been kept up for decades. The British government appointed a viceroy in India as the representative of the queen, reporting to a secretary of state in London who in the last resort could impose ministerial authority, though it would never be easy for the secretary of state to claim to know better than the viceroy and his officials. In any case the viceroy, who invariably came directly from Britain and had had some political experience, would always understand the point of view of the British government much better than his civil servants or army commanders, who were apt to become committed to an increasingly conservative official point of view.

The reorganisation in 1858 also tried to make it possible for Indians to enter the Indian Civil Service, in the strict sense of the thousand or so men who ruled districts or directed policy. Although administration in India could not have functioned without tens of thousands of Indians who held government posts, the Indian Civil Service was determined to retain a monopoly of decision-making, and its members gave only the coolest of welcomes to Indians who passed the appropriate examinations and qualified to join this elite group. This coolness was part of a chill in relations between British and Indians in the second half of the century, often attributed to British memories of the Indian Mutiny. On the other hand, improved arrangements for travel and for British women to live in India were sometimes blamed for the deterioration. People argued that British men and Indian men could meet easily enough but that respectable Indian women did not emerge in public and could not easily meet women from Britain. It was also suggested with a nudge and a wink that British men had learnt a lot about India in earlier decades by arranging durable but informal relationships with less respectable women, and this was said to be impossible once ladies came to India quickly and comfortably by the Suez route. In fact, British women and their families had been in India at the time of the Mutiny. Perhaps the change was simply part of the rising tide of concern about respectability that swept over Victorian Britain.

The widening of the gulf between British and Indians was accompanied by a shift away from the reforming policies of governors like Dalhousie and the abandonment of his policy of 'lapse'. This was entirely understandable; popular support for rebellion had come from people who had been disturbed by the pace of modernisation and in particular from those who were worried by the threat to princely power. The politicians who made the queen's involvement in Britain's rule over India more directly visible hoped that this would improve links with the princes and turn them into noblemen of a Whiggish type, ready to undertake administrative duties and help run the country efficiently. This was not the way the princes saw their destiny; in England the Marquess of Hartington might move on from his well-known affair with 'Skittles' (otherwise Catherine Walters) to a decorous life of yawning at his own political speeches, but the Indian princes saw very little point in such a sober way of life. This left the way open for new groups of Indians to mount their own challenge to British power in later generations.

The move away from radical action suited Britain's overseas policy in the 1850s and 1860s, which rested on an aggressive defence of the status quo rather than a desire for expansion. The Crimean War against Russia (1853–56) was fought a long way from Britain or any British possessions, in alliance with France which was reinventing imperialism under Napoleon III. The war brought Lord Palmerston to office, who expressed very well the mood of readiness to exercise power at a distance without having any territorial objectives in mind. He was of course committed to holding on

to power in India, but at the same time his government was on bad terms
with China. Disputes over trading posts, including the British port at
Hong Kong, and over the rights of merchants under the protection of
European powers led to a war in which Lord Elgin marched into Peking
at the head of a victorious Anglo-French army in 1860. The Chinese empire
was so weak that it would have been easy enough to launch a policy
which took the first steps towards repeating some stages of the earlier
conquest of India, but Elgin was content with a treaty that gave Britain
only a few coastal concessions. This was clearly regarded as satisfactory,
for he became viceroy of India a couple of years later.

Palmerston felt so confident that British power could be exercised anywhere within easy reach of the sea that he was perfectly ready to hand
over to Greece the Ionian Islands, acquired at the end of the Napoleonic
wars. While the power that he wanted Britain to assert had very little to
do with imperial expansion, the world altered in the course of the 1860s
in ways that meant his light-hearted political interventions no longer made
such good sense. By the end of the decade Italy and Germany had changed
from being mere geographical expressions for areas made up of dozens
of uncoordinated and quarrelsome little states into nations ready to play
their part in world affairs. Bismarck's skilful unification of Germany under
Prussian leadership had reached its last stage in 1870–71 when France was
defeated and reduced to a position where it could never again be seen or
feared as the dominant power in Europe. The United States had maintained
its unity in a bitter civil war won by the ability of the northern anti-slavery
states to mobilise their industrial power for military purposes. Russia
was making some unsteady attempts at reform and reorganisation after
its defeat in the Crimean War, while Japan launched a well-planned
programme of modernisation in 1868.

Egypt was nominally part of the Ottoman Empire, but by the 1840s it
was clear that the sultan of Turkey could only exercise effective control
there if he had outside assistance. In the late 1850s the khedive of Egypt
was persuaded to accept de Lesseps's plans for a Suez Canal from the
Mediterranean to the Red Sea. Earlier on this might have been of strictly
local concern to people in the Red Sea and at the east end of the Mediterranean, because sailing ships would have found it so hard to get through
the canal that they would not have used it as an alternative to the ocean
routes from Britain to India and Australia. By the middle of the century
passengers were crossing the Suez isthmus overland and travelling down

the Red Sea by steamship, and it was clear that steamships could steer their way through narrow channels so easily and quickly that a canal through the isthmus would soon become very important for British imperial trade. Palmerston, who could see the trouble that this could cause with Egypt and probably with France, did his best to obstruct the building of the canal, but successive khedives stood firmly behind de Lesseps. By 1869 the canal was open and Britain had to adapt to the new situation. At the end of the 1860s a punitive expedition to Abyssinia to rescue some British missionaries was successful enough, and popular enough, to show that Palmerstonian assertiveness, combined with a lack of interest in expansion, was still the dominant force in British policy. In the following decades the Conservative Party adopted his policy of assertiveness, while the Liberal Party tried to maintain his lack of interest in territorial expansion.

Within the empire the British colonies in North America united themselves in the 1860s in a way that opened up new possibilities for self-government. In 1864 the three small colonies on the Atlantic sea coast were planning a local union when they found themselves interrupted by something more ambitious – a deputation from the two Canadas wanted to discuss a much wider union on a federal basis. The 1840 Act of Union had led on to a government responsible to a majority in the assembly, but holding majorities together turned out to be very difficult. This was nothing unique to Canada: in Britain each of the first five governments which won general elections after Victoria's accession in 1837 was forced from office before the next election because its parliamentary majority had disintegrated; and in the Australian colonies governments were even less stable. The issues in the two Canadas were more serious: so much mid-century emigration from Britain had gone to Canada West that it had become resentful that it did not have 'representation by population', while Canada East was afraid that any movement away from equal representation for the two sections would be followed by legislation discriminating against the Roman Catholic and French-speaking minority. The question of Canada East against Canada West was always liable to destroy governments, and might even tear the colony in two. A federal constitution would ease the problem by separating Canada West and Canada East and giving each of them control of issues linked to religion, education and their different codes of justice, while a central government handled issues of communications, general economic development and relations with the British government. Bringing the three eastern colonies into the scheme would help the process by reducing the risk that the central government would become a battleground between Canada West and Canada East, and by opening a wider field for economic development. Ambitious Canadians could look further afield and hope to bring the newly-launched colony of British Columbia into the scheme, and then try to show that the federation (or confederation, as it has always – a little imprecisely – been known in Canada) could take on responsibility for all the land between Canada West and British Columbia. At the same time, the eastern colonies had not really looked forward to a local union, which had simply seemed to be forced on them by economic logic. A federal arrangement would allow them to go on looking after things that concerned them directly, while transferring some economic problems to the central government. They could always hope that easier access to a larger market and larger fiscal resources in Canada would help solve their problems.

There were external questions as well. The United States was bringing its Civil War to an end, which would leave it with an enormous army at its disposal and no friendly feelings to the colonies to the north. The British government had felt in the earlier stages of the war that the South was 'making a nation' of its own,[3] and in the later stages Confederate supporters had attacked the northern states from Canadian soil. Washington declined to renew the reciprocity treaty, easing trade between Canada and the United States, that Lord Elgin had negotiated when he was governor-general in the early 1850s. Canadian eagerness for confederation was due in part to a desire to be able to provide the best possible defence against the United States. The British government was ready to support confederation mainly because it agreed that uniting the British colonies in North America was the most effective way for them to prepare to defend themselves. The British could even hope that, once Canada was united, British troops could be withdrawn and less money would have to be spent on imperial defence.

By 1867 the first negotiations were complete: the two Canadas (renamed Ontario and Quebec), Nova Scotia and New Brunswick had joined together in a federal system. The title of the new state, the Dominion of Canada, drawn from the phrase in the Psalms, 'He shall give them dominion from sea to sea',[4] indicated what would be undertaken next; British Columbia was persuaded to join Canada by the promise of a railway across the prairies, and Canada negotiated to get the Hudson's Bay Company to give up its claims to rule the immense stretch of territory between British

Columbia and Ontario. The company was perfectly ready to give up political power and stick to its commercial activities. Rash prophets might easily have thought that the extinction of the East India Company in 1858 and the disappearance of the political role of the Hudson's Bay Company showed that chartered companies no longer had any place in imperial affairs.

The company might be ready to go, but it did not follow that the population of the immense Hudson's Bay Company territories was going to welcome the change. A small rebellion in the Winnipeg region was suppressed by sending part of the remaining British garrison out to the west, but its leader, Louis Riel, escaped and remained a hero for people all the way from the Great Lakes to the Rockies. The British returned to their policy of withdrawing troops with an alacrity that suggested that they wanted to get rid of colonies when possible. In New Zealand, this attitude was made more explicit. Responsible government usually went with some assurance that local assemblies could handle the problems of dealing with the local population. In Australia the original population was too weak to resist pressure from the colonists. In Canada relations between colonists and the local population had been arranged by treaties for well over a hundred years and, as the United States spread across 'the West' in a combative and assertive way, the advantages of negotiation became clearer and clearer to everybody north of the 49th parallel. While expansion in New Zealand had to take place within the terms of the treaty of Waitangi, the Maoris had a tradition of warfare, and in the 1850s and 1860s they resisted the colonial government effectively. The latter had the advantage of being able to call on the British garrison for support; by 1870 Maori resistance was being worn down and both sides were taking a more peaceful approach. The Liberal government in Britain was not pleased to find its troops used for local wars which, it strongly suspected, only broke out because the colonists were pressing the Maoris too far. It went on to suggest that, if the colonists could not follow a more peaceful policy, the troops would be withdrawn and the New Zealanders might think about separating from the British Empire.

This was not popular in Britain. Taxpayers would no doubt have preferred not to spend money on troops overseas, but they certainly did not want to see the New Zealanders abandoned. More generally, it would never be easy to carry out a withdrawal which left people of British descent, or even of recognised European descent, in danger from the local population. While withdrawing from a colony was very difficult, expansion had not returned to the agenda at the beginning of the 1870s and the British government was still looking for ways to withdraw and cut costs. Cape Colony, which depended for its export trade very largely on the Victorian fashion for ostrich feathers, could hardly be expected to find the money to pay for an army of its own. When diamonds were discovered at what became Kimberley – one of the modest perquisites of the secretary for the colonies was to have towns named after him – the British government noted with pleasure the effect of the discoveries on the colony's revenue. The governor had ruled in the old style while the British government had kept up troops at the Cape, but the diamonds meant the colony could pay for its own troops, so executive authority passed from the governor to a ministry responsible to the local assembly. Further north in Africa explorers like Burton, Speke, Livingstone and Stanley had drawn a reasonably accurate map of the continent by 1870 or 1880 but their activities were not at the time seen as laying foundations for imperial advance.

When it resumed in the 1870s, expansion took place at first in regions where it seemed hard to avoid. The Conservative government which came to office in 1874 was faced with the desire of the Fijian ruling house to become part of the British Empire. Europeans and Americans were moving into the islands and looked as if they might soon become strong enough to push the existing rulers aside; it seemed much safer to swear allegiance to Queen Victoria and become subordinate rulers under her authority. The Conservatives – concerned to avoid expenses because they were committed to reducing income tax to 2d. (less than 1p.) – hesitated, but decided that it would be beneath their dignity to let any other country help Fiji. It is quite possible that the Liberals would have done just the same. In southern Africa Cape Colony's diamond wealth contrasted sharply with the poverty of the two Dutch republics further inland. The confederation of Canada had been so successful that it looked as if this device might solve other colonial problems. When the Transvaal, or South African Republic, was in financial difficulty in 1877, the governor of the Cape hurried to Pretoria and announced that the Transvaal was to be united with Cape Colony. This step seemed very natural to the white minority in southern Africa; if government broke down under financial pressure, the Transvaalers would be unable to organise to defend themselves against the Zulus to the south east, and other states and colonies would have to come to their help.[5]

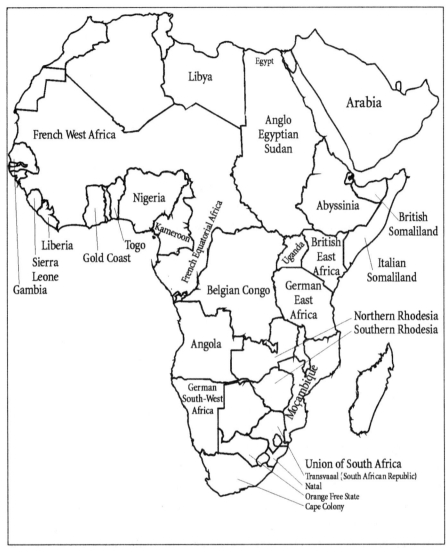

The Partition of Africa

In opposition the Conservatives had sometimes talked about empire in terms of resisting the apparent desire of the Liberals to see it fade away. In office they found themselves involved in another stage of the disintegration of the Ottoman Empire in Europe when a revolt of Christians under Muslim rule brought Russia back in the expansionist role it had tried to play at the time of the Crimean War. Nobody could maintain the Ottoman Empire intact this time, and the 1878 settlement was based on the principle that Russia should not be the only power to gain from Turkey's shortcomings. If Russia was to acquire Bulgaria as a satellite, Austria's claims in the region had to be acknowledged by giving it Bosnia, and Britain's claims required that it should receive Cyprus as a British colony. Disraeli acquired Cyprus as a symbol that showed that Britain was not to be ignored; the same enthusiasm for symbols led him in 1875 to buy the khedive's shares in the Suez Canal Company to show Britain's concern about the canal, and in 1876 to give Queen Victoria the title of empress of India to underline Britain's involvement in India.

Symbols like this may have affected the spirit in which policy was made. In the late 1870s policy became more aggressive in southern Africa and in India. The danger of war with the Zulu kingdom of south-east Africa was not met by prudent diplomacy, nor by building up an overwhelming force, but by a challenge which allowed the Zulus to parry and counter-attack. One British force was wiped out at Isandhlwana; another much smaller force saved itself by a heroic defensive action at Rorke's Drift. Eventually the Zulus were brought to battle in a position where British firepower could destroy their army, but by then the Zulu War had had its effect in the Transvaal. Afrikaners, who did not want to be absorbed into an incipient federation of South Africa, saw the initial British defeats as a sign of British weakness and the subsequent destruction of Zulu power as a sign that it was safe to repudiate the 1877 agreement that put them under British protection.

On the north-west frontier of India the events of forty years earlier repeated themselves exactly enough to remind us that we learn from history that people learn nothing from history. In 1878 the British began to worry that Russia was going to turn Afghanistan into another useful piece in the collection of disorganised states it was acquiring to the south of its Siberian territories. The government of India insisted that the Afghans accept a British mission in Kabul to watch affairs there and give advice. The following year the Afghans attacked the mission, which was stormed with very few survivors. The British were by this stage established on the frontier between Afghanistan and British India – 'the North-West Frontier', a location for stories of adventure for over fifty years – and it was easy enough to send an expedition forward as had been done in 1842 to show that Britain could assert itself if necessary, but this was more a matter of marching round the countryside than any serious attempt at conquest. It was once more accepted that the sensible policy for Afghanistan was to leave it alone, intervening only to make sure that its ruler could maintain his independence from the Russians as well.

In 1880 Disraeli's government was defeated. Gladstone formed a Liberal government after an election campaign in which enough was said about the military and moral disadvantages of Conservative policy in southern Africa, and in India, to show that the Liberals were not going to be drawn into imperial expansion by symbolism or a readiness to pick up territory just because it was easy to do so. It was during Gladstone's time in office that Sir John Seeley wrote, in his *The Expansion of England*, that his country 'seemed to have conquered and peopled half the world in a fit of absence of mind'. Seeley entirely approved of the development, though he wished that more thought had gone into it and that those who held power in Britain had paid more attention to cooperation with the people, mainly of British descent, who populated the self-governing colonies – the illustration he used was that they should be no more different from people in England than people in Kent are different from people in Yorkshire.[6] Opinion in Britain had been moving towards taking more interest in the empire for some time years before Seeley published his book. Sometimes the arguments ran in favour of paying more attention to British settlements overseas, as in Sir Charles Dilke's *Greater Britain*, and sometimes they took directly expansionist form, as in Ruskin's Slade lecture in 1870, when he told his Oxford audience that 'England ... must found colonies as fast and as far as she can, formed of her more energetic and worthiest man, seizing every piece of ground she can get her feet on'. Ruskin seems to have been taken aback when he found this led to imperial expansion, but it is very hard to see what else he could have expected.[7]

The Liberals were at first able to resist pressure in this direction and stuck to the principles they had put forward in the election campaign. They withdrew from the Transvaal, despite complaints that it made Britain look weak, and set about devising terms with the Dutch republics to keep friction to a minimum. In 1884 the London Convention gave the republics authority to run their own affairs, on condition that they continued to forbid slavery and observed the provision against making treaties with foreign powers to be found in so many other imperial agreements. Very few economic interests were involved in this settlement; the government of Cape Colony persuaded the British government to retain a strip of land west of the Dutch republics and east of the Kalahari Desert, but at the time this was seen primarily as a road to enable missionaries to go north in the footsteps of Livingstone.[8]

When economic interests were involved, the government had to respond to conditions in the areas where people wanted to trade or invest. In the middle of the century, traders who ran into trouble overseas usually did so in countries like Argentina or the Ottoman Empire whose governments would pay attention to protests from London, and Palmerston's policy of assertiveness without expansion had suited the situation very well. By the later decades of the century traders were going into less settled areas in Asia and Africa whose governments had relatively little control over their own people and had no idea what protests from London involved. While passing a law forbidding traders and missionaries to go into such places would have been difficult, the British government could not give them diplomatic support as it would have done in more peaceful areas. So it returned to the seventeenth-century practice of giving charters to trading companies to endow them with some of the powers usually exercised by the government. The British Borneo Company, which wanted to carry on wood-cutting operations in Sabah, the northern corner of the island, was the first organisation to benefit from this revival of the old policy. Delegating powers to the company was all the more natural because of the curious arrangements for government along the north-west coastline of the island. The Brooke family, landowners in Kent, had installed themselves as rajahs in the 1840s and set up a government which was fairly rudimentary by Colonial Office standards but did better than the previous rulers in the Sarawak region at establishing law and order. The British government was pleased to have piracy on the Borneo coast reduced, without any cost to the taxpayers, but had enough doubts about the Brooke approach to mean that the arrangement remained unique. The Borneo Company charter provided a precedent for policy elsewhere. In the last twenty years of the century British involvement in Africa relied heavily on companies with charters, at a time when improvements in medicine, including the use of quinine, and developments in transport and in weapons made it much safer to penetrate what had been known as 'the Dark Continent'. In the first half of the century fevers had inflicted unacceptable loss of life on expeditions inland, and the weapons of Africans were not so inferior to European muskets that they could easily be defeated. By the end of the century technological development made it possible to move inland much more easily than at mid-century.[9]

The French had begun advancing from their coastal bases in west Africa in the 1870s. Military men played a very large part in French imperial activity. Germany's victory over France in 1870–71 had provoked a response in which a desire to build up a pool of potential soldiers who might later on allow France to win revenge was combined with a desire for glory, which meant good prospects for active service and promotion. Napoleon III had allowed France to lose touch with the European countries that might have made alliances with her. Politicians in the Third Republic could see the advantages of good relations with Britain, though many of them thought Britain was too closely linked to Germany to make it likely that France would gain effective support by such a policy. French interest in Egypt went back at least to the time of Napoleon's 1798 expedition, and the links had been strengthened because the de Lesseps company which built the Suez Canal was established in Paris and had raised a good deal of its money there. The canal had made communication with India much easier and had helped trade with Australia and China, but it had not done much for Egypt. In the early 1860s Egypt's cotton crop commanded much higher prices than usual because of the dislocation caused by the Civil War in the United States, so it looked as if the country could shoulder the burden of providing the balance of the money needed to build the canal. After 1865 cotton prices fell back. Khedive Ismail had to finance his schemes for modernisation with money borrowed at rates of interest that rose higher and higher as it became clear that he could not handle his national finances with the firm hand needed to stop development costs from running out of control. This had forced him to sell the Egyptian government's Suez Canal shares to Disraeli, though the proceeds did not keep him going for long. In 1878 Ismail suggested that there should be joint French and British control of Egyptian government finance. As he did not cooperate with this system once it had been set up, in the following year the French and British governments persuaded the sultan of Turkey to revive his theoretical power over Egypt and depose Ismail. The French and British now hoped the new khedive would listen to their advice carefully and follow it obediently.

The trouble was that, as had happened in Bengal in the days of Clive, a docile ruler was unlikely to be able to control his subjects. His army rebelled, partly because it was the most modern and the most nationally conscious part of the government, but mainly because measures of economy imposed by the French and British were likely to mean reducing its size and cutting its pay. Arabi Pasha, who rose to command the army revolt, was more of a native Egyptian than anyone who had ruled in Egypt for a very long time, and could call on nascent national feeling to support him. Unless the cost of running the army was reduced, Egypt was not likely to be able to reassure the bondholders, who were predominantly French despite an important British minority, that the interest on the debt would be paid; or to convince the British, with their trade connections with India, that the canal would be kept open and properly dredged. Gladstone's government acknowledged that France was better informed about Egypt and more deeply concerned in its financial affairs but, as the two powers drifted towards naval and military action, the British grew more ready to protect their position in the country. In 1882 anti-European rioting broke out in Alexandria and British ships bombarded the coastal defences. The French government could not win parliamentary support for joining in these operations. Later in the summer it was held back by fears about what would happen in Europe if it became deeply involved in Egypt. These fears meant that eighty years in which France had been culturally and diplomatically the dominant European power in Egypt went for nothing. France was outraged by the way that Britain took up an aggressive policy, so that for twenty years afterwards French diplomacy was hostile to Britain because of the Egyptian question. But the canal was the main British concern and, after the bombardment of Alexandria, this led them to land an invading force and destroy the Egyptian army. The British established what they called a 'temporary occupation', and created a system in which the khedive was expected to follow advice given by the British agent general as obediently as an Indian prince would follow advice given to him by a British resident officer. The agent general would try to give advice as infrequently as possible, because constant pressure would show how powerless the khedive was, yet British involvement could not be concealed. British control of Egypt was sensible and humane, but incipient Egyptian nationalism did not disappear.[10]

At about the same time as the British were moving into Egypt from the Mediterranean, a rebellion led by the Mahdi, a religious leader who preached the need to return to the purity of the Koran, was sweeping the Sudan, the southern province which Egypt had ruled for nearly sixty years. Egypt clearly could not reconquer the Sudan, but British instructions that the province was to be abandoned only underlined the fact that the British agent general in Cairo was dictating the policy of the Egyptian government. Withdrawal might be prudent but carrying it out would not be easy. The British government made a great mistake in entrusting it to General Charles Gordon, a man so completely free from respect for his superiors and from any sort of fear that he very soon decided that withdrawal was unnecessary and that Khartoum, the capital of Sudan, could be defended successfully. For ten months he held out against a steadily tightening siege. When a relief expedition finally marched south towards Khartoum, the Mahdi's forces stormed the city and Gordon was killed early in 1885. Gordon may have thought that his heroic defence would force the British government to follow a policy of reconquest, but Gladstone was as determined to avoid imperial expansion in Sudan as in southern Africa and the Mahdi was left in control.

Gladstone tried to avoid expansion even though his restraint earned him hatred and contempt, yet he was not always able to maintain this approach. In West Africa lobbying by traders in palm oil, used for making soap, pushed the government into declaring a British protectorate to cover the area of their scattered trading posts to the east and west of the delta of what they called the Oil river (now the Niger). When Bismarck had a brief moment of enthusiasm for imperial expansion in 1883 and 1884, he established a German colony of Kamerun just to the east of the Oil River Protectorate and he also set up German East Africa, with its capital at Dar-es-Salaam on the mainland, close to the British island dependency of Zanzibar, though British merchants persuaded their government to declare its interest in the coastline around Mombasa and a little way to the south. The German government enquired whether Britain had any plans for the coastline north west of Cape Colony, and had to wait an inconveniently long time for an answer. The British certainly did not want to occupy the sandy shore of the Kalahari Desert, but the government of Cape Colony disliked the idea of German neighbours and hoped Britain would take over what is now Namibia. Eventually the British government decided that it was not interested, leaving Germany disgruntled about being kept waiting and Cape Colony annoyed that the London government did not pay attention to the wishes of its colonies about areas close to their borders.

The Australian colonies were beginning to think of themselves as a nation; there were no political institutions to unite them but their cricket team had no problem about calling itself Australia. When it defeated England at the Oval, in 1882, English cricket was declared dead and a stump duly cremated; all subsequent matches between England and Australia have been played for the 'Ashes'. When Germany showed some interest in the Pacific Ocean, the Australian governments asked the British to annex everything in the area south of the equator, which would have included Samoa and a whole range of other small islands, and also the non-Dutch half of New Guinea, a little way north of Cape York Peninsula in Queensland. The British, who would have had to pay for all this, drew back. Queensland tried to annex New Guinea on its own account, but was disavowed by the London government. The colonies saw Britain as invulnerable because of its naval supremacy, which no doubt was the case in the Pacific; the British reflected that the colonies paid none of its expenses of keeping up the navy and did not realise the problems that disagreeing with other European powers about colonial issues raised for British diplomacy on other issues. In 1884 the eastern half of New Guinea was divided between Britain and Germany, but the Australian colonies began to think of uniting to have a stronger voice in telling Britain about their concerns in the Pacific region.

While Cape Colony and the Australian colonies were annoyed by the British response to Germany's interest in overseas expansion, Canada was concerned with internal expansion that raised some of the same questions. British Columbia was waiting for the railway line across the continent that had been promised to persuade it to join Canada, and many Canadians looked forward to the new land that would be opened up for farming and forestry as a result. The expense of the project was so large that it was hard to get it started; nevertheless, once construction began in 1881, the lines of rail were pushed ahead at great speed and the main line from east to west was complete by late 1885. The thinly scattered population between Lake Superior and the Rockies, which depended on hunting and trapping, could see that its way of life was about to be destroyed and Louis Riel, the hero of the 1870 rebellion, came back to rouse them to revolt. The Canadian government used the new railway to hurry troops to the scene, the rebellion was defeated and the west was made safe for wheat. During the earlier rebellion at the Red River, Riel had exercised the sovereign power of ordering a man, Thomas Scott, to be executed; now he in turn was executed for what was judged to be murder. It might have been wiser to make it clear how unbalanced his mind had become by 1885 and not to punish him for what he had done in 1870: Riel became a martyr, though more of a martyr for French-speaking Canada than for the west, which chose different heroes when it was dissatisfied with its position in Canada.

In the later 1890s Canada was faced with the problem of an ill-defined border. The United States had bought Alaska from Russia in 1867, but nobody had been very interested in tracing the southern end of its eastern border, defined by the Anglo-Russian treaty of 1826, until gold was found in the Klondike in 1897. It then became important to decide who owned the coastal strip of land from which the gold miners would be supplied. Canada, which looked to Britain to defend its claims, declared that this strip was very narrow. British official maps, and books in print at the time, supported the American case and Britain was unenthusiastic about taking Canada's side on the issue. The Canadians, who felt that they were entitled to more loyal assistance from Britain, resolved to take a more active role in defending their own interests in future.

Canada had had internal difficulties about 'peace, order and good government',[11] and external problems about defining frontiers, but did not confront both issues at the same time or in a way that linked them together. When interest in Africa rose in the 1880s, European countries constantly found that they were negotiating with one another about the frontiers of the territories they proposed to govern. At the same time they were trying to reach satisfactory political arrangements with the African states within the boundaries that their diplomatic negotiations had defined. Some general rules for the game were laid down at the Berlin Conference of 1884. If a government claimed a piece of territory in Africa, it had to show that it had 'effective occupation' of the territory. This meant that Europeans who went into the territory could complain to a recognised authority if they were treated badly by the Africans of the region or by other Europeans. Except in empty areas like the Sahara or the Kalahari desert, frontiers were not defined by taking lines of latitude or longitude, as had been done for most of the boundaries of Canada. Most of Africa was densely enough populated to mean that authority could only be established by reaching some relationship with local African rulers. While it was always possible that the relationship would be that of Kurtz's cry, 'Exterminate all the brutes', in *Heart of Darkness*,[12] this sort of policy made no moral or even commercial sense. The normal British practice of negotiating treaties which committed their partners in North America, in India and in the Transvaal to accepting British control of their foreign policy met their needs in tropical Africa almost as well. In North America it had been easy for the existing population to see the expanding British settlements and assess the advantages of well-defined relations with them, and in India rulers had had a straightforward choice between their existing loyalty to the Great Mogul and the rising power of the East India Company, but in Africa there was more danger of misunderstanding. Any local ruler who was asked to sign a treaty by a government official, or the representative of a chartered company, could tell that people who were able to assemble armies of hundreds of Africans to carry their belongings as they made their way through the continent must be in the service of a very powerful ruler, with whom it would be prudent to have diplomatic relations. In this calculation it was obviously irrelevant whether Queen Victoria was an ordinary human being or existed in the way that Marianne existed as a symbol of the French Third Republic. It was less easy to understand that, once a treaty had been made, a European power would be able to unleash overwhelming strength to enforce it in a strictly literal way and, in exceptional cases, might even welcome a breach of the treaty which enabled it to extend its power more fully.

By this stage the palm oil traders concerned about the Niger Protectorate had united as the Royal Niger Company. In 1886 the company was able to build on the Borneo precedent and obtain a charter from Gladstone's government, which allowed it some autonomous power in dealing with states and rulers in the basin of the River Niger. It had a small army, and some boats on the river, so it was a powerful force in local affairs, but it relied on the British government to handle relations with European authorities. In Borneo no rival European authorities had disputed the position but almost everywhere in Africa European countries kept up vague claims in case they might be useful in future, so no company could expect a free hand. The government was unlikely to try to stop British traders who wanted to go about their business. Giving them charters which saved the government from having to deal directly with local rulers was the easiest way to handle the situation. In 1888 Lord Salisbury's Conservative government gave the Imperial British East Africa Company a charter to operate in what are now Kenya and Uganda, and in 1889 it gave the British South Africa Company a charter to operate in what are now Zambia and Zimbabwe, although for several decades they were named Northern and Southern Rhodesia after the company's presiding genius Cecil Rhodes, who created the two countries.

These three companies were responsible for much the larger part of British expansion in Africa during the years of what became known as the 'Scramble for Africa'. The only real interest the British government had in Africa was in Egypt and in Cape Colony, the areas which controlled the routes to India, Australia and eastern Asia. The three companies had limited capital; their shares were worth something like one-sixth of the construction costs incurred by the Canadian Pacific Railway. They transformed the political map of Africa only because this transformation took place in areas where change was relatively easy.

The Royal Niger Company was a straightforward trading company: some of its shareholders were concerned with getting a steady supply of palm oil for their soap manufacturing; others that the palm oil should be provided at a profit – but for all of them it was a business operation. Its leading director, Sir George Goldie, undoubtedly enjoyed the diplomacy and the occasional outbreaks of warfare in the Niger basin more than the strictly commercial activity, but he always knew that the company's political existence depended upon its financial stability. The company was able to handle its negotiations with local rulers successfully. In the south it had to deal with a large number of chiefs ruling over states so small that they were in reality tribes held together by a belief in a common ancestor and in family connections linking all the members of the state; and in the north it negotiated with a relatively small number of Muslim rulers whose states were rather larger. Very few rulers were overthrown or crushed in the process, as the company was happy to run a system rather like the British network of treaties with the princes in India, acting as an overlord with a number of vassals who owed it allegiance rather than the direct obedience a modern state expects from its citizens.

Rivalry with the French in Dahomey, just to the west of the basin of the Niger, led to the end of the company's political powers. The company and the French had competed to persuade chiefs in the area between the two colonies to sign treaties; it was the decisions of the chiefs which fixed the line of the boundary. But the pressure put on chiefs to persuade them to sign, and the danger that chiefs might decide to sign treaties with both sides, opened up the possibility that the company's policy might lead Britain into war with France. Although the British government had no objection in principle to going to war with France, it certainly intended to make such a decision for itself rather than let the company precipitate trouble. So in 1899 the charter with its political powers was revoked and the British government took over the work of government in the new colony of Nigeria, though the company continued to trade profitably (existing to this day as a subsidiary of the Unilever fats and soaps company).

The two other companies were less single-mindedly concerned with trading profits. The Imperial British East Africa Company was based in the area round Mombasa which had been kept as a British sphere of interest when Germany was establishing a colony around Dar-es-Salaam, but it was ready to go a long way inland. It was committed to the idea that 'legitimate trade' (the term that missionary-explorers like Livingstone had used to point the contrast with the Arab slave trade which took Africans across the north-western part of the Indian Ocean to the Ottoman Empire) was the way to fight slave-trading, and that 'legitimate trade' could be carried on profitably enough to support a company with a military and administrative structure of government. Palm oil exports could pay for all this in the Niger basin, but the British East Africa territory had no useful product to be exported overseas and the company simply lived on its capital for three or four years. It started its operations very far inland, involving itself in the complicated politics of the Bugandan kingdom in the west of what is now Uganda. This suited the diplomatic needs of the British government, happy to see the pro-British Protestants at the kabaka's court triumph over the pro-French Catholics and the kabaka's own pagan supporters, but it did nothing for the shareholders. By 1892 the company had to consider withdrawing, although it was not clear that even this would save it from bankruptcy, but the recently-elected Liberal government kept the company in Buganda as its agent until early in 1894 it declared a protectorate over the whole of the East Africa Company's territory. This was clearly a triumph for the foreign secretary over his prime minister, Gladstone, but it is harder to say why Lord Rosebery was so devoted to keeping the territory when it was demonstrably a source of expense rather than profit. He may simply have felt that it was humiliating to withdraw from a territory once it had been occupied, or that the empire ought to expand into areas that might be useful in future, but he may also have shared the Foreign Office's peculiar notion that control of the headwaters of the White Nile was vital for the prosperity of Egypt. This may explain why the government bought out the company a couple of years later, saving the shareholders from losing their investment. Subsequently it paid for a railway from Mombasa through what soon became known as Kenya and Uganda. In reality so much more of the water that flows to Egypt comes from the Blue Nile, which starts in Ethiopia, that damming the White Nile in Uganda would not have had much effect. Any state that could afford to build a totally unprofitable dam to divert the headwaters of the Nile could no doubt have marched an army into Egypt and conquered it.

Further south, the British South Africa Company (seen so much as the leading example of this sort of activity that people simply called it 'the Chartered Company') was part of a larger story. Cecil Rhodes, an English settler in South Africa who combined business, politics and imperial expansion, had done very well out of the diamond mines at Kimberley; he had gone to Oxford, where he is said to have been inspired by the ideals of Ruskin's lecture on imperial settlement; he went into politics in Cape Colony, setting out to reconcile the interests of the diamond mining companies and the Afrikaner farmers. When gold was discovered in 1886 on the Witwatersrand, just south of Johannesburg in the Transvaal, he invested in it successfully, but he never reached anything like the dominance in diamond mining he attained when he unified the Kimberley mines as de Beers Consolidated in 1888. The gold of the Witwatersrand stabilised the finances of the Dutch republics, making it possible that the Transvaal would become the dominant region in the politics of southern Africa. It also suggested that more gold could be found north of the Transvaal. Rhodes obtained a charter for his company in the first instance because he had obtained from the Ndebele ruler Lo Bengula permission to dig for gold in his territory north of the River Limpopo. The British government may have thought it would be unreasonable to impede anyone who wanted to prospect for gold, and it may also have thought that establishing British territory north of the Limpopo would cut the Dutch republics off from the outside world in the way that the establishment of Natal had done fifty years earlier.

With his charter, and the road for missionaries west of the Dutch republics which the British government had retained in 1884, Rhodes assembled an expedition of miners who hoped to find gold and farmers who hoped to acquire fresh land which moved north in 1890. The expedition tried to stay away from the centre of Lo Bengula's realm, but the fact that farmers, who had not been mentioned in the charter or in the royal permit to dig for gold, had been encouraged to move into the new territory with the miners was bound to lead to the sort of trouble that allowed the company to claim that the treaty was not being observed. In 1893 it duly came: when the Ndebele raided the farmers' cattle in 1893, the settlers organised a small army and overthrew Lo Bengula. Rhodes was away in Cape Colony, where he had become prime minister; opening up the prospect of new land in what became Rhodesia was popular in the Cape where well-watered land had become expensive. Although this was only one of the ways in which he gained supporters, it showed Rhodes's dexterity in dealing with a large number of groups in the colony, providing most of them with a reasonable amount of what they wanted.[13]

In the Transvaal Rhodes's plans for British expansion went less well. The Afrikaner government remained firmly in command; it levied taxes on the gold mines, and it set about making sure that the newcomers to the Witwatersrand – or Uitlanders – should not acquire the right to vote. In other states in southern Africa adult white men gained the franchise immediately; the Transvaal declared that it wanted permanent residents and would not give votes to the mining community, which was very often transient. Taxation and the right to representation had caused trouble elsewhere; the Uitlanders grumbled and talked of rebellion. Rhodes encouraged this by smuggling arms to the grumblers and placing a small force of armed police west of Johannesburg on the missionary road to the north. When it became clear, late in 1895, that the grumblers were not really prepared to do much more than grumble, Dr Leander Starr Jameson, the leader of the police force, tried to stir up rebellion by advancing on Johannesburg, but he and his force soon had to surrender to Afrikaner commandos. Rhodes realised that he had forfeited the support of the Afrikaners in Cape Colony and resigned as prime minister. The British government now faced embarrassing questions about how much Joseph Chamberlain, the secretary for the colonies, had known about the arrangements for rebellion in the Transvaal. From the late 1880s onwards British policy had been to rely on Rhodes to use his wealth in diamonds and gold and his power in Cape and Rhodesian politics in a way that would make the area secure for imperial interests. The Jameson Raid involved the British government much more directly in the affairs of southern Africa: it had no effective allies in the region after the raid, and it now had to work out a policy to deal with the position of the Uitlanders and the rising power of the Transvaal.

# 6

## *The Too Vast Orb*

A short-lived mood of rising imperial enthusiasm made it all the harder to handle the situation in South Africa calmly. The diplomatic moves of the 1880s had taken place against a background of general indifference, broken only by public protests at the death of Gordon. The 'absence of mind' about which Seeley complained still persisted, even if there were solid reasons why the British might have taken more interest in their empire. In 1887 Queen Victoria's Golden Jubilee had been primarily a British celebration, although some distinguished figures from the colonies had come for the ceremonies and had held discussions with British ministers. Hofmeyr, Rhodes's main Afrikaner ally, had suggested that all imports into the empire should pay a 2 per cent duty and that the proceeds should be used for imperial defence. While this suggestion was never put into effect, it brought together two important features in the discussion of 'closer union' of the empire that went on for the next twenty years. The British were aware that they paid almost all the defence costs of the empire; most of this money would have been spent even if there had been no colonies, because naval supremacy was worth having for its own sake, but it did mean that, when colonial politicians made proposals for imperial activity which were unwelcome, the British government could always respond that the British taxpayer was already heavily burdened. On the other hand, the self-governing colonies were aware that Britain was their best market and argued that they could do even better if Britain gave them a tariff preference; they could see that their own countries were not such good markets for British products, but they pointed out that on a per capita basis their relatively small populations were Britain's best customers.

The great changes in communications in the nineteenth century made a united and self-sufficient empire look more possible than it had done fifty years earlier. Messages and orders for imports or exports could travel on electric cables at a speed which meant that trade was no longer a matter of guessing what would please people thousands of miles away. Wheat could be brought to Britain from the Canadian prairies via the newly-built railways. Steamships made of iron could carry refrigerators which would have generated too much heat to be safe on wooden ships. This made it possible to export butter from New Zealand and lamb from Australia to Britain.[1]

Britain had never possessed as complete a dominance of the commercial shipping trade in the days of sail as it gained during the first hundred years of the steamship. Until 1850 British supremacy in naval warfare had depended more on artillery and discipline than skill in ship-building. In the last decades of sail the Americans built faster 'clipper' ships than the British, and while even early steamships were very useful for going up rivers, a difficult task for sailing ships, they were not able to compete in the great seagoing trades. By 1860 ironbuilt steamships could travel much more reliably than sailing ships, and up to 1939 half the world's shipping was British-owned.

Victorian self-assurance was often punctuated by predictions that Britain's place in the world was in danger, and one portent of doom was often taken to be the way that the country could be seen to import more than was exported. In practice the profits of shipping and of the worldwide insurance of shipping through Lloyd's of London paid for part of what was imported, but the most important element of the unseen or invisible exports that paid for the flow of easily visible imports was the return on overseas investment. From the beginning of the nineteenth century the City of London had arranged loans for substantial amounts overseas, initially in the form of government bonds and then as railway bonds and other types of more direct investment. Money had gone at first to the Continent of Europe, and a little later to the United States, but in the second half of the century the amounts invested in the empire rose faster than money invested anywhere else. Indian railways were financed with government bonds, and so were most Australian railways; the private companies that built railways in Canada also had to raise their capital in London. The British government approved of this and, as one contribution to the 'closer union' discussed at the end of the century, legislation was passed to make bonds issued by the self-governing colonies as acceptable for investments by trustees as the British government's own National Debt.[2]

Substantial British investment and the improvements in communications meant that for some commercial purposes the empire was more united at

1. Sir Francis Drake (1540?–1596), the first British circumnavigator of the world, by an unknown artist, *c.* 1580–85. (*National Portrait Gallery*)

2. Robert Clive, first Baron Clive (1725–74) ('Clive of India'), studio of Nathaniel Dance, 1772–73. (*National Portrait Gallery*)

Geo: Dance
May 31st 1794

CAPt BLIGH

3. William Bligh (1754–1817), captain of the *Bounty* and governor of New South Wales, drawing by George Dance, 1794. (*National Portrait Gallery*)

4. Richard Wellesley, Marquess Wellesley (1760–1842), governor-general of India and brother of the duke of Wellington, by J. Pain Davis. (*National Portrait Gallery*)

5. Horatio Nelson, Viscount Nelson (1758–1805), the victor of Trafalgar, by Lemuel Abbott, *c.* 1797. (*National Portrait Gallery*)

6. David Livingstone (1813–1873), missionary and explorer, chalk drawing by
Joseph Bonomi, 1857. (*National Portrait Gallery*)

7. Horatio Herbert Kitchener, first Earl Kitchener (1850–1916), by Sir Hubert von Herkomer, 1890. (*National Portrait Gallery*)

8. Queen Victoria (1819–1901), as empress of India, bust by Sir Joseph Edgar Boehm, *c.* 1887. (*National Portrait Gallery*)

the end of the century than it had been in the days of the 'old colonial system' of tariff restrictions and preferences before 1846. The self-governing colonies, except for New South Wales, used their freedom of action to move towards tariff systems of their own when Britain was adopting complete Free Trade. Hofmeyr's 1887 proposal of a universal tariff for imperial defence costs would not have involved any new principle for them. For Britain any tariff meant reversing the decisions taken in the 1840s, and a imperial tariff meant committing the British economy to concentrating on the relatively small imperial market and turning away from the rest of the world. While this was not going to be done without a lot of thought, and Liberal governments clearly would not make the change, by the 1880s a few Conservative politicians thought protective tariffs might solve some of the problems of the domestic economy and could usefully be combined with measures of imperial preference to encourage the development of an empire that was closely united for purposes of defence and foreign policy.

Enthusiasm for the empire was slow to build up. Even in 1895 Oscar Wilde had expressed a light-hearted view of the colonies when Ernest Worthing was told 'I don't think you will need neckties where you are going ... Jack said you would have to choose between this world, the next world and Australia'.[3] Later in the year, Chamberlain's decision to take office as secretary for the colonies had surprised people who expected him to ask for a more important position in the cabinet. Queen Victoria's Diamond Jubilee in 1897 was, however, a great moment of imperial enthusiasm. Troops came from all over the empire; politicians came from all the self-governing colonies, and from a number of the Crown Colonies ruled directly from London; a great naval review off Portsmouth demonstrated the strength available to defend the empire; and the secretary for the colonies held an official conference with the prime ministers of the self-governing colonies. The prime ministers argued in favour of a system of imperial tariff preferences and their case was greatly strengthened by the decision taken by the Canadian government earlier in the year that it would give tariff preferences on some imports to countries which admitted Canadian imports free of duty. Only Britain (and New South Wales) qualified for the preference, so it was seen as a clear step towards 'closer union'.

In Australia in the 1890s 'closer union' might have referred to a different change, as the separate colonies moved towards a federation. New Zealand

## Richard Seddon

Richard Seddon (1845–1906) emigrated from Liverpool to Melbourne in 1863, and moved on to New Zealand soon afterwards. He rose quickly from running a pub to be mayor of Kunara and was elected to parliament just as the disadvantages of the Vogel policy of heavy borrowing for expansion were becoming visible. In 1891 a Liberal majority was elected and set out a policy designed to help industrial workers and small farmers. In 1893 Ballance, the first Liberal prime minister, died and Seddon won the fight for the succession. Seddon's rivals for the leadership were more radical than he was and also better-educated, a fact which they explained perhaps a little too often. They pressed for temperance legislation and for votes of women, neither of which looked to Seddon like a vote-winner. He was probably right in thinking that temperance was a vote-loser but votes for women was accepted without doing the Liberals any harm. It proved to be the beginning of a wave of reforming legislation. Seddon's own main interest was old age pensions, and he eventually forced the legislation through against stiff resistance to increased government spending. Factory legislation, laws to help small farmers set up cooperatives and the creation of an arbitration court to settle industrial disputes peacefully all helped to make New Zealand into a showcase for state intervention. While a reformer, Seddon was a strong supporter of the empire; like most New Zealanders he wanted Britain to occupy any South Pacific islands which were unclaimed and, although his appeal to the 'crimson thread of kinship' made him sound like a sentimental imperialist, his country was certainly going to feel safer if Britain took an interest in the Pacific. His support for an 'Imperial Council' looked at the time like the quickest way for New Zealand to gain influence over imperial policy. Seddon's policies were ambitious enough and diverse enough to mean they required a well-organised political party of a type that had not been seen before in New Zealand. By nineteenth-century standards he behaved autocratically, often selecting candidates himself instead of leaving it to local associations, and his nickname of 'King Dick' was not meant entirely kindly. Although he was not able to prevent the emergence of a Socialist Party, his modernised Liberal Party was very successful: his thirteen years in office remains the longest premiership in New Zealand's history, and his party remained comfortably in office after his death.

took part in the earliest discussions but it was too far away from Australia and too involved with rather different problems for any formal links to be useful. New Zealand had gone through a difficult period of dealing with a large debt run up in years of optimism. It then moved on to adopt a programme of social reform based on breaking up large enterprises and great estates to open the way for small cooperative businesses, with a heavy emphasis on dairy farming and meat production for export. In the early twentieth century New Zealand was seen as a model for social reformers, but it was not a model that would have been easy to follow in Australia; large estates might not be popular there, but they were accepted as a necessary part of sheep-farming; just as large mining companies were accepted as a necessary part of mineral development once the individual prospector with his sieve and his shovel was no longer enough to keep a whole industry going. Australians saw themselves as egalitarians living in a country where large-scale organisation was essential; New Zealanders were glad they lived in a country where a more human scale of development was possible.

Even uniting the six Australian colonies was not easy. The United States and Canada provided examples of federalism to be followed or avoided. Australians wanted each of the existing colonies, or states as they now became, to have the same number of seats in a senate which, as in the most democratic of the American states of the day, was to be elected by voters rather than chosen by state assemblies. They also wanted the government to be responsible to the lower house, elected on a basis of what very soon became universal adult suffrage. By the last years of the century the major difficulty to be resolved was New South Wales's commitment to a free trade policy which suited the needs of a colony which did well out of exports of wool and of minerals and wanted to keep its production costs low. The five other colonies all used tariffs to obtain revenue and also to protect uncompetitive industries against imports from overseas. When the question of federation was put to the colonies in referendums, five were in favour but New South Wales voted against. New South Wales had the sentimental importance of having been the original colony and the practical importance of being a useful counterweight in a federation that would otherwise be numerically dominated by the large population of Victoria; the other colonies were not going to give up their protectionist policies but they wanted to conciliate New South Wales. As a result, it was conceded that the capital should be in New South Wales, though not too close to Sydney. Eventually, Canberra was chosen as the site. This persuaded New South Wales that it ought to join in what had become a popular movement all over Australia, and the Commonwealth of Australia became a united country on the first day of 1901. As with Canada in 1867, there was in theory no change in the constitutional relationship between Britain and the new country: in 1900 there were six colonies with responsible government whose foreign policy was controlled from London, and in 1901 there was one colony with responsible government whose foreign policy was controlled from London. In practice the opinion of Australia had to be taken more seriously than the diverse views of half a dozen colonies, some of whose populations were so small that nobody could think of them becoming independent, even in a world where small nations like Norway were emerging as sovereign states.

The self-governing colonies were not nations in the same sense as Norway. Nationalism they certainly felt, but it made sense to call it 'colonial nationalism', because some of it was an attachment to Britain expressed in terms of what the secretary to one Canadian prime minister on his first visit to London called 'pride and exultation that I belonged to a country of so much glory and greatness'.[4] People in the colonies who were devoted to Britain were occasionally irritated that the British government seemed to have relatively little idea of what the colonies wanted or how they managed their affairs. On the other hand, leaders like the first French-Canadian prime minister of Canada, Sir Wilfrid Laurier, who might possibly have shown some reserve about the imperial connection, spoke in terms that suggested a fervent desire to strengthen the political and even the parliamentary links that united the empire.

In the last years of the century, events in Africa helped open the road to an attempt to give closer union a definite form. In the years just after the Diamond Jubilee imperial enthusiasm helped to push expansion forward. In Egypt the debt had been handled so frugally and payments had been made so regularly that the rate of interest had been brought down to less onerous levels, forced labour and the lash had been abolished and some modest prosperity was visible. The British directors of policy in Egypt felt they had done enough to stabilise its finances and improve its army to justify an advance up the Nile to subdue the Sudan; Egypt could afford to pay for a military campaign, and the army had been sufficiently modernised to make sure that the Sudan would not be able to offer effective resistance. In 1898, after a well-organised march south, the heirs of the Mahdi were

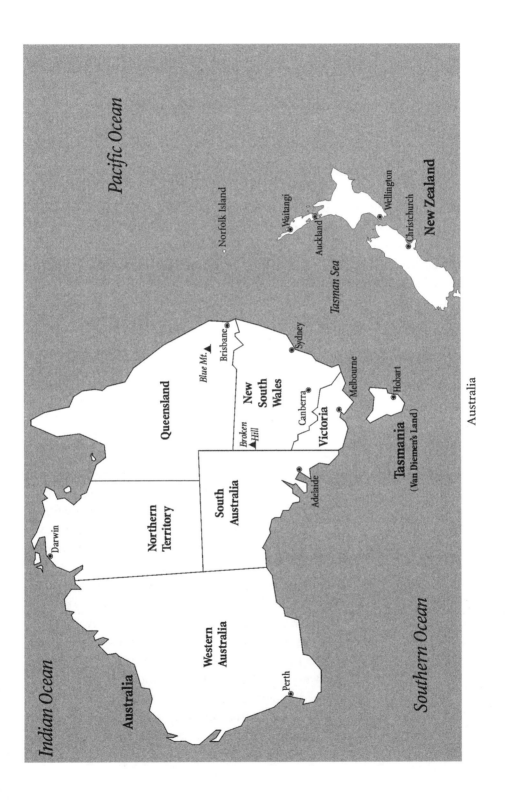

Australia

wiped out at Omdurman by machine-gun fire and artillery with the type of slaughter seen when English archers confronted French knights at Agincourt. This was welcomed in Britain as revenge for the death of Gordon a dozen years earlier. Pleasure at the victory was heightened when the triumphant army moved further south up the Nile to Fashoda and encountered a small French expedition which had made its way there across the Sahara. The French were received politely but were told firmly that the British had made it clear that they would regard any challenge to their position on the Nile as a threat of war. Salisbury, who had returned to office in 1895, had made his diplomatic preparations carefully; France found that even Russia, her ally acquired half a dozen years earlier, accepted Britain's claims. The slaughter of the Sudanese was followed by the humiliation of the French.

It was clear that people in Britain felt no great need to pay attention to the warning against 'frantic boast and foolish word' that Kipling had included in his poem for the Jubilee the previous year.[5] In the same spirit the British government moved forward to push the government of the Transvaal into giving Uitlanders the right to vote. If enfranchised, they would certainly use their votes to defeat the backward-looking government of Paul Kruger, who had come to prominence when leading the resistance to the 1877 attempt to unite the Transvaal with the British colonies. They might even reverse Kruger's policy. The Afrikaners could see the pressure mounting, and they could also see that the British were building up their military strength in southern Africa. In mid 1899 they asked the British to stop bringing in soldiers and to reduce the number already brought in. Lord Salisbury's government was hardly likely to think it was the business of the Afrikaners to decide how Britain should position its troops. By October Britain and the two Dutch republics were at war.

The Boer War offered two large lessons for twentieth-century warfare, though nobody showed much sign of having learnt them. In the first months of the war the Afrikaners showed that riflemen in defensive positions could inflict heavy casualties on any force that tried to attack them directly without a devastating preliminary bombardment by artillery. The British then brought in generals who understood how to advance without launching a direct attack on prepared defensive positions, and they moved forward fast enough to capture the main Afrikaner army and the capitals of the two republics. By mid 1900 the British had recovered from their initial setbacks and expected the Afrikaners to acknowledge that they had been defeated. The remnants of the Afrikaners then provided a second lesson. Once they fell back on guerilla operations, they were very hard to locate and bring to battle. For people brought up on the short European wars of the 1860s, the long drawn out last phase of the war was a great anticlimax. It was taken as proof that the British army was inefficient rather than a warning that the Boer War could provide useful lessons for the wars of the new century.

In 1902 the last Afrikaner commandos accepted inevitable annexation by Britain of the Dutch republics, but the treaty of Vereeniging contained an assurance that Britain would not use its position of imperial power to settle the question of the right to vote of the African majority, and would leave it to South African voters to decide after the return of self-government. British taxpayers certainly would not have paid to go on fighting simply to get Africans the right to vote, but as a matter of policy the failure to obtain voting rights for a small number of propertied Africans was likely to endanger Britain's long-term aims in South Africa. Rhodes knew that the British had to have allies in southern Africa and in his last years had seen that it had become hard, to a large extent through his own fault, to make an alliance with the Afrikaners. In this situation perhaps the best the British could do was to ask – as Rhodes had done – for 'equal rights for all civilised men south of the Zambezi'.[6] But the amount of support for this to be found among the British in southern Africa was limited. The British government may have been wise in its generation to rely on the alliance between the British and the more pro-British of the Afrikaners. That, as things turned out, brought South Africa into two world wars on Britain's side.

The end of the war clearly did not solve all the political problems of the white rulers of southern Africa, but it had a wide range of effects on imperial policy. The self-governing colonies had strongly supported Britain in the war and had sent troops who fought so well that imperial cooperation became a more lively political issue than ever. When the prime ministers of the colonies came to London for the coronation of Edward VII in 1902, they were fewer in number, because the six Australian colonies had been merged in a single country, but they were more unanimous than ever in saying that tariff preference for imperial products was the way to build up imperial unity.

The British government remained as uncommitted as in the past to any idea of changing the Free Trade arrangements of the 1840s, but Joseph Chamberlain as secretary for the colonies had been impressed by what was said.

### Lord Kitchener

Horatio Herbert Kitchener (1850–1916) was unlucky enough to be described in the last phase of his career as 'not a great man, but a great
poster', because of the effectiveness of his picture with the accusing
forefinger and the slogan 'Your Country needs YOU'. But as an imperial
general Kitchener was much more than a poster. The public saw him as
a great organiser of victory, and people closer to the centre of power
knew that he also had considerable dexterity in diplomacy and intrigue.
He served in the expedition that conquered Egypt in 1882, but his career
took off in 1892 when he became commander-in-chief of the Egyptian
army that was steadily being improved and modernised under the
undefined British rule that followed the 1882 campaign. Plans were already
being made for a march south into the Sudan to avenge the death of
Gordon at Khartoum in 1885, and to secure British control of the upper
Nile. In 1896 the advance began. Kitchener kept expenses as low as
possible, even though he had to lay a railway track to maintain his supply
lines with the north, and always remembered that the Egyptian taxpayer
could not, and the British taxpayer would not, pay heavy imperial
expenses. In 1898 the advance reached its logical conclusion when all the
efficiency of modern weapons was used to slaughter the Sudanese army
at Omdurman, just north of Khartoum. Kitchener then had to move
south to Fashoda to neutralise a French expedition which had made its
way across the Sahara to the Nile. He courteously advised the expedition's
commander that its position was completely untenable, while the British
government made it clear that the Royal Navy's supremacy meant that
no external support would reach the French in Africa.

The year after Omdurman the British generals in South Africa did
badly in the opening months of the Boer War. Roberts, the most trusted
general of the older generation, was summoned to take command and
Kitchener, the rising man of the new generation, was appointed second-
in-command. After Roberts had forced the Boer armies in the field to
surrender, Kitchener was left with what turned out to be the harder task
of encircling and capturing the Boer guerilla forces organised in commandos. It took months and months to marshal a much larger army
than had been expected, and to lay miles and miles of barbed wire
entanglements to reduce the mobility of the Boers. Eventually he brought

them to negotiation. Once he had done so, he was ready to assure them (perfectly accurately) that their interests would be safe if they surrendered: the government in office in London would soon lose office and its Liberal successor would restore self-government in South Africa sooner rather than later. With this in mind, the Boers made peace in 1902.

Kitchener was already looking forward to becoming commander-in-chief in India, the highest military position in the imperial system. He promptly set out to concentrate military authority in his own hands and reduce the power of the viceroy and his council. He handled his arguments and his contacts with cabinet ministers in London so skilfully that the viceroy, Lord Curzon, was defeated and felt obliged to resign. As the Indian military system worked very badly in the First World War, Kitchener's concentration of power must take some of the blame. He was aware of his lack of capacity for delegating authority to trusted subordinates, and he declined to become Chief of the Imperial General Staff, the head of the entire British military system, imperial and European, a post which obviously involved close cooperation with other commanders. He hoped to become viceroy of India, the supreme autocratic position in the British Empire, but he had to be content with becoming consul-general (which, under a thin veil, meant the same as governor) of Egypt in 1911. This looked like the last stage of a great career in imperial positions, but in August 1914 he was made secretary of state for war. This appointment was a splendid success in attracting volunteers, and helped the British to raise 2,500,000 recruits while he was in office, but Kitchener was no more able to delegate responsibility than in the past. He could see that Britain would have a important role in the First World War only if it lasted for three years, and that a very large army would have to be prepared for use in France, but he was not able to follow up the implications of his insight. His cabinet colleagues transferred some of his powers to Lloyd George and some of them to General Robertson. They were distinctly relieved when Kitchener was lost at sea when going to inspect conditions in Russia in 1916, but the wider public was dismayed and for months believed that reports of his death were untrue and that he would return, like King Arthur, at a moment of deep national peril.

At the conference he had suggested that Britain was suffering from what has recently been called 'imperial overstretch', which he expressed more grandly in Matthew Arnold's words about 'The weary Titan ... bearing ... the too vast orb of her fate' when he asked the self-governing colonies to go on supporting Britain's military and naval position.[7] Faced by the colonies' requests for imperial preference, he expressed mild sympathy and went to southern Africa to examine the position after the war.

When he returned in 1903 he was convinced of the case for imperial preference. In this decision imperial sentiment was reinforced by his own political background. He had gone into politics after making a fortune as a manufacturer, but he had kept in close touch with Birmingham industrialists who declared that British industry was being overwhelmed by imports from countries which sheltered their own industries behind tariff walls, and that Britain needed tariff protection against this sort of attack. Chamberlain's conversion to imperial preference opened new avenues for imperial enthusiasm. It also won him support from farmers and manufacturers under pressure from imports, who were attracted by the idea of tariffs and saw the imperial side of the programme as of secondary importance.

This did not provide a broad base of support. Only about 60 per cent of adult men in Britain had the right to vote, but enough of them were so close to poverty that the price of food was of vital importance to them. Anything that drove food prices up, whether by protecting British farmers or by giving imperial farmers a privileged position against low-cost farmers from the rest of the world, was unwelcome. Chamberlain and his supporters tried to rally support by pointing to fresh prospects for industrial develop-ment in the phrase 'Tariff reform means work for all', but only a minority of the electorate was attracted by it. The British liked the idea of having an empire for its own sake and did not expect to grow rich out of it, but there was not going to be much support for the idea that the reward for victory in an expensive war in southern Africa should be an increase in the cost of living. Balfour, the Conservative prime minister, tried to obscure the issue and to put off an election for as long as he could, but early in 1906 the Liberals won an enormous majority on the issue of Free Trade. Imperial preference – however popular it might be in the self-governing colonies – looked like a millstone round the neck of anyone in British politics who supported it.

The Liberals may have been helped towards their success by the appearance of one of the most influential of all the books to be written about imperial expansion. J. A. Hobson's *Imperialism*, published in 1902, offered a plausible explanation of imperial expansion and of the problems of the British economy which Chamberlain tried to cure by protective tariffs. Hobson pointed to the large amount of money the British had invested overseas in the last quarter of the nineteenth century, and to the vast stretches of territory brought under British rule in the same period, and asserted that the two were directly linked. The British domestic economy, he argued, was not running well enough to absorb all the capital available for investment. As a result the surplus had to be invested overseas, and the British government had acquired territory to protect these investments. This explanation attracted the attention of Lenin, who put it into a more deterministic form and said that it was the nature of capitalism to generate surplus capital, which led to imperialistic expansion. Because he hoped to evade the Tsarist censorship, Lenin said very little about the position of pre-1914 Russia, but it would have been interesting to see how he would have explained its expansion into central Asia in the nineteenth century, when Russia was generating too little capital to meet its own needs and had to borrow abroad, mainly in Paris, for large-scale enterprises like the Trans-Siberian railway.[8]

Hobson was not committed to the idea that expansion was inevitable or that all imperialist expansion took place because of surplus capital; he was concerned only with the British experience. His argument was that, if the British economy was arranged properly and an adequate level of domestic demand maintained, there would be no surplus of capital. This may have been true. It was often argued that the City of London was much more ready to supply capital overseas than to provide it for firms inside Britain, though the suggestion was usually that this was a failure on the City's side rather than a deficiency of demand. But the imperial question was whether expansion and investment were linked. The answer seemed to be that the great bulk of investment went to foreign countries, mainly the United States, which were fully able to look after themselves, or to self-governing colonies which were becoming more ready to have policies of their own as the century drew to a close. Most of the imperial expansion of the late nineteenth century took place in areas too poor to offer any attraction to investors and too unstable for trade to be conducted without imposing a greater level of law and order than had existed previously. Even nowadays there is no general agreement on the

moral question whether outsiders are entitled to come into an area of
disorder and impose a minimum acceptable level of law and order, but
law and order for the sake of trade, rather than law and order for the
sake of investment, was obviously what underlay the activities of the
chartered companies which took over so much of Africa, much as they
had taken over India and most of Canada in an earlier period. Scholarly
studies showed there was very little connection between areas of investment
and areas of expansion, but the linked ideas that investment caused
expansionist policies and that the Empire was necessary for capitalist
prosperity became established in people's minds for half a century or
more. Later on, part of Hobson's analysis returned to favour when it
began to be suggested that overseas lending had led to neglect of
domestic investment and that, while 'it may well be that ... the Victorians
did right to channel such a large part of their savings abroad, it is
difficult to avoid the conclusion that they must have contributed thereby,
to an unknown extent, to the deterioration of the British economic growth
rate'.[9]

Southern Africa, where money had been invested in the gold mines and
imperial expansion had taken place by force of arms, stood out as the
place where Hobson's theory had most plausibility. Even there the British
would have been unlikely to go to war if the position of the Uitlanders
had not enabled the opponents of the Dutch republics to put the question
in terms of defending the rights of Englishmen. The Boer War and its
great expense, which undid all the patient work of thrifty Victorians in
reducing the National Debt after the long wars with France, decisively
checked some aspects of the imperial enthusiasm of the late 1890s. The
great change in patterns of British emigration in the early years of the
twentieth century suggests that in other ways imperial attachments had
been strengthened: between 1900 and 1913 emigration to colonies of British
settlements rose to three times its previous level and became distinctly
more popular than emigration to the United States, which went on at the
same rate as in the nineteenth century.[10]

In 1907 the Liberal government organised the first conference with the
prime ministers of the self-governing colonies held entirely to discuss
matters of common interest and not as an adjunct to a royal jubilee or
coronation. The Liberals respected the position of the self-governing colonies and arranged that they should be distinguished from that of other
British territories by being called Dominions, but on the substantive issue

they made it clear that the 1906 election had 'banged, barred and bolted' the door against imperial taxation of food imports.[11] While this eliminated the topic that really interested the Dominions, they could still explore questions of imperial organisation. In 1897 Laurier had raised issues about consultation and, while he had now grown more detached about the issue, the Australian prime minister Alfred Deakin brought it forward. As with imperial preference, the interests of Britain and of the Dominions ran in different directions. Britain would have liked to see a larger overseas contribution to defence spending at a time when Germany was mounting a challenge to her naval supremacy, while the main concern of the Dominions was to be informed about British foreign policy and to have some opportunity to influence it in the regions closest to them.

The British government was more immediately concerned about what to do with southern Africa. It moved quickly to make the former Dutch republics self-governing colonies, which was really the way that the British had seen them in the second half of the nineteenth century. While this may have been no more than a desire to keep away from a complicated situation, it gave the pro-British Afrikaners their best chance to argue that the Boer War should be forgotten and that the Afrikaner majority in the electorate should not use its power in a way that went against the feelings of the prosperous British minority and their supporters in the rest of the empire. The four self-governing colonies of southern Africa then went on to discuss how they could join together. Although the British and the Afrikaners probably had less in common with one another than the populations of Canada or of Australia, they nevertheless set up a much more tightly integrated union in which the constituent provinces were left with very little autonomy. This was partly because they wanted a strong central government to maintain white supremacy in the event of an African challenge to it, partly because the British and the Afrikaners were geographically so closely intermingled in the large and rich provinces of Cape Colony and the Transvaal that federalism would have done very little to protect the position of either group.

The British would have liked the Union of South Africa to have moved towards the gradual extension of the right to vote (which had made up a large and generally welcome part of their own political history in the nineteenth century), but the debates about unification made it perfectly clear that the influence of the Transvaal, where people drew strict and stern colour lines, was going to prevail over the milder approach of the

Cape, where some Africans had for decades qualified for the right to vote. In Britain some Liberals asked the government to apply pressure to the South Africans and to refuse to pass the legislation needed to give effect to the Union unless better provision was made for the position of the Africans, but the government was convinced that it had no effective way of bringing pressure to bear and that unsuccessful pressure would only make things worse. The legislation contained provisions to make it hard for the South African government to reduce the tenuous rights of the Africans any further, which seemed to be the best that the Westminster parliament could do when it passed the Act of Union in 1909.

South Africa was represented by the pro-British Boer leader Louis Botha at the 1911 conference, when it was New Zealand which took up the theme of a central organisation for imperial affairs. The other countries at the conference felt that it was enough to hold frequent conferences at which the British government could keep them fully informed about world affairs. The British government explained how it saw the diplomatic situation in a degree of detail that later on – when people were discussing angrily how much information the British cabinet had had in the years before the outbreak of war in 1914 – led to comments that the Dominion governments had known more about British foreign policy than British cabinet ministers outside the foreign secretary's inner circle. The Dominions recognised the principle that Britain was now spending much more on defence than in the nineteenth century and discussed ways of increasing their own spending, though they worked this out in terms of preparing for local defence rather than making contributions to a central imperial defence organisation.

When discussing problems with the Dominions, the British government was dealing with people who still for the most part felt a deep attachment to it and its way of looking at the world. Sir John Macdonald who, as prime minister of Canada, had played a leading role in the original confederation negotiations and the main role in bringing other provinces into confederation and arranging the building of the Canadian Pacific Railway, was a devoted British subject of the generation that believed the desire to run their own local affairs was entirely compatible with Seeley's idea that people in the Dominions should be no more different from people in England than people in Kent are different from people in Yorkshire. By the early years of the twentieth century Dominion politicians were becoming aware of ways in which their interests and feelings were different from those of the British. Sometimes they thought it would be useful to have a permanent organisation in which the Dominions and the British government were represented. More often they felt that the best approach was for British and Dominion prime ministers to meet for regular discussions, though this did not mean that they thought their governments stood on a basis of equality with the British government. Some of the politicians still thought of themselves as British, and undoubtedly many of their voters thought themselves British, if only because recent immigrants from Britain made up a large minority of the population of the Dominions. Possible lines of political division could easily be seen in Canada and the South African colonies, where many voters had no direct links to Britain and did not speak English as their mother-tongue; and in Australia there was an Irish minority, mainly poorer than the British-descended majority. An appeal to an Australian identity was the natural way to reduce the influence, internal and external, of the British and those who saw themselves as British. People in the Dominions who had never seen Britain, and who knew that their interests did not always run in the same direction as those of Britain, were naturally likely to pick up the idea of national identity, though in the years before 1914 this had not overtaken the dominant force of British sentiment.

The Liberal government in Britain had also to face the growth of national feeling within a small section of the population of India. There was no reason to question the view of the administrative rulers of India that almost all Indians still thought about politics in terms of personal loyalty; their great-grandparents had been loyal to the Great Mogul or to an Indian prince and that loyalty had been transferred to Queen Victoria and her descendants. It might be transferred easily enough to a new ruler, but it would be a much larger step for personal loyalty to be replaced by the type of political devotion to a nation that was becoming so widespread in Europe. The minority of Indians who had learnt about British political ideas in the course of preparing for jobs linked to the government of India had, however, reached rather a different position. Very few of them were able to enter the central elite, the Indian Civil Service, but many of them obtained other government positions or else, as teachers, lawyers and journalists, had jobs that depended on the new system of government that the British had developed in India.

The Indians who benefited from the new arrangements would have lost ground if there had been a return to the old system of personal loyalty;

## Sir John Macdonald

John A. Macdonald (1815–1891) was born in Glasgow but his family moved to Canada five years later. (Canadian politics were sufficiently dominated by Scotsmen to mean that he needed the A. in his name to distinguish him from John Sandfield Macdonald, a man of considerable importance in mid nineteenth-century politics in Upper Canada.) He served in the militia against Mackenzie's rebellion in 1837, but never mentioned the divisive subject in public. He first held office in one of the ministries of the 1840s installed and supported by the governor of the day. Once it was established that governors should choose ministers simply on the basis of their ability to put together a majority in the lower house, he settled down as a Liberal Conservative, determined to keep up political and economic links with Britain but ready to end the privileged position of the Anglican Church in Canada. This gave him a flexible enough position for him to be able to base a long political career on the firm foundation of an alliance between the Orange Order in Upper Canada (later Ontario) and the religiously-minded Catholic majority in Lower Canada (later Quebec). Distances were great enough to mean that ordinary members of the two groups rarely met. Their leaders worked together in parliament to resist their common enemies; they had to face the weak opponents of clerical influence in Lower Canada, also known as Les Rouges, and the more numerous Liberals under George Brown who claimed a right to representation by population, which meant that Upper Canada should have more seats in parliament than Lower Canada. Macdonald and his allies saw behind the Rouges and the Liberals the general menace of the anti-British, anticlerical United States. Cross-pressures of religion and regional loyalties made it harder and harder for anyone to hold together a government in the late 1850s and early 1860s. Macdonald was a patient politician ready to back 'myself and Time against any two men', and confident that voters would prefer 'me drunk [which he often was] to George Brown sober'; but when the idea of a federal solution was put forward, he could see that it would solve many problems and welcomed it eagerly. He dominated the discussions between 1864 and 1867 because he understood the fears of so many of the groups taking part.

His skill in finding something to satisfy most of the groups involved meant that by the time agreement was reached on Confederation it was natural for him to become the first prime minister of the new country. Most of the issues that caused passionate division on religious lines, such as education, were entrusted to the provinces, so when Macdonald went to the new national capital in Ottawa in 1867 he found it easier than before to maintain the parliamentary alliances on which his power depended. He went on to persuade other British colonies and territories in North America to join those that had already formed the Dominion of Canada. British Columbia agreed to join on the condition that two thousand miles of railway line were built to link it to the east, a great opportunity for nation-building, and also for collecting money for the party funds. Macdonald's government was heavily defeated in the 1874 election after it was known that, in the previous general election, he made several calls on the firm that had been given the contract to build the railway for financial help, ending with the fatal telegram 'I must have another ten thousand. Will be last time of calling.'

Macdonald was lucky that the Liberals arrived in office just in time to be blamed for the severe depression of the mid 1870s, and by 1878 voters were ready to forgive him and support his National Policy: this time he would get the railway built honestly to open up western Canada, and he would establish a protective tariff for the industries of Quebec and Ontario. The 1880s were still a period of economic difficulty, but the National Policy was popular enough to keep him in office until his death in 1891. Opening up the Canadian West for wheat farming led to a rebellion by the hunters and trappers of the region which could have been anticipated, and to trouble for his French-Canadian allies that was harder to foresee. When the rebel leader Louis Riel was captured, Macdonald had him executed to satisfy his own Ontario supporters, but this weakened the position of the Quebec politicians who worked with him. The Liberals had been bold enough to choose a leader, Wilfrid Laurier, from the French-Canadian minority who naturally rallied to him. Macdonald was able to hold his supporters together in his last election in 1891, and to express his view of the imperial relationship by declaring in his election address 'A British subject I was born, a British subject I will die', but after that the Liberals settled down as the dominant party in Canada on a basis of solid support in Quebec and shifting alliances in English Canada.

but they would lose nothing if the British left India, provided the new system of government survived. The change would be dramatic, but some of the people who helped run the new system undoubtedly were Indian nationalists, preparing to challenge the position of the British rulers of their country. Others might think this an adventure in irrelevance, but would agree with the nationalists that they should organise to explain their position and defend it against anyone who threatened it.

As viceroy Lord Dufferin behaved as a gentleman should: when a number of associations of Indians who worked in government, or in jobs connected with the British system of government, held an All-India National Congress in 1885, he expressed pleasure that he would be able to learn their views. When their second annual meeting took place in Calcutta, he held a garden party for them. He could see that they were a group of legitimate importance in India, without whom the British would find it very hard to rule the country, and he felt that the best way to handle them was to show that their importance was acknowledged. While Congress soon became the focus for the activity of Indian nationalists, most of the original members found this development far from welcome. While they hoped to advance quietly and peacefully, they could see that assertive agitation by nationalists might deprive Congress of its usefulness as a lobbying organisation for improving their position inside the system. From 1885 until the First World War the opponents of nationalist agitation controlled Congress most of the time and tried to go about their business on a basis of cooperation. It was imprudent for Curzon, the great interventionist viceroy at the turn of the century, to say in public that he hoped to see Congress pass into obscurity, but he was right to see that the British had allies, at least on a short-term basis, with whom they could work in the years to come.

Some of the British in India could see the way things might turn out, stigmatising Indians who benefited from the new system of government as 'baboos', a term which, according to the *Oxford Dictionary*, was 'occasionally used of a Bengali, with a superficial English education'. Indians might have questioned the words 'occasionally' and 'superficial', but the British in India who used this term in a hostile way had grasped the point that Indians with an English education were the only real threat to the British position. Bengalis they might well be, because Bengal was the area that had been under British rule longest and had taken to English education most readily. It was also noticeable that Hindus had taken to English education more readily than Muslims; and men from Hindu families –

though they might themselves profess modern or secularist views on religion – were an even larger majority in Congress and its leadership than in the country at large.

There were people in Britain who felt that British rule was not always fair to the Indians. One point was the 'Drain', the comprehensive term used for the transfer of funds from India to Britain over and above payments for imports.[12] Some of this was the return on investments such as the building of railways, but some of it was the cost of the British conquest of India, and it was questioned whether the conqueror ought to charge the defeated with expenses of this sort. This made little impression in Britain: the Indians had simply been treated in the same way as the French, who had been made to pay some of Germany's expenses for the Franco-Prussian War of 1870–71, an example still remembered fifty years later when statesmen at Versailles were discussing the settlement of reparations for the Great War. But in India the question of the 'Drain' suggested that nationalists who debated about relations with Britain were talking about something of more than merely theoretical interest.

In the 1890s local assemblies had been set up in India, mainly on an appointed basis, although it was possible for members to be elected. The Liberals took a further step in the same direction in 1909 when they gave these assemblies authority to debate a wider range of issues, and opened many more seats to election; what was created was rather like the mixed assembly that Carleton had arranged for Canada under the 1774 Quebec Act. These assemblies were for the authorities to consult, much as medieval monarchs had consulted assemblies that represented important communities in their kingdoms. There was no idea that they should control the executive government in the way that parliaments in Britain and the Dominions had relatively recently acquired the right to control their governments.

As the assemblies were meant to represent communities, it was natural to treat Muslims as a separate group with representation of their own. When it was pointed out that seats reserved for Muslims might become the monopoly of Muslim candidates selected by and then elected by the Hindu majority, the British government agreed to set up communal electoral rolls, so that the Muslim representatives should be elected exclusively by Muslim voters. This came to be seen as a step of immense importance for the future by supporters of Congress who could not believe that anyone, even a Muslim, could feel ignored by the Congress majority. The British tended to underestimate the seriousness of Congress nationalism and to

## Lord Curzon

As the nineteenth century went on the British government became less and less willing to appoint anyone as viceroy who had held a subordinate post in India, which meant that few viceroys knew much about the country. George Nathaniel Curzon (1859–1925) was a brilliant exception; he declared from early in his life that he intended to be viceroy of India, as a natural stepping-stone on his way to 10 Downing Street. His ambition was so obvious that it sometimes seemed like self-parody, for which he had a capacity that was not always recognised. He was talented enough and well enough placed in the minor aristocracy to win a Conservative seat in parliament at the age of twenty-seven, and for the next nine years he combined the House of Commons with a series of journeys through dangerous and important areas, concentrating on the land of the 'Great Game' north of India. He became under-secretary of state for India and then moved up to be under-secretary of state for foreign affairs. In 1898 his energy and his application were rewarded when he became one of the youngest men ever to be appointed viceroy. By then he had married the immensely rich and charming Mary Leiter, now remembered only for the lightly-curried soup named after her but until her death in 1905 able to conciliate many of the people who found her husband too pompous or too upright.

Curzon earned himself a good deal of honourable unpopularity by his determination that Indians should be treated fairly by the British, but this sometimes came with a faint hint that everybody in India was so deeply inferior to him that he could not imagine why any of them should claim to be superior to anyone else. The civil servants in India, who were used to viceroys who listened to their suggestions and responded with prudent advice about what the British government and British public opinion would accept, now faced a flood of detailed and well-informed proposals. Many of Curzon's policy departures were undoubtedly desirable; his concern for Indian monuments and antiquities rescued many crumbling buildings, and visitors to the Taj Mahal can still see the acknowledgement of how much he did to save it. Some of his proposals roused anger at the time but made a great deal of sense: he partitioned Bengal amid an outcry from the Hindu professional classes around Calcutta. Although this step was reversed a few years later, it was based on an understanding of the deep division between the Calcutta elite and the Muslim peasants further to the east: if his policy had been maintained, the 1947 partition in Bengal would have been carried out less destructively and the original rulers of Pakistan might have understood the position of what is now Bangla Desh rather better.

Curzon's foreign policy of activity in the Gulf, close involvement with Afghanistan and assertion of British claims in Tibet at the expense of China eventually drove Balfour, the Conservative prime minister, to warn him that the British Empire could not afford, militarily or diplomatically, to have two foreign policies, one made in London and one made in Calcutta. When his five-year term as viceroy was drawing to a close he asked to be reappointed; the government was uneasy but acknowledged that he was so completely master of the Indian scene that it was hard to refuse him.

He came to grief early in his second term after Kitchener, revered as the victor in the Sudan and in the Boer War, became commander-in-chief in India and suggested changes in the way the viceroy's council handled military questions. Curzon resisted the change but resigned in August 1905 when, to his astonishment, the cabinet supported Kitchener. It was hard for him to regain a position in his party because imperial issues in politics were focused on tarriffs rather than India, and it was really the First World War that revived his career. Lloyd George disliked him but, realising that he was hard-working and well-informed, made him one of the five ministers in the 1916 War Cabinet. After the Versailles conference Curzon moved to the Foreign Office, and rose in the peerage to become a marquess; he was willing to follow Lloyd George's lead on European issues but became uneasy about his policy towards India and Asia Minor when problems developed in the area he really knew about, the western half of Asia. Curzon's resignation in October 1922 strengthened Lloyd George's opponents, and he returned to the Foreign Office in a new government and in 1923 narrowly missed becoming prime minister. It was explained that he was passed over because he was in the House of Lords, an acceptable enough reason, but some people suggested that the real reason was that he had never shaken off the reputation as a 'superior person' he had first acquired as an undergraduate.

feel that it was all a matter of manipulation by a handful of agitators; in turn, Congress tended to underestimate the seriousness of Muslim uneasiness and to feel that it was all a matter of manipulation by the British. Undoubtedly there were British officials who thought that divisions between Hindus and Muslims strengthened the British position, but they were hardly likely to imagine that they could create divisions where none had existed previously. The lobbying for the creation of communal electoral roles in 1909 was carried on by the Muslim League, a body of men inside Congress who felt sufficiently worried by the Hindu background of the majority to set up their own pressure group inside Congress to remind the majority about the feelings of the Muslim minority. At the time of the creation of new representative bodies, the admission of Indians to the viceroy's council, and the reversal of Curzon's sub-division of Bengal into a mainly Hindu western section and a mainly Muslim eastern section, seemed to be enough to satisfy most Indians of the politically active class that they were making progress.

In the years after 1906 the Liberal government found it much easier to avoid territorial expansion than its predecessors had done in the 1880s and 1890s. Africa had been almost completely divided up among European powers. Abyssinia remained independent because it had defeated an invading Italian army in 1895, and Liberia was understood to be in an informal United States sphere of influence, but everything else had been swallowed up. There was some ambiguity about the French position in Morocco, which led to tensions in relations with Germany, but in twenty-five or thirty years the continent had been partitioned so completely that the Liberals had no difficulty in pursuing a policy of peaceful development of what they already possessed. Their general attitude was one of hostility to government involvement in economic affairs, one of the reasons for the vehemence with which they opposed Chamberlain's proposals for protective tariffs. Chamberlain had said that Crown Colonies under direct British rule should be seen as 'undeveloped estates' that needed economic encouragement. The Liberals were not comfortable with this view and were not sure that the government should intervene to promote development in colonies. In the event governors in the new African colonies found themselves behaving like the rulers of India; the treaties with local rulers which were the legal and diplomatic basis of their position meant that the rulers had to be given some of the limited autonomy of the Indian princes. One of the greatest of governors in Africa, Lord Lugard, worked out a whole theory of 'indirect rule' to justify this in a much more elaborate way than was usual in British imperial activity. At the same time economic development in Africa could not proceed very far without establishing some sort of infrastructure, and the government was the only possible source of authority for anything of the sort. While the government had originally built its railway from Mombasa to Nairobi and on to Entebbe for reasons of imperial strategy, it soon served as a basis for British settlers to take up farming on land in Kenya high enough to be reasonably cool even though it was on the equator, and for local agricultural development of cotton and coffee in Uganda. In West Africa export trade in the palm oil of Nigeria and the cocoa of the Gold Coast was handled by private companies, but the colonial governments provided some of the infrastructure for development out of local revenue.

During the decades when Africa was being divided up among half a dozen European states, the islands in the Pacific Ocean were being divided up in the same way. The United States acquired the only large colony to be transferred in the process, the Philippines, while Britain, France and Germany concentrated on sharing out the South Sea islands, and Portugal and the Netherlands were content to keep what they had. The distances were even greater and the populations far smaller than in Africa. While there might be no advantages to expansion in the Pacific, the imperial powers were carried forward by their own momentum and a belief that ill-organised communities would be all the better for becoming part of an empire.

The Chinese empire of the late nineteenth century showed little sign of being better able to defend itself or reform itself than it had been in 1860. By 1900 the imperial powers were making their preparations for its collapse, acquiring coastal bases and negotiating with each other for spheres of influence which could serve as guidelines to be followed if the question of partition arose. A resistance group which called itself the 'Fists of Righteous Harmony' (briskly abridged to 'Boxers' by westerners) ignored their own government and besieged the western embassies in Peking (now Beijing). A western alliance raised the seige and the Boxers faded away, but the weakness of the Manchu dynasty was all the more obvious. Its fall in 1911 was followed by the creation of a republic which offered some prospect of reform. The imperial powers realised that advancing into China would be very expensive and saw no reason for doing anything so drastic if they could negotiate with an effective government for rights to trade and rights to build railways. In its early years the republic looked like an improvement on the empire. By the time its weaknesses became visible there were other inhibitions against imperial expansion.

In the rest of Asia, Afghanistan survived as a possibly impregnable area of no man's land between Russia and British India, and Siam, now Thailand, was maintained as a useful buffer state between Indo-China (which the French had acquired as a colony in the 1880s) and the British colony of Burma, which had expanded inland at the same time. Persia, now Iran, might have hoped to play a similar role but European diplomacy in south-western Asia was more directly assertive. In 1904, Britain and France drew together because they were becoming increasingly worried about the rising power of Germany, and because Britain wanted to reduce the European complications that might be caused by its recent alliance with Japan. They resolved a number of colonial problems left over from the disputes of the past two centuries, from Egypt to the question of Newfoundland fishing rights. Britain then went on to work out a number of problems with France's close ally Russia. Persia was divided into three zones, a Russian zone in the north, a British zone in the south east and a central zone in the middle. As the capital, Tehran, was in the Russian zone, these terms favoured the Russians; but the British were not really concerned about this because they were thinking in terms of the defence of India. Their south-eastern zone served much more to keep the Russians at a distance than to provide anything that the British wanted for themselves.

In the nineteenth century people had been ready to predict that the Ottoman Empire would disintegrate and be partitioned; the Ottoman sultans ruled over Christians and Muslims in the Balkans and over Arabs to the south and east of their Turkish-speaking heartland. For most European statesmen the problem was to find a way to get the Turks out of the Balkans without giving either Russia or Austria too strong a position there. The Arab areas aroused less immediate interest, but European powers showed signs of being ready to absorb the outer edges of the Ottoman Empire by slow degrees. Egypt remained under firm British control, despite the absence of any permanent legally defined basis for this arrangement, and Kuwait and other small states in the Persian Gulf were becoming distant satellites of the British Empire in India. Germany was creating a sphere of influence based on sponsoring railway lines stretching to Basra on the Persian Gulf, and France had a long-established interest in Syria. Europeans had managed to divide up Africa without going to war with one another. It was hard to see why the division of the Ottoman Empire should cause any more trouble than Africa had done.

# 7

# *The Two World Wars*

The Ottoman Empire in Europe broke up in 1912, and in 1913 several Balkan countries fought among themselves about the division of the spoils. The more important countries of Europe did a certain amount to bring about settlements in these two related struggles, but in 1914 trouble returned to the Balkans when the Austro-Hungarian Empire declared that it was intolerable that members of the Serbian government had been involved in the assassination of Archduke Franz Ferdinand at Sarajevo. Serbia appealed to its ally and supporter, Russia, and a war began which eventually involved all the imperial powers of Europe, the United States, Japan and several smaller countries. The First World War was at its bloodiest in Belgium and north-eastern France, and the battles there decided what happened elsewhere, but its effects were worldwide. It had an immediate impact on empires in Europe, and a long-term impact on empires throughout the rest of the world. To justify the war, and to show that they were inspired by higher standards than Germany, Britain and her allies adopted a new moral stance which was hard to reconcile with maintaining imperial power for an indefinite period of time. When they spoke of 'the rights of small nations', they were thinking of countries like Belgium and Serbia which had been attacked by Germany and her ally Austria. When they put forward 'the right of national self-determination', they were thinking of people in Alsace-Lorraine which Germany had taken from France in 1871, or of people in eastern Europe who were ruled by the Habsburg, Romanov or Ottoman empires when they might have preferred to live in nation states of their own choosing, but ideas of this sort were later applied outside Europe in a way that directly challenged all imperial rule. Very few people in 1919 thought that everybody in the world ought to have a nation state to belong to, or that nationalism was a political emotion that everybody could feel. While policies of imperial expansion considered normal and beneficent before 1914 went less unquestioned after the war, this did not imply a general retreat from overseas empire.

Suspicion of Germany's aggressive policies made the British eager to help their ally France and, despite some moral doubts about Tsarist rule, they were glad to have as powerful an ally as Russia on their side. Prewar discussions of the position of the Dominions produced results as good as any British politician could have hoped. While the British Empire was a single entity and all of it was legally committed to war with Germany when Britain decided to oppose the German advance through Belgium, the self-governing colonies were free to decide whether to take any active part, as they had been at the time of the Crimean War or the Boer War. In 1914 all of them followed the path of active involvement they had chosen in the Boer War, partly because of the eagerness of men from the recent wave of emigration from Britain to return and fight for the country of their birth. In South Africa there was a minor Afrikaner revolt, but Botha's government had no difficulty in suppressing it. At first the Dominions raised very few questions about accepting British leadership and took it for granted that the British knew more about warfare, if only because they were closer to the fighting and because their troops had been involved in the first battles of the war. As it became clear how different the First World War was from anything that happened earlier, Britain's experience in relatively small imperial wars seemed less relevant. British governments had been less involved in economic development than Dominion governments which had had to launch their countries' railways, handle the problems of immigration and encourage new industries. Although it improvised a new munitions industry successfully enough, the British government had no established skill in organising the country for modern warfare to pass on to the Dominions, and its generals were as baffled as everybody else by the problems of trench warfare.

All over the empire young men volunteered because they felt that they were British and that Britain was in danger, but they were organised by their own governments and fought as Australians or as Canadians. The Australian and New Zealand Army Corps took part in the operations at Gallipoli in 1915, which immediately reproduced the conditions of trench warfare and stalemate that had developed in France; Anzac Day became a day of national significance in both countries, and the reputation of the British high command suffered because so little was achieved. By the end of 1915 the Dominion governments were uneasy about British leadership, and Asquith's government was not able to reassure them. There were doubts about Asquith in Britain as well and, while he was able to lead a united government into adopting military conscription, he was overthrown by his ministers at the end of 1916 and replaced by Lloyd George. The new government was run by a war cabinet of half a dozen ministers. Lloyd George invited the Dominion prime ministers to London for meetings of what he called the imperial war cabinet, although the members were responsible to their own domestic legislatures and could not be committed to any sort of cabinet solidarity. But they were obviously agreed on their policy objective – to win the war – and were sufficiently in sympathy with one another to try to work together as much as possible. They agreed to rely on a process of 'continuous consultation' to work out a common policy by exchanging information and by holding conferences in which they met on something like a basis of equality.

Seen from the outside, the British Empire was a united body of considerable war-making capacity; seen from the inside, it was an alliance of six or seven governments working closely together for a common objective, despite occasional moments of tension. Lines of party loyalty were strained in Britain and in the Dominions as governments were formed on a basis of cooperation among groups united more by their enthusiasm for the war effort than by the policies they would support in peacetime. The Canadian government obtained legislation for conscription; the Australian government lost two referendums in which it asked for conscription; the South African government knew that conscription would be very divisive and never raised the question. The Indian government was still legally under the direct control of the secretary of state for India, and for practical purposes of waging war the viceroy still had the powers of an autocrat. The country raised a large army, conducted military operations in Mesopotamia (now Iraq) which were conspicuously unsuccessful and supplied troops for operations in Egypt and Palestine and in France. At the beginning of the war loyalty to the crown and king emperor dominated the Indian response. As the war went on, national pride in India's contribution increased, reinforcing the nationalist approach already taken by Congress. The British government, realising that the situation was changing, issued in 1917 a carefully phrased declaration (attributed to Montagu the secretary of state and Chelmsford the viceroy) that India would in due course advance to responsible government. This was an ambiguous phrase. Was it to be responsible government as originally meant in the 1840s, or in the way it had developed by 1907 when the colonies that already had responsible government became called Dominions? Or did it mean that India would have the same powers as the Dominions? Some Indians believed that the government had undertaken to put their country on the same footing as the Dominions, and the external role of the government of India encouraged this view. Representatives of the British Empire went to Versailles for the peace conference at the end of the war, and the British government had to explain to the other countries at the conference that the Dominions were entitled to a role in peacemaking because they had made important contributions to the war effort by providing troops and equipping them, had put large armies in the field and had suffered heavy losses. The other countries recognised the claims of four of the Dominions (Newfoundland was regarded as too small to have a right to take part), and the government of India was also allowed to attend despite its position as a British colony. The Dominions and India were grouped with Britain as the British Empire delegation, but each of them signed the treaty and became a member of the League of Nations after signing. The implication seemed to be that Dominions had a right to run their own foreign policy, and that 'responsible government' meant, as in the nineteenth century, that a colony had a government which ran its internal affairs and was responsible to an elected assembly.

The four land empires of central and eastern Europe had collapsed and broken up in the last years of the war. The Irish Free State broke away from Britain in 1921 after two years of civil war. While it accepted a close relationship with Britain by remaining a dominion for almost thirty years, its advance towards independence showed the force of the principle that empires were to give way to nation states. Most of the territory in the Hohenzollern Empire in Europe was so German in national feeling that it was not going to break up, but Germany had to surrender the land it had acquired in Alsace-Lorraine and in Schleswig-Holstein in south Denmark fifty or sixty years earlier, and most of the land it had annexed in the eighteenth-century partitions of Poland. Germany was also made to give up all the colonies Bismarck had acquired in the 1880s. Several Dominions showed that they were victorious sovereign states by acquiring some of the territory Germany lost. As the idea of gaining colonies by conquest was no longer respectable, the victorious powers took these colonies under mandates to rule them for the benefit of the local population. Australia obtained a mandate for the north-eastern quarter of New Guinea it had wanted Britain to acquire on its behalf in the 1880s, New Zealand obtained a mandate for Samoa, and South Africa obtained a mandate for the territory in south-west Africa that Cape Colony had hoped would be kept out of German hands in 1885. Britain acquired mandates for German East Africa, renamed Tanganyika, and for part of Kamerun, though most of this colony passed to France.

Much of the time of the Versailles conference was taken up with trying to draw boundaries in eastern Europe, where the Habsburg Empire was shattered into fragments and the boundaries of the Russian or Romanov Empire were forced back hundreds of miles to the east. The newly-established Communist government, which managed to retain all the old Tsarist possessions on its southern and south-eastern borders, was not reconciled to the loss of the territories to the west. The Ottoman Empire had lost virtually all its land in Europe in the years just before the outbreak of the First World War. Defeat in the war led to the loss of the Arabic-speaking lands to the east and south, the replacement of the sultan by a modernising republic firmly based on the Turkish-speaking heartland, and a brief Anglo-French occupation of the area around the Dardanelles and the Bosphorus.

During the war the British and French had worked out an agreement in relatively general terms for handling the Arab territories. The British government had also given assurances to Jewish representatives about 'the establishment in Palestine of a national home for the Jewish people' in the Balfour Declaration.[1] With an effort the Balfour Declaration could be reconciled with the Sykes-Picot agreement with France, but it was very hard to make these two commitments effective without repudiating what British officials in Egypt had said to Arabs under Turkish rule to encourage them to rise in rebellion. After the war the Arabs in the sands of Arabia were left to govern themselves, the French were given a mandate over Syria, while the British gained mandates for Iraq and for Palestine. In 1921 the land east of the Jordan was divided from Palestine and became a third mandate territory with the name of Transjordan. These three mandates spread the British Empire wider than ever, yet it was clear that imperial strength was in many ways more limited than in the nineteenth century.

The British government worked out a scheme to give effect to the Montagu-Chelmsford promise of eventual responsible government for India. A new elected assembly 'at the centre', as officials chose to refer to Delhi, would be able to question ministers and debate their policies but would not be able to force them out of office. Some ministers in the provinces would now become responsible to the existing elected assemblies, while others would go on being responsible to the British authorities. This arrangement, known as dyarchy, would give Indians a chance to gain experience, position by position, as the British gradually drew back from power. Such a proposal might in the days before 1914 have been seen as the ideal way for Indians to move slowly towards the exercise of authority that in the nineteenth century had been transferred to self-governing colonies without any conscious preparation. Indians after the war were not so convinced that they needed to be trained and given experience, and they mobilised for political action to ask for independence or, at the very least, the position of a Dominion.

Congress was ready to become a mass movement and, during the war, it had acquired a leader with the qualities to enable it to do so. Mohandas Gandhi had lived for twenty years in South Africa, where he had learnt how to unite the Indian community there to enable it to lobby for improvements in its position. When he went back to India he had some reputation as a leader, combined with a useful detachment from local rivalries. As part of his strategy for convincing people that problems large and small would be easier to resolve if India was free to look after its own affairs, he intervened in a number of disputes in different parts of the country as people struggled with the dislocations of war. In these conflicts he offered a form of passive resistance based on the pacific element to be found in Christianity and in Hinduism; the authorities would have had no difficulty in meeting any attempt at violent revolt with a brisk display of force, but the limitations of force were shown at Amritsar in 1919. The city was disturbed but was hardly in a state of rebellion. When Reginald Dyer, the general in charge, ordered his soldiers to fire on an unarmed crowd and about 380 people were killed, the British in India saw this as a praiseworthy pre-emptive measure to maintain law and order, whatever the cost. Indians might possibly have seen it in this way, or at least been cowed by it in the short run, if the British had been united in supporting such methods, but the British government and public opinion in Britain saw no reason to approve of such an overreaction to a crisis. In 1920 Congress was able to launch a formidable campaign against British rule, but eventually the strain of keeping their movement non-violent was too much for its organisers. In 1922 Gandhi, who could see that events were drifting towards violence which would give the authorities a good reason to respond forcefully, declared that the campaign had to be ended. He was arrested and convicted of sedition, and for the rest of the 1920s the system of dyarchy worked much as intended, though Indian politicians who chose to work within the system always had to remember that Congress might challenge them from a more radical nationalist position.

At the beginning of the 1920s 'continuous consultation' between Britain and the Dominions operated successfully. Choices had to be made, but the Dominions were consulted about them. Britain accepted naval equality with the United States at the 1920 Washington conference, and ended its prewar treaty with Japan, a step opposed by Australia and New Zealand (though approved of by Canada), but the Dominions knew what the British had in mind and why a desire for good relations with the United States had led to the termination of the treaty. The British government did not see any such need to consult the Dominions about the problems it faced as it helped to oversee the break up of the Ottoman Empire and encouraged Greece to carve out territory for itself in the areas of substantial Greek population on the western coast of Turkey. In the summer of 1922 the Turks pulled their forces together, drove the Greeks into the sea and marched north to confront a British force at Chanak, across the Dardanelles from Gallipoli. At this point the British government sent out urgent messages to the Dominion governments to ask for assistance, and released the messages to the press at the same time. This was at best ill-mannered. At worst it looked like an attempt to build up a wave of opinion to push the Dominion governments into agreeing to express support. Australia and New Zealand accepted the British position, perhaps out of loyalty to Britain, perhaps out of concern for their trade route though the Suez Canal, but Canada and South Africa declined to join in and made it clear that 'continuous consultation' was not likely to work in future, and that the politicians had to find a new way for the British Commonwealth to handle problems of foreign policy. People in Britain were not happy that they had come so close to war with Turkey, and Lloyd George's government was driven from office.

As the term British Commonwealth came into use in the 1920s, it indicated that Britain and the Dominions made up a community of nations rather different from the British Empire. The Empire was ruled from London; the members of the British Commonwealth were much more independent, but they wanted to work together even though they realised that this might not always be possible. The British government expected to pursue a relatively active policy in Europe and would be unlikely to discuss every step with Dominion governments; and Dominion governments had policies of their own – at least in the realm of trade – and would not want to have to refer every proposal to British diplomats. The Dominions began appointing representatives in foreign countries, starting with the United States, and the British government signed the 1925 Locarno agreements with an explicit disclaimer to say that Dominion governments were not bound by these treaties, which meant that they could stay out of any wars that might follow from them. In 1926 the countries of the Commonwealth set out to define their position and, in words attributed to Arthur Balfour, described their position as 'autonomous communities within the British Empire, in no way subordinate one to another in any aspect of heir domestic or external affairs, though united by a common allegiance to the Crown and freely associated as members of the British Commonwealth of Nations'.[2] This described the situation in terms that everybody could accept and provided a practical definition of the phrase 'Dominion status', but it left legal implications still to be examined. Previously Britain could legislate for everybody in the Empire because all of them were British subjects, while the Dominions could legislate only for what happened inside their own territories. The Colonial Laws Validity Act of 1865, which defined these rights, had originally been passed to strengthen the position of the self-governing colonies by enabling them to make laws that could not be challenged simply because they did not agree with British law, but it took the general supremacy of British legislation for granted. Now that this was no longer to be accepted, the Colonial Laws Validity Act would have to be replaced. Some Dominions wanted to go much further.

British legislation was the foundation of the legal existence of all the Dominions, and most of them had constitutions which could be amended only by an Act of the Westminster parliament. South Africa and the Irish Free State wanted to have the right to amend their own constitutions without any question of involvement with Westminster; in contrast, Australia, New Zealand and Newfoundland liked the process of going to London for formal ratification of constitutional changes, and asked that, whatever might be done for other countries, the legislation should retain the authority of the Westminster parliament for them; and Canada found this a useful way of dealing with a political problem. When Australia had established its federal constitution, it had laid down the procedure by which Australians could decide to change it. Westminster's involvement was strictly ceremonial, because it was unthinkable that the British parliament would reject something approved by the Australian people in the referendums required by the constitution. But when Canada had drawn up its federal constitution, a generation earlier, it had expected that the British parliament would want to debate any subsequent changes. No procedure had been set up that would have had the same binding effect as the referendums in Australia. Before Canada could ask for the right to change its constitution without any reference to London it would have to work out a procedure by which the federal government and the provinces could agree on changes to their powers, and arranging the procedure would have taken up far more time than was available in 1931. So Canada for practical reasons adopted the approach which Australia, New Zealand and Newfoundland had adopted for reasons of sentiment, and these four Dominions left the formal right of amendment with Westminster. The 1931 Statute of Westminster gave legal definition to the 1926 political declaration that the countries in the Commonwealth stood on a footing of equality; but, while the position of Britain was becoming less dominant, the Commonwealth connection was not becoming weaker at this point.[3]

Under the pressure of the worldwide depression of the 1930s the Dominions again raised the question of imperial preference. This time the British government accepted the idea. The Conservatives had fought a general election on the issue in 1923 and had once more been defeated, but persistent unemployment in the 1920s, followed by an alarming drop in international trade in 1930, had undermined much of Britain's traditional support for Free Trade. When the Labour government collapsed in 1931, under the strain of supporting a weakening pound, it was succeeded by a Conservative-dominated coalition which won an election on a platform of having a free hand to do whatever was needed to pull the economy together. It then used its freedom of action to impose short-term tariffs as a prelude to the creation of an imperial system.

At Ottawa in 1932 Commonwealth leaders, and representatives of some colonies, met to work out trade concessions with one another, largely on a bilateral basis, which would turn the empire into something rather more like a detached and self-sufficient trading unit. The most ambitious supporters of imperial unity had hoped for empire free trade, with tariffs against imports from outside the empire and no tariffs between the countries of the empire, but this was never politically possible. The British expected the conference to be a triumph of imperial sentiment. They had been

touched by the fact that it was Joseph Chamberlain's son Neville who had
brought forward the legislation taking the first steps towards tariff reform
at the beginning of the year, and they felt that they had received so much
encouragement to set up imperial preference from the Dominions that the
discussions would be simple and friendly. They were unpleasantly surprised
to find how cool a welcome was given to their proposals and how fiercely
the experienced protectionist Dominion delegations bargained with them.
It has been suggested that the British government wanted the Dominions
to be able to export more than they imported, so that they could earn a
surplus and keep up payments on all the money they had borrowed from
Britain, and as a result was inhibited about responding aggressively to this
pressure.[4] Under Free Trade the British had had very little experience of
this sort of discussion, or of the problems of organisation required inside
the country by tariffs. The Dominions already had tariffs of the ordinary
type and only needed to negotiate how large a preference they would give
to their partners; the British wanted to avoid imposing tariffs on food, and
instead offered guarantees that they would purchase set amounts, or quotas,
from Dominion farmers. The British were virtually the only people in the
world who were ready to run an economic policy that depended on
importing food. On the other hand, they wanted the Dominions to buy
their manufactured products, and plenty of other countries were ready to
sell manufactured products, sometimes at prices that benefited from government subsidies to exporters. The Ottawa Agreements gave some help to
all the participants, mainly at the expense of other exporting countries,
who in turn started negotiating with Britain or with the Dominions to
mitigate the effect of the Ottawa Agreements. Britain was making a larger
change of policy than any other country involved, because moving away
from Free Trade was such a big step, but it was taken for granted that the
change would be made by establishing imperial preference rather than a
simple tariff wall around Britain without any regard for other countries.
The agreements probably helped stabilise Commonwealth relations in much
the same way as the passage of the Statute of Westminster had done. The
Dominions had negotiated with Britain on a basis of equality, but the result
was that economic links with Britain which had been weakening since the
outbreak of war in 1914 were strengthened.

Although India was represented at Ottawa, Britain could not restore the
old economic and other links with it. India had gained enough autonomy
after the first war to have some freedom of action in imposing tariffs, and

its government knew that what people wanted were tariffs against imported textiles, to improve the prospects of the Indian cotton industry. When Gandhi said that India should turn away from industrialised imports, and that all loyal members of Congress should spin a little cotton every day, he was striking a blow at the connection with Britain and he was also endearing the party to the Indian textile manufacturers. Gandhi presented himself to his followers as a peaceful and ascetic man of God, a type of leader that they understood, and he was also able to find points of conflict with the British which everybody could understand. In the 1920s Congress was a sophisticated and ingenious opposition party in representative assemblies at Delhi and in the provinces, but its political leaders did not always manage to explain to the Indian public why its activities were relevant. When a Labour government was elected in Britain in 1929, the viceroy, Lord Irwin, consulted British party leaders privately and then declared that the objective of British policy was that India should move towards Dominion status, which meant equality with other Commonwealth countries as defined in the 1926 Balfour Declaration. But no timetable was given, and Gandhi set out to press for independence as soon as possible. He chose the salt tax as the focus of a massive exercise in civil disobedience: since the time of the Mughals salt had been a government monopoly providing revenue through a tax which was regressive because everybody consumed roughly the same amount of it. In the spring of 1930 Gandhi announced that he was going to march to the sea and ignore the government monopoly by making salt from sea water. The proposal caught the attention of millions of Indians. Many thousands of them joined in variations upon this theme in civil disobedience. At the peak of the campaign about 60,000 opponents of the salt tax were in prison. But the government was able to keep control of the situation, and it was agreed that 'round table' (to show that all parties were speaking on terms of equality) discussions should be held about the way to approach Dominion status.

These discussions had to face the problem of princely India, and a council of princes was set up to take part in the political debate. But it was one thing for princes to enter a debate under the sway of the viceroy and another thing for them to acknowledge that effective rule was going to pass to Indian politicians. They felt certain that the king emperor would respect the monarchical principles which gave them their power, but they were not nearly so sure that Congress would accept their position if it held

## Mahatma Gandhi

M. K. Gandhi (1869–1948) came from a family rich enough and ambitious enough to send him to London to qualify as a barrister, but he was ineffective in court in India and in 1893 went to South Africa to practise in the Indian community in Natal. Discriminatory legislation had already been passed there, though with little of the perverse precision that later characterised it, and Gandhi set out to organise resistance. He could see that violent action would not help an insecure minority, so he brought together the diverse elements of the Indian community to lobby the British and colonial governments. The peaceful protests he organised, sometimes employing civil disobedience, made an impression on the white ruling minority and left him convinced of the effectiveness of non-violence.

In 1914 he returned to his native country. In many independence movements a prominent figure returning after long years away with a political reputation built up elsewhere could become a leader detached from local ambitions and jealousies, but Gandhi could expect no easy path to the top. After a year spent watching Indian affairs carefully and silently, he began applying his non-violent methods to a number of local problems and was successful enough to win a position in national politics. By 1920 he had gained temporary control of Congress and had committed it to a programme of protest that he said would bring freedom within a year. The government was able to hold this challenge back and, when the campaign began to dissolve into violence, Gandhi said early in 1922 that it was time to abandon it. Tried for sedition and imprisoned for two years, he took no part in the parliamentary activity of the 1920s after his release. He came to be seen as a man of simple and austere habits who could be taken for a saint, an approach that may have weakened his position among the Muslim minority as much as it widened his appeal to the Hindu majority.

At the end of the 1920s interest in politics reawakened. When Lord Irwin, the viceroy, declared that India's political development was going to lead to Dominion status, Indian parliamentary parties began to discuss ways of reaching this objective. Congress was afraid that moderate politicians were going to dominate the situation, and it decided that, to regain the position as the effective leader of Indian national feeling that it had held just after the Great War, it would have to encourage Gandhi to come back. Once Congress acknowledged his leadership, Gandhi offered a new challenge to the government's authority by setting out to the coast to make salt by evaporating seawater. Making salt had been a government monopoly for centuries and the salt march of 1930 attracted attention as a form of civil disobedience to protest against a form of taxation that affected everybody. Congress supporters were roused by this and won new recruits. For a time Gandhi emerged as the only national leader in the country, though the regional leaders of other parties remained important. When the viceroy and Gandhi negotiated an agreement in 1931 to bring the salt tax protests to an end, the imperial rulers conceded very little but Gandhi's position as the leader of nationalist politics was established by the role he had played. He dominated Congress in the many-cornered negotiations that led up to the Government of India Act of 1935, but the Act brought India back to parliamentary politics. Younger leaders, including Nehru, were prominent in the 1936 election campaign and Gandhi withdrew into non-political detachment. When war broke out, Congress realised that its leaders would have to assist military activity in a way that would split the organisation if they held on to the ministerial posts they had gained after the 1935 Act. They resigned their posts and Gandhi's influence revived with the swing back to extra-parliamentary politics. At first he recommended a pacifist approach which suggested he did not realise what Nazism was about, but after Japan entered the war he took the lead in the mid-1942 campaign to make the British 'Quit India' which rallied large numbers of Indians. The imperial authorities responded with mass imprisonments which led to most of the Congress leaders being out of politics while the Muslim League gained ground rapidly. At the end of the war elections and negotiations among party leaders opened up the road to independence and partition, but Gandhi had no part to play in this. When massacre struck just after independence he went to Bengal, forced the politicians to come forward and by personal example and political influence did more than anyone else could have done to subdue violence. The following year he was assassinated by a religious enthusiast who imagined he was betraying the Hindu cause. The murder of Gandhi was a dramatic contrast between true religion and misguided fanaticism.

power in India. The problems of people at the bottom of the caste system, or untouchables, and the possibility of protecting them by giving them special representation were also discussed. The religious differences of Hindus and Muslims were not expected to have major political implications; separate electorates, a reasonably well-established feature of the political landscape, were thought to be all that was needed.

The British government emerged from these discussions with a Government of India Act that passed into law in 1935. It took the idea of dyarchy a long step towards Dominion status by making all ministers in provincial governments responsible to elected assemblies, and making most ministers in Delhi responsible to a national assembly. The viceroy continued to run defence, police and foreign policy (and could intervene in financial affairs), and had emergency powers to remove provincial governments if they ran into difficulty or caused the central British authorities trouble. Granted the premise that the way to train people for ruling themselves was to let them gain experience by first running the less vital parts of the government, the 1935 Act was a logical step towards the transfer of power at some point in the next dozen years or so.

When elections were held on the basis of this new constitution in the cool weather at the end of 1936, Congress did well but the Muslim League did much worse than it had expected. When, after the election, its leaders made it clear that they expected to be asked to nominate Muslims to serve in the provincial cabinets which were being formed, Congress replied that, while Muslims would certainly be included in the new governments, chief ministers in provinces had the right to choose their own cabinets. The Muslim League left the discussions with a grievance. Its leaders felt that they had to transform the League into a mass party and for this they turned to Mohamed Ali Jinnah, a Muslim who had left Indian politics because of his concern about Hindu domination of Congress and had only recently returned from London, where he had a successful legal practice. Jinnah undertook the task of mobilising Muslim feeling. Congress was slightly handicapped by the fact that the Gandhian approach of non-violence and civil disobedience had much deeper roots in Hindu or in Christian belief than in Islam. While Muslim voters could appreciate Gandhi as a political leader, they were unlikely to see him as a saint who deserved unquestioning allegiance. But it was clearly going to be difficult to mobilise opposition to Congress when it combined the prestige of leading the national movement against imperial rule with all the practical opportunities of holding office in most of the provinces.

While the British were withdrawing gradually from involvement in India, they were becoming if anything more deeply involved in Africa. There were no suggestions of moving towards independence here. The three British mandates in what had been parts of the Ottoman Empire were clearly designed to lead to independence in the near future, and Iraq did become independent in 1932, though it remained closely linked with Britain for another thirty years. The African mandates had no such provisions, though the British government saw itself as the guardian of the interests of the Africans. When the governor of Kenya said that the interests of the British settlers should be paramount, the secretary for the colonies found a suitable moment to declare equally publicly that the interests of Africans should be paramount. This dismayed the settlers, who had invested sizeable amounts of money in the colony's agriculture and understandably saw themselves as the main force for economic growth, but British officials, who had been ardent modernisers for much of the nineteenth century, were now becoming conservative and were not always sure that they wanted economic growth. They were afraid that it might lead to exploitation of the African population, though this left the question what the alternative might be. A few years later President Franklin Roosevelt of the United States landed briefly at Bathurst in the Gambia, noticed the poverty and declared that 'It's just plain exploitation of these people'.[5] If he had been able to find an airport at Monrovia in Liberia he could have seen poverty which was quite as bad, in a country that had never been under imperial rule although it had always been closely involved with the United States. If people wanted development at all, they had to consider the possibility that it would be development by capitalists from outside.

Some officials felt that Africans who had come into too much contact with Europeans were harmed by the experience; they were better and happier as noble savages than as imitators of a more complex and corrupt way of life. This attitude could be found in many colonial administrators; in India it led to preference for the 'martial races' who made up most of the recruits to the army, while the 'baboos' were seen as failed Europeans. British administrators and authors who went to the Arab world were apt to express admiration for the solitary and dignified Arabs of the desert but contempt for the Arabs who had moved to cities like Cairo. The politicians in London noted with approval the economic advance that was taking place in the Palestine mandate, which was attracting well-educated people with enough capital behind them to help them develop it, much as emigrants who had gone to Canada or Australia had developed those countries with money from metropolitan investors to help them. But administrators in Palestine saw the discontent of the local population (apart from those who had sold their land to immigrants) at the expansion of the Jewish population, and regarded the change as dangerous and disturbing to a political balance that looked as if it would be perfectly stable, were not for the newcomers.

African kings and rulers were able to make satisfactory arrangements with the British, acknowledging the king of England as their superior in a dignified relationship reminiscent of feudalism in Europe or the position of the princes in India, but Africans who had been to Europe or America and returned educated and aware of the way government operated were apt to be less respectful; they might even think that they could replace the colonial administrators if the opportunity arose. Lugard, as the theorist of 'indirect rule' with its care for the established order of things, had shown considerable respect for what existed in Africa before imperial expansion, but he claimed that it was possible to carry out sensible development in a way that benefited both Europeans and Africans:

> European brain, capital and energy has not been expended in developing the resources of Africa from motives of pure philanthropy; Europe is in Africa for the mutual benefit of her own industrial classes and of the native races in their progress to a higher plane; the benefit can be made reciprocal; and it is the aim and desire of civilised administration to fulfil this dual mandate.[6]

The compromise was too subtle for some administrators. Others saw the simple fact that development was likely to weaken the power of existing kings and rulers and leave nobody to take their place as buttresses for British rule.

Colonies in Africa, like all the other colonies in the British Empire, were expected to be financially self-supporting. The British government had long ago given up the idea of collecting revenue from colonies, but it saw very little reason for making financial contributions to their budgets: if Britain was not to make money out of them, they were certainly not going to make money out of Britain. Some governors found money for building roads and railways from their budgets, and some governors were uninterested in such things, but they were unlikely to be pushed very far in either direction by the London government. Late in the 1930s it was realised that the West Indies had done very badly in the face of competition from slave-grown sugar from other places which grew cane sugar and, later in the nineteenth century, from subsidised sugar grown from sugar beet by European countries. People might assert that Africans would do better in their traditional societies than under modernisation, but nobody concerned about the West Indies had a comparable traditional society to look back on. The Royal Commission which called them 'the slums of the empire' left no doubt that economic development was the only way to deal with the problem.

Gradual modification of the empire, probably in a way that involved providing more direct signs that it was economically beneficial to all concerned, was undoubtedly expected in the 1930s. There seemed to be no reason to expect any drastic change. The monarch continued to offer a solid central figure, even if loyalty to an individual was being replaced by national sentiment in more and more places. Queen Victoria had been a distant figure of majesty, well suited to an age when people outside the capital city did not expect to see their rulers. Her son Edward VII had social gifts which in 1903 undoubtedly helped the British and French to overcome their disagreement about Egypt and renew an alliance which ran smoothly for over fifty years, though he took little interest in the empire. His son George V was able to visit some parts of his empire, and in the 1930s the minority of his subjects who had access to radios could hear him give well-received Christmas addresses to the empire. His eldest son, who reigned briefly as Edward VIII, was enormously popular in the Dominions. When he abdicated late in 1936, to marry a woman who had been divorced, people wondered if the empire would survive the shock. Divorce and remarriage were not acceptable by the standards of the period, yet Edward seemed to be the unifying force needed to draw the empire together. He was in reality bored by royal duties, and it was hard to tell whether this mixture of glamour and idle detachment could have sustained him permanently as king or as the centre of the empire. His younger brother George VI possessed all the virtues that Edward lacked and performed all the royal duties conscientiously; his stability and even dullness served to reassure people that the monarch would never do anything unworthy of his empire, but added no positive force to it.

Germany's desire to overthrow the Versailles settlement in eastern Europe had been made effective by Hitler's successful diplomacy in 1937 and

1938, when the Dominions had strengthened the British government's desire to avoid, or at least to delay, any conflict. When German expansionism made this impossible and Britain and France declared war in defence of Poland in 1939, the empire supported Britain more readily and more completely than might have been expected. The Crown Colonies were committed legally and practically by the British declaration of war. No Dominion governments considered formally entering the war but then refraining from taking an active role. The Irish Free State remained neutral. Its prime minister, Eamonn de Valera, had taken part in rebellion and civil war against the British in the years before the creation of the Irish Free State and owed some of his prestige and popularity to his record in the struggle, and he had never been reconciled to Britain in the way that some of the Afrikaner leaders had been. In South Africa, there was a direct political clash between two surviving generals from the Boer War, in which the pro-British Smuts was able to gain a narrow majority in parliament over the unreconciled Hertzog, leading to the formation of a pro-war government. The government of Canada paused briefly before entering the war, to underline the fact that the decision to declare war had been approved by the Canadian parliament, and also to allow some purchases of munitions from the United States which would not have been possible for a belligerent. Australia and New Zealand took it for granted that they would enter the war as part of the empire. The viceroy declared war as ruler of India. Some Congress supporters were relieved at this because they were aware that the Nazi government in Germany was deeply and consciously racist in a way that no British government had been, yet they realised that it would have been very hard for Congress to endorse going to war. The pacifist wing of the party, led by Gandhi, would inevitably have been distressed by the idea of any sort of fighting, and would have been supported by people who disliked the idea of fighting for the British Empire. Very few opponents of British rule went so far as to hope for a German victory, but the central organisers of Congress called on all Congress politicians in provincial governments to resign from their positions. Some of them were reluctant to do so, more because they felt their work in government offered an opportunity for improving their country than because they wanted to join in preparations for war or realised the political problems that their resignations would cause Congress later on. After the most powerful political organisation in the country had withdrawn from office, the British authorities were left to search for allies.

The Muslim League and the princes were the obvious choices, though the Muslim League was building up its mass organisation by developing a national spirit of its own. In 1940 it declared that it was in favour of Pakistan, the creation of a separate state for Muslims in north-western India.

For the first nine months of the war very little happened. Germany and the Soviet Union partitioned Poland while Britain and France stayed immobile on Germany's western flank, and operations ceased for the traditional winter pause from fighting. In the spring of 1940 Germany conquered half a dozen western Europe nations in as many weeks, then briefly considered an invasion of England. As the Royal Air Force maintained control over the English Channel in the Battle of Britain, this idea was laid aside and Germany turned to preparing an advance into the Balkans and an attack on the Soviet Union. Britain's immediate involvement in fighting was confined to North Africa and a successful struggle with the Italian colonies there, but in late 1940 and early 1941 there seemed to be no way for Britain to make any impression on Germany. When Germany attacked the Soviet Union in June 1941 and began a rapid advance into Russian territory it was even harder to see what Britain could do, but at the end of the year the Russians were able to counter-attack in winter conditions for which the Germans had made very few preparations; and when Japan attacked the American fleet at Pearl Harbor, in December 1941, Germany came to the aid of her ally and declared war on the United States. While this decision, and the subsequent American decision to concentrate on fighting Germany, saved Britain from probable disaster, the war in East Asia and the Pacific greatly weakened Britain's imperial position.

Japan had prepared a plan for swift advance into south-east Asia and the islands of the eastern Pacific, which involved the capture of British possessions in Hong Kong, Malaya, Singapore, Burma and Borneo. The loss of Singapore, which had been built up as a great imperial fortress during the years between the wars, was a heavy blow to British pride and to Britain's reputation in India, in Australia and the whole region. The Australian government gave the impression that it thought Britain had deliberately lost Singapore without caring about its effect on Australia's security, which would in future have to depend on the United States. In India the results were even more serious: Britain's reputation as an invulnerable military power had survived two years of set-backs against Germany but was suddenly exposed by this defeat. Indians who had seen Britain as obviously preferable to Germany were not nearly so sure that Britain ought to be supported against another Asian power. In the summer of 1942 the British government entered negotiations on the basis of giving Dominion status to India after the war was over; Congress dismissed this as, in Gandhi's words, 'a postdated cheque on a failing bank'. After negotiations came to an end, Congress organised itself for a campaign to compel Britain to 'Quit India'. At a time of acute external danger, the British authorities now faced an internal challenge as fierce as anything seen in 1930.[7] The authorities responded by using their emergency powers to an extent that was only to be expected in wartime. Congress supporters were arrested in sufficient numbers for the British to remain in control, and the crisis strengthened the position of the Muslim League. It had been placed on an equal footing with Congress in the 1942 negotiations; its leader, Jinnah, took care not to be too closely associated with the British, but the British need for mass support made them put up with a great deal from him as long as he acknowledged that India should go on fighting as part of the British Empire. As a British decision to 'Quit India' would have left India in the hands of Congress and buried all hope of an independent Pakistan, the League was forced to work with the British just as the British were forced to work with the League.

The British were able to assert themselves as imperial rulers in India while the war was on, declaring that this was a temporary emergency. They acted in the same way in Egypt, Iraq and other countries in the Middle East. Britain and Egypt had made a treaty in 1936 under which the British withdrew from their ill-defined position of control over the country, but they retained rights to occupy the area round the Suez Canal, and to re-enter Egypt in the event of an emergency. War with Germany could reasonably be seen as an emergency, and Italy's entry into the war on Germany's side in June 1940 raised the immediate threat of invasion from Italy's colony in Libya. This became the focus of British military effort for the next two or three years, and at one point the ambassador reached the point of advising King Farouk to abdicate on the grounds that he was not sufficiently fully committed to the Allied cause. The king was able to convince the British that he would do better in future. In Persia (now Iran) the shah was less fortunate, and was sent into exile, and in Iraq British troops suppressed a pro-German rebellion. These acts of authority could all be justified on the grounds of necessity, yet it was most unlikely that anything of the sort could be done after the war.

Just before the Battle of Britain Churchill said that 'if the British Commonwealth and Empire lasts for a thousand years',[8] 1940 would still be its finest hour. The reference to a thousand years may have been no more than a comment on some of the grandiose ideas of a thousand-year Reich Hitler had put forward. Churchill probably revealed more of his own assessment of the situation when he declared that he had not become the king's first minister to preside over the liquidation of the British Empire.[9] Liquidation became steadily more likely as Britain had to draw on its credit, moral as well as material, to keep making its immense wartime efforts. Defeat, during the last three years of the war, was very unlikely but victory was bound to be accompanied by exhaustion, debt and the emergence of new forces and new powers that would not be easy to reconcile with empire.

# 8

# *Towards Decolonisation*

The British emerged among the victors when war in Europe and in eastern Asia came to an end in 1945, and they regained their colonies in Asia and the Pacific. They were not returning in the awkward role of mere beneficiaries of the victories of others (like the Dutch in the Dutch East Indies, which very soon became Indonesia, or the French in Indo-China, which broke up into Cambodia, Laos and Vietnam over the next ten years), yet their position could never be the same after the defeats of 1941 and 1942.

Many pressures weighed upon the British Empire in the decades after 1945. It is hard to say that any one of them was decisive but, without an awakening of national consciousness in a great many colonies, several external pressures would have lost much of their importance and the British might have found it relatively easy to face their other imperial problems.[1] The war did a great deal to encourage national feeling all over the world; colonies in which the main political sentiment had been loyalty to a distant monarch became much readier to see themselves as nations with a right to become independent states. The war also made people much readier to believe in the universal applicability of the idea that everybody had a right to belong to an independent nation state. In 1919 world opinion had been ready to acknowledge that people in Europe and the Americas had a right to national self-determination, but had not thought this principle applied to Africa or to most of Asia. By 1945 national self-determination was seen as a principle that applied all over the world, though it was unlikely to arouse much attention in countries where the local population showed no sign of interest in it. The tension of the Cold War, which set the United States and its allies against the Soviet Union and its allies in Europe in the late 1940s, and then turned into rivalry over most of the world from the early 1950s until the late 1980s, meant that almost any movement for national independence could hope for sympathy from one side or the other. A well-organised movement would get material support from both sides. The Soviet Union was helped by its links to a Marxist ideology which allowed it to accuse its opponents of a policy of almost automatically exploiting their colonial empires. When the political empires were brought to an end amicably enough, but without any noticeable increase in the prosperity of the newly-liberated colonies, Marxism was adapted to produce a doctrine of neo-colonialism which asserted that a change in political institutions made no difference to economic realities.[2] At the level of theory, this argument did not explain why people had taken the trouble to build up empires if capitalist exploitation could go ahead without them. In practice many governments accepted the loans western bankers thrust upon them lavishly in the late 1970s but, when they were asked to keep up the interest payments, complained of financial oppression.

The United States had its own tradition of hostility to imperial rule. This enabled it to stand aside from its European allies and press for movements for national independence to be recognised quickly, to stop them being diverted towards the Communist system. On the other hand, the United States was ready to help oppose any independence movement that fell under Communist influence, even when the old imperial power had lost interest in the struggle. In British Guiana (now Guyana) the British were ready enough in the 1950s to depose an elected prime minister who declared himself a Marxist, and to produce a new electoral system to reduce his chances of returning to power.[3] By the 1980s they were willing to accept much more disorderly revolutionaries in Grenada, but in this case the United States sent its own forces to bring a rebellion to an end. In Africa many leaders of independence movements had been educated by Christian missionaries and were likely to be repelled by the atheistic side of Marxism, even if they were attracted by socialism in the sense of government planning to promote equality.

The war greatly reduced Britain's economic strength. It had lost touch with some of its prewar customers, and it had had to sell many of the investments that provided the interest and dividends it had used to pay for imports for many decades. Some members and supporters of the 1945 Labour government accepted the idea that the empire was a source of profit, so they were left disapproving of imperial rule but afraid that ending it would leave their voters in Britain worse off.[4] As Britain withdrew from almost all its colonies over the following twenty-five years, and its standard of living rose faster than usual, even if not as quickly as that of other

European countries, the idea that owning colonies was essential for the country's prosperity became much less plausible.

People in Britain who had no desire to make money out of the colonies, and believed that they had been acquired in order to end local warfare and enable their subjects to live peacefully with one another, might all the same not want to spend money on possessions overseas. The British taxpayer had paid very little for conquering half the world, apart for the money spent fighting for national survival in wars with other European powers which had brought in some colonies as one of the rewards of victory. When the British colonial authorities were unchallenged in the territories they ruled, the costs of government were kept low. If they went up the British treasury asked awkward questions, which became even more pointed if a colony could not balance its budget and called on London for assistance.

Resisting nationalist challenges to the British imperial position cost much more money than had been spent on colonies previously, and the British saw no reason for bearing those costs for any length of time. Possibly the Britain of 1900, so rich compared with many other nations, might have tried to find money to pay for an empire that actually drained money from the taxpayers' pockets, though the decline in imperial enthusiasm as soon as it faced the costs of the Boer War casts doubt even on this. Britain's position in 1900 had been so impressive that local nationalists could not easily imagine complete independence; they were attracted by the idea of local autonomy to manage their own affairs, within the security of Britain's universal naval supremacy and reputation for unique skills in the art of government. Neither of these forces mattered nearly so much by 1945, and as a result nationalists wanted independence rather than local autonomy.

British emigration to the Dominions, which had done so much to keep them attached to Britain up to 1914, had remained high in the 1920s, but the flow went into reverse in the 1930s. The discomforts of unemployment in a strange land convinced recent emigrants that they would do better if they went back to a place where they had friends and family to help them. Emigration revived after 1945, with prospects opening up in Kenya and the Rhodesias which were understood to be especially attractive to those worried about finding servants in postwar Britain. For ten or fifteen years after the war Canada and Australia maintained immigration policies that concentrated on attracting people from Britain, and emigration to Australia was as high as at almost any point in the past. But by the 1960s both countries were ready to welcome people from all over the world, and British

emigration changed its emphasis.[5] Some people who went overseas from
Britain in the past had expected to emigrate permanently, but others had
always expected to return to their native land after a period abroad,
sometimes attached to some aspect of British imperial authority or commercial supremacy in India or in other colonies. The end of imperial
authority in the second half of the twentieth century did not affect the
idea of going abroad and coming back home sooner or later, but people
who went overseas in this way were now referred to as expatriates, distin-
guishing them from emigrants who went overseas on a more permanent
basis.

Britain's economic difficulties in 1945 had a direct effect on Commonwealth relations. In 1930 American trade policy had been highly protectionist,
and this had come to be blamed for at least part of the depression of the
1930s. By 1945 the United States was strongly committed to Free Trade,
and was determined to use its new-found strength to press other countries
to follow the same policy. It insisted that, to get a loan for postwar
reconstruction in 1945, Britain must accept free trade and do nothing to
extend its existing preferential tariffs. The British government was not so
wedded to imperial preference that it thought accepting the General Agreement on Tariffs and Trade was a great sacrifice, and it was greatly relieved
to find that the United States was not going to return to protectionism.
The effect of the change was that the Ottawa Agreements could be extended
to promote closer connections among Commonwealth countries only if
they were ready to set up an Empire Free Trade Area without any internal
tariffs.

Relations with the Dominions would in any case have had to be conducted
in a different way after 1945. Canada and Australia stood briefly in positions
of considerable importance. As Germany, Japan and Italy had been conquered and disgraced, and France had been weakened and divided by defeat
in 1940 followed by four years of German occupation, the Dominions
stepped forward into something of a vacuum. They had fought throughout
the war, they were victorious, and they looked forward to a wider audience
for their views. Between the wars they had rarely expressed their opinions
about foreign policy to any audience wider than conferences of Commonwealth prime ministers, but now they felt ready to speak to the United
Nations and to expand their diplomatic representation to cover a wide
range of countries.[6]

In the late 1940s most of the Dominions had governments of the centre-left which felt some sympathy for the Labour government in Britain, but Britain's relations with the Dominions, after they had gained power to look after their own affairs, had never been merely a sentimental matter of friendly feelings. The prospect of imperial preference, and its reality during the 1930s, had helped unite countries moving towards independence and equality, and the Royal Navy and the investment resources of the City of London had provided other reasons why practical men unaffected by deep feelings of loyalty might have thought it made sense to keep in close touch with Britain. After 1945 it was clear that the United States was much richer and much stronger militarily than Britain, though it took some time for the size of the disparity to be fully appreciated, as people at first thought that part of Britain's weaker economic position was a merely temporary result of wartime strain and exhaustion.

One large imperial problem had to be faced at once. Wartime emergency powers could no longer be used to control India, and the British had to think about establishing Dominion status quickly. The Labour Party had accepted this approach before war broke out. When it formed the new British government in 1945, it may have reflected that at the time the 1935 Act was passed nobody would have been surprised if India had advanced to Dominion status in a dozen years or so. In those dozen years the situation had changed because the Muslim League had won a stronger position and adopted a more extreme programme during the war than it had had in 1939. In British politics Labour tended to see Congress as the party most favourable to socialism, while some Conservatives thought the Muslim League was the true descendant of the 'martial races', but these preconceptions had more effect on rhetoric than on events. Elections were held in India at the end of 1945, and the results showed that the Muslim League had turned itself into a mass party and had won almost all the seats reserved for Muslims 'at the centre' in Delhi. Congress remained much the largest single party, but its strength was now based on the devotion of the Hindu majority rather than the support across all of India that it had attracted in 1936. It was clear that Muslims wanted some degree of autonomy but it was uncertain whether this had to involve separation. A cabinet mission from Britain examined the situation and suggested a possible framework, in which provinces would elect their own governments. The Muslim League provinces of the north west and north east would then organise a second-tier government while the Congress provinces in the rest of the country would set up another second-tier government; after which the two second-tier governments would cooperate in choosing a third-tier government for the whole of India, which would run defence and foreign policy and a few nationwide services. This arrangement might have held the country together, at the cost of giving it an unwieldy system of government, and the Muslim League might have held back from pressing demands for an independent Pakistan. Nehru, the dominant figure in the younger generation of Congress leaders, made it quite clear that he thought the proposal was impracticable. It was laid aside and the viceroy, Wavell, an intelligent but taciturn soldier who lamented the inveterate tendency of politicians to think about things in terms of politics, told London that the British community was in grave danger and that he was going to prepare a scheme for it to withdraw from India.

The government was alarmed to hear so pessimistic an assessment, though it realised that law and order were breaking down in the face of ever-sharper hostility between Congress and League supporters. If the British community was in some danger, Hindus and Muslims caught in the developing struggle were in a much worse position, with some risk that the whole structure of government would be torn apart as soldiers and police lined up with one religious community or the other while the politicians tried to find a safe way forward. The British government realised that it would be blamed for whatever went wrong if it stayed on indefinitely, and that this meant Indian politicians were under no real pressure to reach agreement. In 1946 it could still expect to negotiate an amicable departure, but its authority was obviously declining. It had to acknowledge that it would soon find it was doing more harm than good if it went on trying to administer a country where its instruments for governing were crumbling in its hands under the stress of religious division. In February 1947 Wavell was dismissed and replaced by Lord Mountbatten, who was given full powers to deal with the situation on the basis that the British would leave India by June 1948. The Muslim League now had a decisive advantage: if no other arrangements were made, it had only to wait and let power fall into the hands of the existing provincial governments. The British then undertook to grant independence well before June 1948, which persuaded Congress to agree to the partitioning of India and the creation of Pakistan.

For a moment Congress seemed ready to give weight to the fears of the Muslims by calling its new state Hindustan, but it sensibly kept the name of India for its truncated portion. The viceroy and his government began the immense task of dividing up the army and the other moveable assets of the central government by August 1947, while a British judge drew up boundary lines for partitioning Bengal and the Punjab; the Muslim League had won narrow majorities in both provinces, but large Hindu minorities in the west of Bengal and in the east of Punjab would be stranded on the wrong side of the border if the entire provinces passed intact to Pakistan. Partition rested on the principle that as few people as possible should be placed under a government that they disliked, but applying the principle involved drawing boundary lines where none had existed before.

The division of the assets of the central government, including one of the world's largest armies, was carried out on time, but the Bengal and Punjab boundaries had still not been announced at the moment of independence. When Nehru, as the first prime minister of India, said on 15 August 1947 'Long years ago we made a tryst with destiny and now the time comes when we shall redeem our pledge, not wholly or in full measure but very substantially',[7] he was referring with obvious disappointment to the division of the country along unknown boundaries. It became all too clear after the event that all the leaders involved had brought independence forward much too quickly when they accelerated it by a full ten months. Millions of people fled across the new boundaries to escape being stranded as religious minorities, and hundreds of thousands were killed while they were fleeing, or in order to force them to flee. Gandhi was able to bring about some sort of peace in Bengal, but in the Punjab trains crawling towards the frontiers with their loads of refugees were held up and people of the wrong religion were slaughtered. India and Pakistan were always likely to be on bad terms immediately after independence, but the blood of the massacres made relations far worse. The position of the princes had also not been settled before independence. Pakistan was not greatly concerned by this because the princely territories lay within India or on its borders, but the Indian government was eager to bring all of them under its control. This caused further trouble on the northern boundary. The maharajah of Kashmir was a Hindu and was persuaded to place himself under the government of India, but his mainly Muslim subjects rose in rebellion, with some assistance from the government of Pakistan. After several weeks of fighting a ceasefire line was agreed. It has remained the temporary and unsatisfactory frontier between northern India and northern Pakistan ever since.

Despite the disasters of the months just after independence, Britain remained on surprisingly good terms with both India and Pakistan. The

British government hoped that India would become a Dominion – or, as people were beginning to say, a member of the Commonwealth – and, while less concerned about what it did, was ready to welcome Pakistan as a member too. Many Congress supporters felt that being a Dominion was not the same as being fully independent; others wanted India to become a republic, which was not consistent with the monarchical definition of the Commonwealth worked out in 1926. Burma made the point in 1947 by deciding to become a republic and not to consider being a member of the Commonwealth. This approach was underlined in 1948 when the government of the Irish Free State declared Ireland was to become a republic, accepting that this involved ceasing to be a member of the Commonwealth. The other Dominions had been so infuriated by Ireland's wartime neutrality that they almost welcomed its abrupt departure, but it did make clear the difficulty in India's case. On the other hand, Pakistan wanted to enlist allies against India, and was ready to accept Dominion status, which made Indian politicians much more reluctant to leave the Commonwealth. If they could become a republic and still stay in the Commonwealth, most of their opposition would be disarmed: they would have asserted their freedom of action and the Commonwealth would have shown its readiness to accommodate them. By 1949 a new form of words had been worked out which declared the monarch to be the head of the Commonwealth but did not require the Dominions to owe allegiance to anyone, although the members of the Commonwealth did require any country becoming a republic to ask to be readmitted after carrying out the change. These arrangements may have seemed to some people to be mere juggling with words, but they had a profound effect on the future of the Commonwealth. In debates about the road to independence in the next two decades the example of India was always of great importance and opponents of the imperial connection had always to acknowledge that, if membership of the Commonwealth was accepted and even valued by India, it could not be dismissed as a disguised form of continued British domination. A Commonwealth without India might have become a club for white people who spoke English, but after 1949 membership was likely to be accepted as a way to become independent that eased a nation's entry into the international community when it left the colonial structure of British protection and control.

Ceylon, now Sri Lanka, became a Dominion at the same time as India and Pakistan, though when it emerged to independence it seemed to have much less difficulty about internal divisions along lines of religion or language. The Commonwealth of the 1950s was changing from an association of countries with white rulers and voters to an assembly of countries in which white rulers were a small and noticeably prosperous minority. Of its eight members in the early 1950s, Australia, Britain, Canada, India, Pakistan and South Africa were of considerable importance in the world. By 1970 the Commonwealth contained many more countries, but most of them were fairly small and relatively unimportant. This became even more obviously the case by 1980.

The position of South Africa raised questions of racial division. Smuts was as racially tolerant as any politician could be while winning the support of the purely white electorate. He knew much more about the outside world than most South Africans. He may also have been led in this direction by his readiness to work with the mine owners of Johannesburg and Kimberley, who would have welcomed an open economy in which Africans could compete for employment on an equal basis and undercut the wages of unskilled white workers who had secured well-paid jobs simply because of the colour of their skin. As wartime prime minister Smuts had directed an economy that flourished and needed additional labour, which had brought a great many Africans into cities to work. His political opponents said he was betraying the Afrikaner way of life to English and Jewish capitalists, and to Africans who were threatening the jobs that enabled 'poor whites' to keep up some sort of dignity. In 1948 Smuts's United Party polled a majority of the votes cast but lost the election because seats in the countryside had always had much smaller electorates than urban seats. The new government was much more purely Afrikaner, and disliked the British minority in the electorate, but it realised that it had to work with the industrial and mining companies. In theory its policy of apartheid would have driven Africans out of the modern economy and back to rural reservations with some degree of political autonomy, but this was not remotely possible. Africans knew that the reservations were miserably poor, that mineowners and manufacturers needed unskilled labour, and that most white people expected to employ African servants. The avowed policy of forcing blacks and whites to live in separate parts of the country made life difficult for Africans living in or around big cities, but it never managed to reduce their numbers. In practice apartheid turned out to be a matter of finding ways of keeping white and blacks as separate as possible when they had to live in the same towns and cities. The 1948 Nationalist government in South Africa looked back to the past, but its legislation was simply a codification of the way people had normally behaved in the 1920s or the 1930s. In the nineteenth and in the first half of the twentieth century most countries in which the population was divided along colour lines had followed similar policies, sometimes enforced by public opinion and sometimes by law. It was Nazi readiness in the 1940s to take racial doctrines to their ultimate conclusion that convinced people in most of the world that racism was something that the human race could not safely tolerate. Apartheid in 1950 may have been no more oppressive than arrangements in parts of the southern United States at the same time, but South Africa was moving in the opposite direction to the trend of world opinion, and this was bound to lead to trouble in the Commonwealth. Asian nations had already become members of the Commonwealth and west African states were likely to become members in the near future, which would be hard to reconcile with South African membership.

The difficulties of the Palestine mandate had been made much more acute by the war. While large numbers of Jewish survivors of the Holocaust wanted to enter the country, the Arabs already in the country felt that they were about to be swamped. The British authorities did not want to take responsibility for letting Jewish immigrants become a majority of the population in the mandate territory. The British tried to deal with the problem in the way that they had handled an apparently similar situation in India, laying down a timetable and declaring that they was going to leave – whatever the state of affairs might be on the appointed day. But in India it was accepted that the British had no further ambitions in the country and had no direct concern about a partition line between the two successor states, and that Congress and the League were free to decide what to do next. The announcement that Britain would give up the Palestine mandate in June 1948 did not help in the same way, because the Arabs saw the Jewish population as a replacement for direct rule by western imperial forces, and Jewish settlers felt that the British hoped that something unpleasant would happen to them once the mandate was over. In India there had been some degree of trust between the British and the Congress and League politicians, but there was no comparable degree of trust in Palestine and boundary lines were left to be settled by war between Israel and its enemies. There was no question of Israel becoming a member of the Commonwealth, and Arab countries which had been under British rule did not join the Commonwealth either.

India and Israel were the visible problems of empire faced by the British government of the late 1940s, but questions about other colonies lay fairly close to the surface. The government was ready to think about preparing other colonies to move along the same path as India, though the Indian example encouraged some policy-makers to think preparation might take much the same time span as the sixty years that had passed from the launching of Congress to Independence in 1947. India and Pakistan had strong enough military and economic foundations to stand on their own feet as independent nations, even though Pakistan had to face the problem of division into two sections, to the north west and to the north east of India. The British government was anxious to make sure that other nations which became independent would be equally viable, but independence movements sometimes felt in the 1950s that this criterion was being used to delay their progress.

The Second World War had not decisively hastened change in India, and this helped support the assumption that change elsewhere would proceed at the same sedate pace. In the mid-1950s it was thought that some of the larger African colonies might take until the 1980s to become independent and that some smaller colonies would never become independent. Even at the end of the 1950s this timetable had not been greatly accelerated.[8] In west Africa the problems were relatively straightforward because no white settlers had come there. The climate in Nigeria and in the Gold Coast was unattractive enough for people from Europe to mean that the imperial connection was simply an administrative structure to maintain law and order; the business of the trading companies was run by managers who took it for granted that they would retire to Britain. The companies might wonder how well law and order would be maintained after independence, and might have reflected that British colonial governments often gave some informal preference to British traders, but they were not seriously worried about what would happen after the end of British rule.

West Africans who had served during the Second World War had learnt something about the world. They realised that their white rulers had problems and failings of their own, and they were much more ready than before to think of Nigeria or of the Gold Coast as nations. India had always been visibly a geographical unity lying south of the mountain ranges, and had at times been more or less united politically before the arrival of the British. Colonies in Africa could not look back to the past in that way, and national feeling existed almost entirely as a response to imperial rule

– Nigerians were the people who were ruled by the colonial authorities whom Britain had installed in Nigeria. They did not possess the linguistic unity of Poles or of Czechs opposing imperial rule in nineteenth-century Europe, though their leaders could work together in English like the leaders of Congress in the Indian struggle for independence.

In 1947 the very moderate African leaders in Gold Coast politics invited the talented and dynamic Dr Kwame Nkrumah to come back from the United States to organise a political party, much as the leaders of the Muslim League leaders had enlisted Jinnah's help. This pattern occurred often enough. Gandhi had gone back to India with some reputation as a leader, combined with a useful detachment from local rivalries, and several other leaders of independence movements, in the British Empire and elsewhere, returned at an appropriate moment and organised their people. Colonial authorities did not always understand the attraction of a leader who came from outside in this way, feeling that he would be out of touch with the local situation. All the evidence suggests that people in colonies wanted a leader who was not involved in their local concerns. They could handle the problems of their own districts, but what they needed was someone from the outside world who could see India, or the Gold Coast or Kenya, as a nation and put the point of view of the nation to the colonial authorities. The colonial authorities had to spend their lives immersed in local detail, so it was natural enough for them to expect other people who cared about the colony to take the same approach. As the effect was to make it look as if they were following policies of 'divide and rule', the unifying force of the national leader in resisting such an approach was all the more welcome.

Nkrumah organised his political party, the Convention People's Party, and pushed the older leaders into the background. In 1948 he led a march on the government offices in Accra which turned into days of rioting, revealing a depth of discontent that had not until then been suspected. The British government accepted the situation calmly enough, and put into effect a commission report which said that representative assemblies should be given wider powers than had previously been intended. Progress towards independence was greatly accelerated by the riots and the realisation that the war had changed a great deal. When Nkrumah was imprisoned, as a danger to the peace of the country, it helped solidify his position as the leader of African opinion in the developed and highly populated south of

Decolonisation in Africa

the colony. The question of the Asante minority in the north remained to be faced in the future.

The Gold Coast had one of the highest incomes per head in Africa, with a prosperity based mainly on cocoa cultivation. It had a population of 6,000,000, about three times as large as that of New Zealand, which had almost the smallest population of any independent sovereign state at that time. British colonies still showed their origins as territories which had grown outwards for imperial administrative purposes from a small initial settlement. The colonies which had not expanded territorially were often so small that they would have difficulty running their own affairs unless a number of contiguous colonies could be brought together. Canada, Australia and South Africa had all been formed by bringing several colonies together in this way, and in the 1950s it was thought that this approach would help a number of colonies that were acknowledged to have prospects of reaching Dominion status fairly soon. Africans in east and central Africa were afraid that so many settlers had immigrated to Kenya and to Southern Rhodesia that other colonies might be merged with them to create new states which had enough resources to let the white minorities move rapidly to independence and then establish a monopoly of power like that in South Africa.

Northern Rhodesia and Southern Rhodesia had been set up in the 1890s as part of a single piece of imperial expansion. While the contiguous colony of Nyasaland had originally been set up by Scottish missionaries, it had survived largely because Rhodes had put money into it as part of his plans for Africa north of the Limpopo. In economic terms unification in central Africa made even better sense than in the three colonies of Kenya, Uganda and Tanganyika in East Africa. The population would be larger and the financial foundation more stable, so it would be easier to attract investment. Unifying the three central African colonies would not involve the consultation with the United Nations which would be necessary in East Africa because of Tanganyika's status as a mandate. The Labour government held a conference to open up the question of a federation of Northern and Southern Rhodesia and Nyasaland, but African dissent persuaded it not to press ahead with the idea, despite its economic advantages, until the concerns of the Africans had been met. Shortly afterwards the Conservatives won the 1951 election and decided that the economic advantages of federation would soon reconcile Africans to the change. The Federation of the Rhodesias and Nyasaland, often called the Central African Federation, set up in

1953, was a useful instrument for economic development, but it operated in a way that made it all too clear what a candid Rhodesian politician had in mind when he said that the federation was to be a partnership between white and black, just like the partnership between a horse and its rider. The constitutions of the three colonies which made up the federation had very little in common. The electoral system in Southern Rhodesia ensured that the assembly to which its government was responsible would have a white majority until many Africans had become much richer, but foreign policy was in theory left to the British government, which also had a veto over legislation affecting Africans. The government of the federation was in much the same position and, as expected, pressed for Dominion status. The governments of the two other parts of the federation were run much more directly from the Colonial Office.[9]

Kenya, Uganda and Tanganyika had already taken some steps to unify their government services, but further discussion of 'closer union' became impossible when a rebellion broke out in Kenya in 1951. The organisation known as Mau Mau never got beyond the first stage of mobilising opposition to imperial rule among the Kikuyu, the largest single group in the colony, by attacking isolated white farmers and killing Africans who worked for white employers or for the government, but the government of the colony could not control the situation with its own resources and reinforcements had to be brought from Britain. Fighting a successful four-year campaign against guerrillas was irritatingly expensive, and the British government began to think that, while it was certainly not going to let Mau Mau acquire any legitimacy, it needed to find Africans with whom it could work. The obvious African leader in the colony, Jomo Kenyatta, had been sympathetic enough to Mau Mau to be convicted of having supported the rebellion. His trial had left elements of doubt open but the government of the colony felt that it could not work with Kenyatta, and other African leaders would not work with the government while Kenyatta was in prison. In terms of economic development and the existence of an educated group to run the government, at the time considered essential for further progress towards Dominion status, Kenya had much stronger claims than either Uganda or Tanganyika. While Kenya was immobilised, nothing could be done elsewhere in East Africa.

In Kenya there had been suggestions without much evidence that Mau Mau had Communist connections. In Malaya tension between the Malay majority and the Chinese minority in the population had led some of the

Chinese to look to the government of China for help. As the long Communist struggle in China had ended in triumph in 1949, this meant accepting Communist leadership. The British government organised itself to fight a guerilla war. Malaya produced enough tin and rubber to be strategically important in the Cold War, and some of the proceeds of these commodities were deposited in London and sometimes used to support the international value of the pound sterling. The war in Malaya involved a large British military commitment, but the British political position was much better than that of the French, who were deeply involved in an unsuccessful effort, with substantial American support, to hold on to their colony in Indo-China. The Malay majority had no desire to see a Chinese minority replace the British as rulers of Malaya, and some of the Chinese were uneasy about the idea of a Communist government. The British were a little uncertain that Malaya was ready for self-government, but promises of Dominion status were clearly the best way of rallying Malay support against the Chinese Communists. By 1955 the danger was over, and the British could prepare to welcome into the Commonwealth a government with which they had worked successfully during the crisis.

In the early 1950s the foreign secretary, Anthony Eden, enjoyed diplomatic successes in two areas linked to imperial withdrawal, which helped him to become prime minister in 1955. He managed the peace conference after the French defeat in Indo-China in a way that limited the damage to the western alliance. He also worked out an arrangement with Gamel Abdel Nasser, the new ruler of Egypt who had come to power some months after a military coup in 1952, by which Sudan emerged as an independent country, with no British or Commonwealth links, but also with no institutional links to Egypt. Britain withdrew from the strip of territory round the Suez Canal, so Gladstone's temporary occupation was over, after lasting a little more than seventy years. The decline in trade with India, and the ending of British rule there, had not deprived the canal of its importance to Britain. In the years after 1945 oil had become more and more essential to the economy of Britain and of most other European countries, and by the 1950s most of the oil came through the canal from countries around the Gulf. The British government had responded favourably to Nasser's proposal to build a dam across the Nile for economic development but when, in the summer of 1956, the United States withdrew the financing on which the dam depended and Nasser struck back by nationalising the canal, the British government and much of British public opinion felt outraged and shared Eden's conviction that Nasser must not be allowed 'to have his thumb on our windpipe'.[10]

At first it looked as if Britain would have plenty of allies to help put pressure on Egypt. The United States said Nasser must be made to disgorge. France blamed Nasser for trouble in its colony of Algeria. Twenty nations which used the canal gave strong support to Britain and France in their efforts to make sure Nasser did not find extra money for his Nile dam by neglecting the dredging of the canal or raising the tolls to impossible heights. Britain and France assembled an invasion force to help persuade Egypt of the strength of their case, and by mid October Nasser had been brought to the point of serious negotiation. But Eden had no desire for a settlement and, without consulting most of his cabinet, he joined a plan that France and Israel had been working out for some weeks: Israel was to attack Egypt, and France and Britain would send the invasion force forward to take over the canal on the grounds that it had to be protected from damage in fighting between Israel and Egypt. In late October the scheme was launched successfully enough, but by the time the invasion force was landing at the north end of the canal, worldwide outrage was being expressed at an attack on Egypt clearly intended to put the Suez Canal back under imperial rule. The United States joined in the international chorus of disapproval at this imperialist and aggressive behaviour. Before the invasion force could move down the canal, American pressure on Britain's supplies of oil, and the weakness of sterling in international money markets, had made the British government decide to end its involvement in the attack. This forced the French to stop as well and Britain and France then found themselves obliged to withdraw from Egypt amidst almost universal denunciation. They could reflect that they were no longer powerful enough to carry out operations at a distance from home unless the United States gave at least tacit support and remained neutral. The British position in the Middle East was weakened; the pro-British government of Iraq was overthrown a couple of years later; and Britain prepared to withdraw from Kuwait, which had turned from a small trading centre in the Gulf – with a dash of piracy – into an oil-rich country which sometimes gave welcome support to the British Treasury.

France was enraged by the British decision to abandon the Suez operation and decided it was time to abandon the alliance with Britain which had survived in one form or another for over fifty years, even if the alternative was an alliance with Germany. The British government was more concerned

with restoring good relations with the United States. Eden was replaced
by Harold Macmillan and the new prime minister made conciliating the
United States his first priority. In his first days in office he also ordered
a broad survey of relations with the colonies to see if they were really
worth the trouble they could cause. The survey reassured the government
that no serious economic inconvenience would follow if the colonies became
independent, provided they were not swept up into the expanding sphere
of influence that the Soviet Union was now organising. It went on to
say 'It was felt that the economic interests of the United Kingdom were
unlikely to be decisive in determining whether a territory should become
independent.' [11]

The survey counted Ghana as independent, saw Malaya just about to be
independent, expected the West Indies and the Central African Federation
to follow in a few years, and listed eleven or twelve other territories which
were likely to have substantial developments in self-government in the next
ten years. Macmillan may have been reassured by the thought that decolonisation would not have adverse economic consequences, and he seems
to have felt by the summer of 1957 that the pace needed to be much quicker
than he could make public at that stage. He knew that after the humiliation
of Suez he could not ask his party to put up with anything that looked
like a forced retreat from empire until he had done something to restore
their confidence, which meant waiting until after he had won a general
election. Apparently he was deeply impressed by the pessimistic, cut-your-
losses advice of a colonial governor who told him that the African colonies
would not be able to manage their own affairs properly for fifteen or twenty
years, but added that they were by this stage so hostile to imperial rule
that the British could not help them learn how to manage their affairs.[12]

The British government was able to show in 1957 that it was not trying
to revive the old imperial system. Malaya became a member of the Commonwealth as a natural development of the Anglo-Malay alliance which had
defeated the Communist Chinese rebellion, and in Africa the Gold Coast
moved to independence, under the new name of Ghana. Nkrumah's party
had won a decisive enough election victory in 1951 for him to be brought
from prison to become chief minister to prepare for Dominion status. Like
many other minorities in the period of decolonisation that was to come,
the Asante asked for assurances for their position. Yet, short of imposing
a heavily decentralised constitution on a country that was already seen as
rather small, the imperial authorities could do nothing for them except

hope that the new government would see the disadvantages of running a policy that favoured one region at the expense of another. When independence for Nigeria was discussed nobody had any doubt that its population was large enough, but it was not as rich as the Gold Coast and it had much deeper regional and linguistic divisions. Nigerian politicians accepted warnings about disunity from colonial officials as reasonable, and acknowledged that independence might have to wait while a federal system was set up to accommodate regional differences. The people of the north had good claims to make up a majority of the population but they were less educated and less organised than people further south. The British were able to slow down progress toward independence while the northerners prepared themselves, and in any case the country was large enough for a tripartite federation of western, eastern and northern regions not to be seen as a source of weakness.

Working out these arrangements took so long that Nigeria did not become independent until 1960. By then changes in French and Belgian policy had transformed the position in Africa. France had for decades treated her entire empire as if it was a single nation. French islands in the Caribbean and the Pacific, and French cities in Africa, were represented in the National Assembly. A few Africans rose to positions of considerable political importance in the Fourth Republic. But when the wartime hero Charles de Gaulle was swept back to power in 1958, as the result of a rebellion in Algeria, he decided that the whole process of ruling colonies in Africa was a waste of time and set out to turn them into independent countries closely linked to France for diplomatic purposes. Financial aid to maintain political and linguistic links could be provided on a very generous per capita basis, because most of the former French colonies in Africa had rather small populations, but their governments would be assessed strictly in terms of their loyalty and usefulness to France. By 1960 it was clear that the French empire south of the Sahara would be independent in a matter of months rather than years. Belgium had never pursued anything like the French policy of assimilation but it tried, with an extraordinary lack of success, to follow the same policy of rapid independence followed by a high level of subsequent diplomatic influence in its only colony of any importance, the Belgian Congo (subsequently Zaire, and now Congo). While it is hard to tell how far Macmillan had got in working out his policy for British colonies in Africa, the French change of direction meant that progress had to be rapid. De Gaulle's decision to turn all the French colonies in Africa

into independent countries made it very hard for Britain to maintain its
position, even if the British government had still wanted to do so.

# 9

# *After Empire*

When Macmillan won the general election in 1959, he reorganised his government to give Iain Macleod the task of accelerating the process of what was becoming known as decolonisation. The old term 'Dominion status' faded away; in 1960 Nigeria became independent. Macmillan went on a tour of Africa which ended with a speech to the South African parliament in Cape Town which made it clear that he did not think apartheid was justifiable in moral or in practical terms, and warned his audience that a 'wind of change' was blowing through Africa.[1] South African voters were not worried by this sign of tension in Commonwealth relations, and later in 1960 they voted by a narrow margin that the country should become a republic. The established practice that countries had to reapply for membership when they became republics had been a formality ever since the decision over India's application in 1949, but no countries had applied for readmission at a time when their relations with other members were under strain. At the 1961 Commonwealth conference Britain, Australia and New Zealand would have accepted South Africa's application for readmission, but the other members protested enough and raised sharp enough comments about the policy of apartheid to lead South Africa to withdraw its application and leave the Commonwealth. The Commonwealth was ready to allow democracy to be laid aside without serious concern – Pakistan had set up a military government and Ghana was moving towards becoming a one-party state – but it was determined to protest against racial discrimination.

The British government changed its criteria for independence soon after it had decided to decolonise quickly. Previously a well-organised system of government and successful economic development had been taken as the best grounds for making colonies independent. In his two years at the Colonial Office Macleod looked for the colonies in east Africa and in central Africa with the smallest white populations, and arranged that they should become independent first. This made perfectly good sense for the British government, as these were the colonies where moving to independence would cause least political difficulty in Britain, but it was not clear that Tanganyika and Nyasaland had been well prepared for the change. It would have required superhuman modesty and prudence on the part of African leaders to say that their countries were not ready for independence, though the history of Africa in the forty years after independence does suggest that the imperial powers were irresponsible to move so abruptly to a policy of 'independence at once'. But Africans certainly said they were ready for independence, and by 1960 they may have been so eager for it that delay would simply have led to wars of national liberation. Once the first colonies south of the Sahara had become independent, denying the claims to independence of other African colonies for any long period would have been very hard. Independence for Tanganyika was unusually easy to arrange: the United Nations was pleased to see one of its trust territories becoming independent; internally there was virtually only one political organisation in the country, the Tanganyika African National Union; and its leader Julius Nyerere was enough of a Christian, from education and from commitment, to reassure investors and western governments that his foreign policy would not lean towards Communism.[2]

Internally Nyasaland was no more of a problem. The population was almost entirely African, and it had been roused politically in 1959 by the return of Dr Hastings Banda. In personal terms Banda had none of the intellectual depth, the devotion to non-violence or the freedom from any desire for wealth or power of Gandhi, but in the political sphere he played much the same role as a leader who came back from abroad to oppose the existing system, to unite the people of his colony around him and – after what was now becoming the almost requisite period of imprisonment – emerge as prime minister. Nyasaland was well on the way to independence but, for this to happen, the Federation of the Rhodesias and Nyasaland had to be broken up, which led on to other problems. Late in 1960 a royal commission had reported the depth of African hostility to the federation, and recommended that the right of secession of the component states should be open to debate. The government of the federation resisted this furiously, but it was unable to stop the imperial authorities holding elections in Nyasaland and then quickly transferring power to Banda. Late in 1962 Nyasaland's right to secede was conceded. Although some supporters of the federation had thought its chances of survival would be strengthened by the removal of a large number of its African opponents, the secession of Nyasaland meant that Northern Rhodesia had to be allowed to choose whether to secede as well. Macleod produced a finely calibrated electoral system intended to push political parties in Northern Rhodesia into running candidates who drew support from both the black and the white communities, but the British government was not going to delay its departure for long in order to establish a racially mixed government.[3] At the end of 1962 an African-dominated government was formed in Northern Rhodesia which in 1963 chose to follow Nyasaland out of the federation, ending its existence. Both Nyasaland and Northern Rhodesia became independent in 1964, when the new countries changed their names to Malawi and Zambia.

By this time the British government had found ways to deal with problems in Uganda and Kenya which might have delayed their progress to independence. Some problems in Uganda had their roots in the days when the Imperial British East Africa Company took over Kenya and Uganda in the 1890s. There were lines of religious division within the educated groups who could hope to rule the country after independence, and the uneasy position of the African kingdoms which had survived under indirect rule had led to the brief exile of the kabaka of Buganda in the early 1950s. The British government decided that Dr Milton Obote was the best man to lead the country, and steered power into his hands. He was not the inevitable choice for ruler which Nyerere (for better) or Banda (for worse) had been in their countries, and there was something a little contrived about his rise to power. British policy was by this stage mainly concerned with finding someone who could hold the country together after independence and, especially when he had formed a partnership with the kabaka, Obote seemed an adequate choice. Uganda became independent a year after Tanganyika. Kenya had originally been seen as the most intractable problem in east Africa because of the importance of the white settlers, but by the early 1960s they had lost some of their influence. They had had to ask for help against Mau Mau, and they had not been able to reach an accommodation with any African group of any significance. No African leader could ignore the influence of the imprisoned Kenyatta. Sir Patrick Renison, an unnecessarily eloquent governor, called him 'a leader to darkness and death',[4] which expressed the settler view accurately enough, but African politicians who did not press for his release were terminating their own careers. His main support lay among the Kikuyu and, although he was able to make some alliances with other groups, his Kenya African National Union, clearly named to remind people of the party that had led

Tanganyika to independence, was seen by non-Kikuyu Africans as a tribal organisation. The Kenya African Democratic Union, designed as an anti-Kikuyu coalition, was able to persuade the British to set up a federal constitution, but when Kenyatta was released he advanced as a matter of course to become prime minister in mid-1963, and led his country to independence at the end of the year. The white settlers found, to their surprise and relief, that he was perfectly happy to see them go on running their farms in a way that helped that national economy, as long as he and a few friends were allowed a generous share of this prosperity.

Between 1960 and 1964 the British government had dissolved the Central African Federation and seen five of the six colonies of east and central Africa become independent. What was done in this region of Africa reflected the irreversible decision to bring imperial rule to an end. Problems emerged elsewhere, as a result of the decision, which were much harder to solve than simply leaving a new country to devise a new flag. Doubts had been expressed in the late 1950s about the viability of Ghana, with a population of five or six million, but no such doubts were to be heard in the case of Malawi, with a population of a little over two million and much worse economic prospects. It moved to independence as if there could be no difficulty about its ability to survive and prosper. Critics of the colonial empires were apt to say they had drawn boundaries in Africa which cut through the middle of African communities, but in fact practically no boundaries in Africa ran along straight lines like those that divided countries and their sub-divisions in North America. Except in the Sahara Desert, boundaries followed lines laid down in the late nineteenth-century treaties, which in turn reflected the decisions of African rulers about which European empire they would join. Attacks on the old colonial boundaries worried African politicians because the imperial powers really had disregarded pre-existing African boundaries when they set about bringing several existing communities together into a single colony. Condemning the boundaries which the Europeans had created was an invitation to secession and dis-integration. The danger could be seen in Nigeria in the late 1960s, when the Ibo of the eastern region of the Niger delta felt that they were being deprived of their share of power and patronage. From 1967 to 1970 they fought an unsuccessful war of secession for the independence of Biafra. The Nigerian government fought the war with a determination which owed a good deal to its concern about what would happen in other regions if secession once began, and the great majority of African states supported its efforts for the same reason. The African boundaries that had emerged in the late nineteenth century from the principles worked out at Berlin in 1885 might not be ideal, but the danger was that any attempt to alter them would lead not to better boundaries, nor to worse boundaries, but to no boundaries at all.

Confidence that boundaries would be respected, or perhaps detachment from what might happen next, may explain the readiness with which the British government saw Bechuanaland (now Botswana), Basutoland (now Lesotho) and Swaziland proceed to independence between 1966 and 1968. These three colonies were so closely connected to South Africa that the British governor-general in South Africa was usually also appointed high commissioner for them; they were sometimes called 'the high commission territories'. There was obviously some risk that they would fall within the South African sphere of influence after independence and turn into models for the nominally independent states, designed 'for Africans only' and nicknamed Bantustans, which the Nationalist Party saw as the fullest expression of its policy of apartheid. The dangers of economic absorption and political interference could not be avoided, but South Africa left the frontiers undisturbed.

If people felt sure that boundaries would be respected, one reason for the fear that some colonies were too small ever to become independent would be removed. In 1956 a Conservative politician had caused some trouble by saying, when discussing the position of Cyprus, that some colonies would never become independent. In 1960 Cyprus did become independent, one of the first colonies with a population below one million to do so, though the real difficulty was not the size of the population but the fact that it was sharply divided between a Greek-speaking Christian majority and a Turkish-speaking Muslim minority. In 1974 the island was, for practical purposes, partitioned between Greeks and Turks.

By then political leaders paid very little attention to the size of the population when making decisions about independence, though some attention was paid to the problem of expansionist neighbours and the chances that they would try to prevent a newly-emerged nation from remaining independent. In the 1950s, when considerations of size had been taken seriously, the British government decided that Jamaica and most of the other British colonies in the West Indies might be able to survive as an independent country if they were made into a single unit, as they now had universal suffrage and the white oligarchies had lost power in most islands. The Federation of the West Indies was launched with responsible government in 1958. Authorities in Britain no doubt thought the West Indian islands were a unit, though they had not been politically united since the seventeenth century. Jamaica was almost as far from the islands of the eastern Caribbean as Perth in Australia was from Melbourne and, while many of the smaller islands were quite close to one another, the colonies of other European nations often lay in between them. Perhaps all that people in England knew about the West Indies was that it had a cricket team which in the 1950s was as formidable as the Australians had been in the 1880s. While sport can help in nation-building, eighteen years passed between the winning of the Ashes and the establishment of Australian unity, with setbacks and regrouping for fresh efforts as the separate colonies struggled with the task. In the heated atmosphere of the rush to independence of the early 1960s, the Federation of the West Indies got only one chance to test its desire for unity. The distinguished Jamaican politician Norman Manley, who supported federation, had conceded that the Jamaican electorate should have a chance to express its opinion of the new arrangements before the West Indies became an independent state. The electoral system of the federation was weighted in favour of the smaller islands, which meant Jamaica's share of the seats in parliament did not reflect the fact that it had almost half the total population, which made it easy for Manley's opponents to say that their island was not being treated fairly. The 1961 referendum repudiated the federation and in 1962 Jamaica and Trinidad moved rapidly to independence as separate states, and the smaller colonies had to make their own way forward.[5]

The idea of federation, as an answer to the problem of small-size colonies and also of external danger, was applied rather more successfully in southeast Asia. The island colony of Singapore and the three British colonies of Brunei, Sabah and Sarawak on the north-west side of Borneo were so small by the standards of the early 1960s that people doubted their capacity to survive, and the Indonesian government which ruled the rest of the island clearly intended to absorb the three Borneo colonies after the British left. The British government and the government of Malaya agreed that Malaya should form a federation with the four colonies, under the name of Malaysia. Most of the people in Borneo were Malays, who would help balance the weight of the Chinese in Singapore in numbers though not in wealth. The financial balance was tipped still further towards Singapore when Brunei decided to remain a colony. The sultan of Brunei was shielded from Indonesian attack by Sarawak, and he did not want to share his oil revenues with the rest of Malaysia. By 1965 Singapore felt confident enough that the city-state could survive as an independent country to withdraw from Malaysia, and the Malaysian government was happy enough to see it leave; maintaining the position of the Malay majority in the face of the highly-educated and commercially-minded Chinese minority in Malaya was not easy, and the Singapore Chinese made the balancing act still harder. Despite this, the creation of Malaysia in 1963 served the purpose of protecting the position of Sarawak and Sabah. When the Indonesian government moved to what it called 'confrontation', the British government responded to a request to provide troops to hold the frontier. The Indonesian government leant towards the Soviet Union, so British involvement was seen as a move in the Cold War rather than a piece of imperial intervention. It was certainly true that the military leaders who overthrew the Indonesian government and then ended the policy of confrontation defended their coup in anti-Communist terms.[6]

At the same time as it gave up political control over so many colonies Britain weakened the imperial connection in another way. It had always been accepted that people who wanted to come to Britain from any Dominion or colony had a right of free entry, although colonies that gained responsible government often used their newly-acquired powers to exclude visitors or immigrants. This right of free entry had mainly been used by people of British birth or descent coming back to the country after a period of absence, though aspiring doctors or lawyers from all the countries of the empire came to Britain for part of their course of study, and there were also a few districts, almost all of them in ports, where Indian and West Indian sailors had settled down. In the first half of the twentieth century very few people would have thought that there was a black or an Indian community in Britain, but after 1945 immigrants from the West Indies began moving to Britain to look for work. This could be seen as an early stage in the late twentieth-century flow of people from the impoverished world into Europe, North America and Australia which matched and then exceeded the nineteenth-century flow of people from Europe to the Americas. In the mid-1950s the influx of newcomers was accepted with relatively little trouble, but in the years 1958–63 about 100,000 people a year were coming from the West Indies, India and Pakistan; there were obvious limits to the number of West Indians who could move to Britain, but emigration from the Indian subcontinent might lead to a much larger inflow.[7] In the early 1960s a slight downturn in the economy roused a hostility to the newcomers which combined fears that they were taking jobs and housing which ought to have gone to natives of Britain with a wider feeling that they were bringing in new ways of life that disturbed the status quo unnecessarily. Immigration was something that people from Britain went and did elsewhere; it was not something that should happen in Britain. Legislation was passed to reduce the inflow to a trickle of people who had special skills or were coming to rejoin members of their families who had already settled in Britain, a change that could be seen as a capitulation to racial feeling inside Britain, or as an acknowledgement that the Commonwealth was now an association of separate countries, each of which had an immigration policy of its own.

The Commonwealth went through a transformation in the 1960s. In the 1950s the entry of two new members, Ghana and Malaya, had done no more than move it a little further in the direction the changes of the late 1940s had indicated, but the increase to twenty-eight members by 1968 altered what it could do, and what it wanted to do, in a way that Commonwealth leaders from twenty years earlier might have found hard to understand. The admission of India, non-aligned in the Cold War, made it clear that the Commonwealth would not have a common policy in defence or diplomacy. In the 1960s one of its main functions was to provide a dignified way for Britain to withdraw from her important colonies in as short a time as could be arranged. While there was little substance to the idea that Britain was not losing possessions but was gaining valuable associates, it made it rather easier for people brought up to think of Britain as one of the world's great powers to adjust to the new state of affairs. The Commonwealth also provided these new nations with a network of immediately available diplomatic links. When French colonies became independent they naturally started off with close ties to France, but this did not give them close connections with other countries of importance, while British colonies at independence were automatically put in touch with a range of other countries from India to Canada which already possessed some position in the world.

This advantage was not valued very highly by the Arab countries which Britain had ruled, none of which joined the Commonwealth. Iraq had emerged from its position as a League of Nations mandate and Egypt had established its independence by negotiating the 1936 treaty at a time when it was not quite clear that Dominion status was compatible with complete independence. In any case the Commonwealth of the 1930s was anglocentric enough to mean that Arab countries would have looked out of place. Sudan became independent at a time when membership of the Commonwealth would have been seen by Egypt as an attempt to maintain a British sphere of influence up the Nile. Aden in 1967 was the most clear-cut case of a local independence movement dictating the timetable of departure to the British by force of arms in the whole process of decolonisation. Relations with Kuwait and the small states on the south-west side of the Gulf were far more friendly; the British sent troops to defend Kuwait in 1961 when Iraq threatened to attack it and, when Iraq troops overran Kuwait thirty years later, Britain provided substantial forces for the United Nations coalition which restored Kuwait's independence. Britain also played a peaceful but prominent role in bringing the small states together as the United Arab Emirates, but these were strictly bilateral relationships, and neither Kuwait nor the UAE showed any interest in having any connection with the Commonwealth. This was very different from the position in Africa south of the Sahara, where every former British colony became a member of the Commonwealth on emerging as a separate and independent state, and other countries were attracted by the idea of Commonwealth membership.

In one way members of the Commonwealth (other than Britain) overestimated its advantages: they thought it gave them some control over British foreign and economic policy, a misunderstanding that was not confined to the countries that had just become independent. At about the same time as Macmillan and his government were taking the decision to give up imperial rule, countries in western Europe were deciding to join together in what was then the European Economic Community (now the European Union), a trading area with complete free trade among the members and, in addition, harmonisation of their tariffs against the rest of the world. The British government could see advantages in the EEC, mainly because it would provide access to a much wider market for trade in industrial products, but it could also see advantages in imperial preference, mainly because it meant food could be imported at the world price rather than paying the EEC variable levy on imports. Briefly it thought it might be able to get the advantages of both systems, but in 1958 this was rejected by France. After his 1959 election victory Macmillan pondered the situation and, once the process of decolonisation was going ahead, his government applied for membership of the EEC, while promising to obtain as many trade concessions for Commonwealth countries as possible.

Commonwealth Prime Ministers did as much as they could to oppose the application at meetings held in 1961 and 1962. The British representatives tried to provide for Commonwealth interests in negotiations at Brussels, and appeared to be making progress when the French government announced, early in 1963, that it would not accept Britain as a member. The British government was left with no obvious alternative policy. Commonwealth countries did suggest that closer trade links with them might help but the General Agreement on Tariffs and Trade, accepted by most trading nations at the end of the Second World War, allowed the Ottawa Agreements to be extended only if they were turned into agreements to set up complete free trade among the countries involved. Britain had proposed a Free Trade Area to Canada in 1958 but it was never quite clear whether Britain was completely serious or simply wanted to point out that speeches by ministers in the Canadian government about increasing the amount of trade among Commonwealth countries could only be made effective by establishing a form of free trade area. The British were conspicuously unsurprised when Canada made no response to the proposal.

The issue of the European Community was handled relatively politely. For the rest of the 1960s Commonwealth relations were dominated by the effects of one of the least successful of all of Britain's arrangements for decolonisation. Once the Central Africa Federation had been broken up, and Zambia and Malawi had become independent, Britain was left to work out what should be done with Southern Rhodesia, which changed its name to Rhodesia after Zambia had dissociated itself from the name of Cecil Rhodes. Southern Rhodesia had had responsible government since the 1920s, and had its own army and air force since the Second World War. Its government often spoke as if it had delayed the country's progress to Dominion status in order to get the Central African Federation working properly. This assertion had no force in law, but it meant that the mainly white Rhodesian electorate thought of the dissolution of the federation as the prelude to constitutional advance. They were apt to judge their position by that of their neighbour South Africa, and they pointed out reasonably enough that they had not set up any system of apartheid. The legislation which held Africans back was mild by mid-century standards, and the main barrier to change was the land distribution which left prosperous white farmers in control of large farms, making it unlikely that many Africans would meet the property qualifications for voting at any time in the foreseeable future.

Macmillan had been sufficiently polite to the Rhodesian government to make it think the Conservatives would, if re-elected in 1964, open the way forward to independence. When Harold Wilson formed a Labour government and made it clear that no steps towards independence would be taken until the African majority had some assurance that it would soon become a majority in the electorate, the Rhodesian government issued a unilateral declaration of independence in late 1965. This was not the way that countries were supposed to become independent. As the step was taken to avoid progress toward racial equality, it was easy to convince the rest of the world that the Rhodesian government ought not to be recognised, and that governments should declare that trade with Rhodesia was illegal. But Rhodesia had realised the dangers of a blockade and had made arrangements with South Africa to deal with it, so the British government had to consider taking stronger measures.[8]

Wilson knew that using armed force against a country in which many of the white minority had relations in Britain – all too often referred to as 'kith and kin', a phrase so out of date that people sometimes ignored the reality behind it – would be unpopular in Britain, and he also knew that Rhodesia was so far away, and so far inland, that bringing military force to bear would be extremely difficult. Some of his critics compared British support for Malaysia with the absence of armed intervention in Rhodesia; suggesting that it was as easy to move an invading force hundreds of miles inland as it was to bring troops to a country at the invitation of a well-organised and sympathetic government was so stupid that it was understandable if the British government failed to take its critics seriously. Irritation at Britain's handling of the Rhodesian question fairly certainly accelerated some natural changes in the machinery of Commonwealth organisation. A Commonwealth secretariat had been set up in 1965 to handle paperwork and exchanges of information instead of leaving such things in the hands of a ministry in the British government. This change turned the official side of the Commonwealth into something much more like the other international organisations that had developed in such large numbers after 1945. A secretariat in which several nations were represented, a wide range of member states and a readiness to settle for a policy which everybody knew would be only the lowest common denominator among members could be found in the United Nations, in the Organisation for African Unity, in the North Atlantic Treaty Organisation and in a large number of other organisations in which countries tried to work together without surrendering their own vital interests. Other organisations, of which the European Union was the most important and the most successful, achieved a much higher level of unity and of willingness to give up some national freedom of action, but the Commonwealth did not possess that sort of unity. The changes reduced Britain's distinctive position in the Commonwealth, though it is hard to say whether they were made mainly for this reason or because so many international organisations had developed after 1945 in a way that provided what the members of the Commonwealth wanted and set a pattern for it to follow.[9]

By the late 1960s twelve of the twenty-eight nations in the Commonwealth were African, naturally deeply concerned about what happened on their continent. They needed to show that they were achieving something, partly because their own positions were not very secure. In 1966 the governments of Ghana and of Nigeria were overthrown in military coups; Nigeria was particularly hard to govern because of the size and the diversity of its population, but in some ways the problems of Ghana were more instructive. To rouse enthusiasm for independence the leaders of the Convention People's Party had spoken about the political and psychological advantages of running one's own country, but they had also suggested, like many other leaders of independence movements, that freedom would lead to prosperity, and they had accused Britain of taking money out of the country. Budget surpluses from the 1950s had been deposited in the London money market and were available for Ghana at independence, but they were not large and certainly could not finance Nkrumah's ambitious development schemes. Hopes of prosperity were dashed, or at least delayed to a distant future, and Ghana, like most countries just after independence, found itself under pressure to do something. African governments which could show that they had pushed the British into taking drastic action against Rhodesia, or even could show that they had fearlessly denounced the British for not taking drastic action, were able to strengthen their positions at home. African governments said that the British were strong enough to overthrow the Rhodesian regime but were holding back for racist reasons; the British reflected that if they were both strong and racist they would not have given up their colonies so easily and so peacefully. Commonwealth meetings in 1965 and 1966 were embittered enough for the British government to indicate that it would not allow any further meetings that set out to tell it how to run its policy. The danger that disputes like this might destroy the organisation led in 1969 to a decision to hold Commonwealth heads of government meetings (CHOGMs, for those who wanted an acronym to puzzle the uninitiated) at regular two-year intervals in appropriate member states, instead of almost always holding them in London at the invitation of the British government.[10]

The British government continued to manage negotiations with Rhodesia, though it always realised that protests and anger would follow if it departed too far from the position of those who wanted no independence before majority African rule, or 'Nibmar'. The British hoped to satisfy the Rhodesian government and the supporters of 'Nibmar' by devising a voting system in which enough Africans would qualify for the vote to gain a majority in the near future but not immediately. This would let the white Rhodesians say that they had achieved independence without surrendering their position of power to the African majority, while giving the Africans control of the government in a few years' time. Arrangements like this might have helped a little in the atmosphere of eager constitution-making and relative good will in Northern Rhodesia or in Uganda in the early 1960s but, half a dozen years later, they were unlikely to do much good. Rhodesia remained officially unrecognised but apparently impregnable.

Rhodesia was flanked by the two Portuguese colonies of Angola and Mozambique. Portugal had not given up any colonies during the period of rapid decolonisation in the early 1960s, and its resources were being stretched by a war against guerillas who wanted to end its rule in Africa, but it was hard for guerillas to conduct any operations against Rhodesia while Portugal kept the eastern and western frontiers closed. The Zambian government could not support guerilla bases north of the Zambezi because it had to work with Rhodesia on so many matters of everyday business. A blockade of Rhodesia had been expected to produce rapid results but it soon became clear that a blockade would have an effect only if the government of South Africa was ready to apply it, and it also became clear that South Africa saw Rhodesia as a valuable outer line of defence. In 1974, when the Portuguese government was overthrown by army officers who recognised that the war in the colonies was a useless drain on national resources, Angola and Mozambique passed into the hands of the guerilla leaders. Their position was far from secure, partly because South Africa supported their internal opponents, but the two newly-independent states gave as much support as they could to Rhodesian guerillas who now had more effective bases from which to attack the white-dominated government.

By the end of the 1970s the Rhodesian government had been forced to turn for support against the guerillas to African leaders who had continued to hope for a peaceful settlement. Finally, in 1980 Rhodesia returned to British rule and a new governor went out from Britain to supervise elections. The guerilla leader Robert Mugabe won the election. He was helped by his record as the most determined opponent of the unilateral declaration of independence and the government that carried it out, but he also benefited because the Shona, the largest African group in the population, supported him. In office he was not successful. Rhodesia had kept going well enough during the fifteen years after its declaration of independence, despite all the complications caused by its lack of international standing, but the newly-named nation of Zimbabwe had great difficulty in keeping its economy going. In Kenya the advantages of retaining white commercial farmers to grow export crops were accepted; in Zimbabwe the white farmers came to be treated as scapegoats for the country's economic troubles.

Several African states had run into similar problems after independence. They had become independent at a time in the 1960s when the world economy was running very smoothly and economists were confident that government intervention would make it work better. This view, which can loosely be called Keynesianism despite the oceans of economists' ink that have flowed in debates over what the distinguished British economist really meant, was becoming generally accepted at just the time in the early 1970s when the world economy began to run less well. Many explanations were offered, from sharp increases in the price of oil in 1973 (and again in 1980) to a drop in new items of general consumption to stimulate new industries, but certainly rates of growth declined and unemployment went up. African countries, which often depended on exporting a single crop or commodity, were in a very exposed position if demand for their single product went down. As more and more people came to believe it was impossible to be too thin, chocolate became less fashionable. At the same time Ghana's cocoa-growers had to face successful competition from other west African countries like Ivory Coast. Zambia became independent at a time when demand for copper was high, but the price declined in later years and the Zambian economy suffered as a result. Tanganyika had a conspicuously incorrupt government, but it could neither promote growth through its own efforts nor trust foreign investors to do the job for it.

French, Belgian and Portuguese colonies in Africa all had comparable problems after independence; colonies in the rest of the world had difficulties after becoming independent, but they did not suffer as frequently or as intensely. African colonies became independent with far less preparation than those which became independent earlier or later. The sixty years of steady diminution of British power in India meant that by 1947 Indians were experienced in politics, in the army and in the civil service. Despite this, the problems of partition in 1947 showed that even wellprepared states might not be able to deal with sudden shocks. In the decades before independence in Africa, officials had not been warned that they had to prepare their states for change in the near future. By the time the imperial powers decided to leave, the fever for independence was raging so fiercely that there was no time to do much in the way of preparation and very little willingness on the part of the independence movements to listen to anything that the old rulers had to say.

More army coups followed those of 1966. Dr Obote denounced the new British prime minister, Edward Heath, so virulently at the 1971 Commonwealth conference that, when the Ugandan government was overthrown immediately afterwards by a coup led by Idi Amin, it became known that Heath was 'not wholly displeased'.[11] Some military interventions were simply attempts to secure increases in pay, or were inspired by what happened in French or Belgian colonies, but some African politicians restricted the expression of public opinion by setting up one-party states which left the army as the only institution which could get rid of a leader who had become unpopular. Some one-party states were created because of the danger of disintegration visible in struggles like the Nigerian civil war. Political parties were often regional groupings and, because the country might break up if one region opposed another along party lines, it was thought that putting all the regions under the umbrella of one party reduced the risk of disintegration. Some one-party states allowed minor disagreements about policy, but this could never be very effective if the governing party could expel its critics and declare that they could not take any further part in politics. Men who had led their countries to independence were naturally ready to see themselves as indispensable and sometimes set up one-party states to protect their own positions. Their followers were apt to think that, because loyalty to the party had been the road to independence, anyone who opposed the party which had brought the nation into existence was disloyal to the nation. Leaders and followers could see a one-party state as the natural way to run a new nation, quite apart from the attractions of the monopoly of power and the monopoly of the rewards of office, legitimate and all too often illegitimate, which went with the elimination of all opposition.

A few episodes in the history of India and Pakistan after independence may have encouraged one-party states and even military seizures of power. Nehru remained prime minister until his death in 1964, and the Congress Party held on to office much longer. After a brief interregnum, his daughter Indira (married, by a happy coincidence, to a man who was no relation of the great Gandhi but had given her one of the most honoured names in India) became prime minister and, with another brief interval in the late 1970s, held office until she was assassinated in 1984 and was succeeded as prime minister by her son Rajiv Gandhi. Even after he had been assassinated in 1991, his widow Sonia retained enough of the family prestige to make her the dominant force in the Congress Party in the 1990s, though she was Italian by birth and upbringing. This prestige was no longer enough to bring the party success in national elections.

Dynastic politics of this sort might show that Indian voters did not reach the levels of sophistication expected of them by political scientists but, except for two years in the 1970s when Indira Gandhi proclaimed an emergency and ruled by presidential decree, political activity was unrestrained, opposition parties could fight elections freely and governments in the states were often strongly opposed to Congress. People in India chose to remain attached to the Congress Party and the Nehru family, but no laws gave Congress or the Nehrus a monopoly of power. This sort of deep respect for established political families also allowed the widows and daughters of party leaders to overcome any prejudice against women that existed in Sri Lanka or in Pakistan. At the same time Pakistan was one of the relatively few Commonwealth countries outside Africa to be affected by military coups. Holding together the two areas separated by the whole width of northern India would have been hard for any government, and the civilian rulers of the 1950s and the military rulers of the 1960s made things worse by favouring the western section at the expense of the eastern half. When the eastern section rose in rebellion in 1970, India was very happy to assist it, in order to break Pakistan up and launch Bangla Desh as an independent country. When Bangla Desh was recognised as a member of the Commonwealth, Pakistan left in protest and settled down to a form of government in which elections were held often enough, but were monitored by an army that was all too ready to nullify the results. Bangla Desh soon slipped into the same sort of government. Few military rulers were as blatant about setting up a dictatorship as Amin in Uganda, or as cruel in running it, and in the 1980s military rulers in Nigeria and Ghana took the same approach as the praetorians in Pakistan and Bangla Desh who were willing to put up with a return to civilian rule as long as they had a veto over the civilian rulers.

Between 1970 and 1983 eighteen new countries became independent and were accepted as members of the Commonwealth, which more or less completed the process of decolonisation. Eight of these states were small islands in the Pacific, and another eight were islands or small coastal territories in or around the Caribbean, the ultimate legacies of two centuries of acquiring small colonies on the basis that the Royal Navy could protect them without difficulty. The distances in the Pacific were so immense that ideas of federation made no sense. Britain had never thought of reviving the Federation of the West Indies, but half a dozen of the smaller states in the eastern Caribbean agreed on a common currency and a certain amount of cooperation. Once national self-determination had been acknowledged, the limits imposed by size had to be faced; but, while their survival depended on the world's acceptance of the rights of small nations, an island or a Pacific archipelago could have compensating advantages. Its boundaries were firm and easily defined, and it might have a homogenous population that reduced the risks of internal division which worried African politicians and sometimes led to serious trouble. Even in a small state trouble could come if the population saw itself as ethnically divided. Sometimes the differences involved were small enough to suggest that they could be solved by the passage of time, but the unusual position in Fiji shows the forces at work when newcomers settle in a country as often happens in an empire. In Canada, Australia, New Zealand and Singapore newcomers came in such numbers that they outnumbered the existing population; in South Africa, Zimbabwe and Kenya (and, in a slightly different sense, in Britain) the newcomers were clearly a minority; in Ireland the newcomers were a minority but were a majority in a small and distinct part of the island. Indians came to Fiji to work on the sugar plantations as indentured labourers in the late nineteenth century. The descendants of those who stayed on after their indentures had expired became educated and commercially successful, and made up over 40 per cent of the total population. Native Fijians became worried that their majority in the whole population was so slender, and in 1987 a conservative revolution was carried out to hold the Indians back. The Fijians went on to declare the country a republic. Its application to be readmitted to the Commonwealth was not accepted at the time, a decision that owed a lot to India's disapproval of political moves against Indians overseas. It also owed something to a growing feeling that coups and policies that overthrew democracy were unworthy of the Commonwealth. Ten years later the application for readmission was accepted, but in two or three years time it became clear that the problems of internal division had not been solved. By this time the Commonwealth was ready to suspend the membership of countries that blatantly ignored the democratic principles it had proclaimed in 1991, though this was not enough to persuade the native Fijians to accept the claims to equality of the Indians.

Some territories that remained as colonies after 1983 did so for local and individual reasons that made it unlikely that they would become independent, even though the British government was clearly eager to see them go. Some of them, like Bermuda which voted to remain a colony in a referendum in 1995, saw no advantages in independence; some, like Pitcairn or St Helena, were too small to pay for even the minimal requirements of an independent state; and some had neighbours all too willing to absorb them. While they usually preferred independence to remaining as colonies, very few colonies saw amalgamation with another state as a satisfactory road to independence. The federations which had been so popular with the Colonial Office for a hundred years no longer had any appeal. Zanzibar joined Tanganyika to form Tanzania in the first months of independence, part of the British mandate territory from the German colony of Kamerun joined the former French colony of Cameroun rather than Nigeria, and British Somaliland was linked with Italian Somaliland to become the state of Somalia, but this was the furthest that independent states went in the direction of voluntary mergers.

If the danger of being taken over by a larger neighbour had been far greater in the imperial past, the position of the Falklands Islands showed that it still existed. In 1982 the military government of Argentina decided to reassert by force its claims to the islands which went back to the eighteenth century. The British government had hinted that in the distant future it might negotiate about the claim without letting ideas about self-determination give an absolute veto over its policy to the local population, which was firmly attached to Britain. Forcible annexation without negotiation was quite another matter. British forces set off to sail the 6000 miles to the South Atlantic, defeated the Argentinians and recovered the islands. This successful reassertion of power at a great distance from any home base helped the British government to persuade Guatemala not to think of pressing its territorial claims on the colony of British Honduras, which was just emerging to independence as Belize. It may also have strengthened the British position when negotiating with China about the status of Hong Kong. The original British colony, acquired in the 1840 and 1850s, occupied a very small area, which had been greatly expanded in 1898 when Britain acquired a ninety-nine year lease on the 'New Territories'. The return of the New Territories to China in 1997 would have left the original Hong Kong as the centre of a thriving city whose suburbs were in another country, so the British set out to negotiate an arrangement which would make all of Hong Kong part of China for defence and foreign policy purposes but leave it autonomous in economic and social affairs for the next fifty years. The Chinese leaders were happy to insulate Hong Kong from the rest of the country, because they admired the city's economic success, but thought its free press and western legal system might have a disturbing effect on a country where the idea of strict limits on government authority had never been accepted. Agreement was reached relatively easily in 1986, and the people of Hong Kong made their arrangements to face partial absorption into China. In the last five years of British rule in the 1990s the constitution of the colony was changed to set up a much more democratic electoral system than it had ever had before. The 1986 agreement had not provided for this, and the Chinese government was annoyed because the change increased the possibility that Hong Kong would have a disturbing effect on the rest of China.

One of the British government's concerns over Hong Kong had been its fear that, if British citizenship were given to most residents of the colony, there might be a flood of Chinese immigration to Britain which would be hard to accommodate and might arouse racial hostility. Once Hong Kong had been transferred to Chinese rule in 1997, the population of the remaining colonies was small enough for the British government to suggest that citizenship should be available for everyone in the colonies, as long as their legislatures harmonised some of their laws with the arrangements in Britain. This would give people in colonies too small to be likely to become independent some sort of place in Britain, though the old idea of representation in the Westminster parliament was not revived.

Commonwealth countries which had wanted to influence British policy on Rhodesia in the 1960s felt the same way about South Africa in the 1980s. Many of them wanted the Commonwealth to impose trade sanctions and end investment, and the African members naturally felt deeply committed to this approach. As most Commonwealth countries had few trade links with South Africa and did not have much money for foreign investment, the first step towards making the policy effective was to persuade the British to adopt it. Margaret Thatcher, the British prime minister of the period, was not easy to persuade, and she felt that hectoring countries to change their policy was something that she should do to them rather than have them do it to her.

In the event, the Afrikaner-dominated Nationalist government of South Africa resolved the problem by moving from a racially restricted franchise to universal suffrage in a dramatic four years of transition from the release of Nelson Mandela in 1990 to his election as president in 1994. This would probably have been accompanied in any case by a return to Commonwealth membership once the policy of apartheid had ended, but the government of Pakistan had pointed the way by becoming once more a member of the Commonwealth in 1989, during a period when the country was making a serious effort to escape from the pattern of military control. While South Africa was going through its great transition, the Commonwealth was acknowledging that the developments in the first generation of decolonisation had not run well. In the Harare declaration of 1991 it committed itself to principles of free elections, freedom of speech and freedom of the legal system from political interference that ten years earlier would have been denounced as intolerable intervention in the domestic arrangements of member states. The British government built up moral pressure for this change by a substantial remission of the debts owed it by several of the poorer states, a step that was almost inevitably attacked as a form of economic imperialism by some leaders who had fond memories of the days when they had enjoyed the security of ruling one-party states. But during the 1980s opinion had turned against one-party states and against military rule; party leaders faced contested elections and generals returned to their barracks. Neither system of government had provided economic gains that made up for the loss of a government responsible to popular complaints, and the disintegration of the Soviet Union exposed the weaknesses that had grown up in one of the most important one-party states.

These changes in the Commonwealth made it rather easier for people singing 'Land of Hope and Glory' to think of Britain as 'Mother of the

Free' than it would have been in the first decades of decolonisation, and it was even possible to imagine that the lines about 'wider still and wider shall thy bounds be set' were not totally irrelevant.[12] Cameroon and Mozambique were admitted to membership of the Commonwealth in 1995, after some scrutiny of their position to be sure that they were moving in the direction of the ideals laid out at Harare. Mozambique had never been connected with the British Empire, which previously had been taken for granted as a qualification for membership, but it was in the unusual position that all six of the nations which bordered on it were members. Cameroon did include a small area which had been a British mandate from 1919 to 1960 and, if it was also a member of *La Francophonie*, the French equivalent of the Commonwealth, so was Canada. These new admissions showed that the Commonwealth kept some vitality as one of the organisations in which countries try to work together without giving way on issues that they consider to be of essential importance. The principles approved at Harare led the Commonwealth to suspend Nigeria's membership in 1995 until 1999, after the way towards a return to free elections had been opened by the death of the military dictator, General Abacha. When Yemen, which included the former British colony of Aden, applied for Commonwealth membership, the suggestion was laid aside until the country could be seen to be moving in the direction of the Harare principles. A military coup in Pakistan in 1999, which in the past might have been received with resigned acknowledgement that Pakistani elected politicians were often their own worst enemies, led to steps to suspend the country's membership of the Commonwealth. This change of attitude was obviously only in part a matter of a change in the Commonwealth; it reflected a larger change which suggested that the world at the end of the twentieth century was escaping from some of the crimes and follies of the century's earlier decades. In any case, international action was not something that the Commonwealth could undertake; when Sierra Leone dissolved in the late 1990s into a unusually cruel civil war, west African states led by Nigeria tried to intervene to protect the stability of the region, the British government sent troops to protect the capital, Freetown, against the worst horrors of the war, and the United Nations provided forces that made some attempt to keep the peace, but the Commonwealth acknowledged that it could not intervene effectively.

While the Commonwealth had turned into a useful international organisation of the second or third rank, the important legacies of the British

Empire were its role in the expansion of Europe, and the spread of the English language. Five hundred years ago the countries of Europe were unimportant little states, not able to run their own affairs very well, and in some danger of being absorbed into an expanding Ottoman Empire. The expansion of Europe and the diffusion of its ideas about government, about nations and about human rights has transformed the world, and in the first instance the expansion of European empires served as the vehicle for the transformation. The Commonwealth was no more than one multi-national organisation in a world full of multinational organisations, but the great change from a world of disconnected units, ignorant of each other's existence, to one in which multinational organisations are able to exist was carried out and driven forward by the European empires. It is easy to say that the change might have been carried out by speechifying majorities rather than by blood and iron, and it is possible to argue that the change should not taken place at all. But the change happened, and it is impossible to understand the modern world without recognising that, China apart, almost all the world has at some time in the last five hundred years been part of one or another of the empires of half a dozen European countries, and has been profoundly altered by the experience. Among these European empires, the worldwide extent, the great variety of people under its rule, and the wide range of different approaches that it took to its problems of government, made the British Empire the most important and the most fruitful.

In 1897, when imperial power and enthusiasm were at their peak, Kipling was afraid that the British Empire might fade out of human memory like Nineveh and Tyre. As the Roman Empire can never be quite forgotten while so much of Europe speaks languages descended from Latin, English as a worldwide language is the British Empire's claim to an immortal memory. The nineteenth-century expansion of the British Empire is of course only part of the reason for this; the twentieth-century rise to world power of the United States is at least as important, and by the end of the Second World War the United States had been an independent nation for just as long as the American colonies were part of the British Empire. English may become more and more regionally divided; perhaps a formal type of English will be used for international purposes, in the way that Latin survived as the language of a universal church, while informal English breaks up in the way that demotic Latin broke up into French, Italian, Spanish and the other Romance languages.

This may happen because English is spoken in so many different places and for so many purposes as a result of the worldwide diversity of the empire. If English breaks up into British-English, American-English, Indian-English and many other languages that are no more mutually comprehensible than Portuguese and Italian, their common origin in the British Empire may be of merely historical interest. But English has already taken such strides to being a worldwide language that it would be a waste of intellectual resources to let it break up in this way, and it will be no bad thing for the world if it is brought closer together by a steady increase in the number of people 'who speak the tongue that Shakespeare spake'.[13]

# Notes

*Notes to Chapter 1: Settling by the Seashore*

1. The *Oxford Universal Dictionary* gives 1586 as the first use of the word in the earlier sense and 1706 as the first use of the word in the later sense.
2. D. H. Willson, *King James VI and I* (London, Cape, 1956), pp. 300–3.
3. Michael J. Braddick 'Government, War, Trade and Settlement', in Nicholas Canny, ed., *The Origins of Empire* (Oxford, OUP, 1998), p. 300.
4. Brian Vickers, ed., *Francis Bacon: Writings* (Oxford, OUP, 1996), p. 407.
5. *Dictionary of National Biography* (London, Macmillan, 1891), entry for John Harvard.
6. R. B. Sheridan, *Sugar and Slavery* (Baltimore, Johns Hopkins Press, 1973), pp. 128–30.
7. K. G. Davies, *The Royal African Company* (London, Longmans, 1957), pp. 316–25.
8. At the very beginning roughly equal numbers of men and women were brought over, but imports of female slaves soon declined. Sheridan, *Sugar and Slavery*, p. 243.
9. K. N. Chaudhuri, *The English East India Company* (London, Frank Cass, 1965); and, for the later period, idem, *The Trading World of Asia and the English East India Company* (Cambridge, CUP, 1978). The tables of exports and imports in appendix 5 show the dominance of textile imports in the whole period down to 1760.

*Notes to Chapter 2: War with France*

1. John Brewer, *The Sinews of Power* (New York, Knopf, 1989), especially pp. 29–33, 120–26.
2. Most accounts of pirates rely heavily on J. Esquemeling, *The History of the Buccaneers*, originally written in Dutch and published in 1684, but translations and revised editions appeared very quickly, and on 'Captain Charles Johnson' (probably a pseudonym; at one stage it was believed to be that of Daniel Defoe), *A General History of the Pirates* (London, 1724; revised edn, 1727). Esquemeling gives more attention to Morgan than to anyone else; the *General History* was written just after Woodes Rogers's campaign

against the Bahamas pirates and owes a good deal to the reports of their trials.

3. *Canada: Treaties and Surrenders from 1680 to 1890* (Toronto, Coles, 1971), vol. i.

4. J. Prebble, *The Darien Disaster* (London, Secker & Warburg, 1968), pp. 93–95, 22, 282–83, 314.

5. W. R. Scott, *Constitution and Finance of English Scottish and Irish Joint-Stock Companies to 1720* (Cambridge, CUP, 1912; reprint 1968), i, chs 20 and 21, and iii, pp. 288–360; J. Carswell, *The South Sea Bubble* (2nd edn, Stroud, Alan Sutton, 1993), pp. 111–12, 119–20, 125–26, explains the mechanics of the 'Bubble'. The book was first published in 1960.

6. Edmund Burke, 'Speech on Conciliation with America', 22 March 1775.

7. R. Koebner, *Empire* (Cambridge, CUP, 1961), chs 3 and 4.

8. V. H. H. Green, *John Wesley* (London, Nelson, 1964), pp. 42–43, 60–61, 119.

9. Philip Woodfine, *Britannia's Glories: The Walpole Ministry and the War with Spain* (Woodbridge, Boydell Press, for Royal Historical Society, 1998). Woodfine makes it clear that neither the South Sea Company nor the Spanish government did anything to help Walpole escape the pressure of public opinion.

10. T. B. Macaulay, 'Frederic the Great', in *Critical and Historical Essays*, selected by A. J. Grieve (London, Dent, 1961), ii, p. 134. The essay was first published in April 1842.

## Notes to Chapter 3: First Moves Inland

1. Abbé Prévost, *Manon Lescaut*, first published in 1731; Daniel Defoe, *Moll Flanders*, first published in 1722.

2. W. S. Randall, *George Washington: A Life* (New York, Henry Holt, 1997), pp. 66–67, 137–39 and map on p. 24.

3. Voltaire, *Candide*, ch. 23, first published in 1759.

4. Several city corporations gave Pitt the freedom of their cities to show their approval of him and, as they usually put the charter for this in a gold box, their support is often summed up in Horace Walpole's phrase 'For some weeks it rained gold boxes'. The situation is analysed in M. Peters, *Pitt and Popularity* (Oxford, OUP, 1980); pp. 1–3, 75–76 are very useful.

5. Pitt was not the inventor of this policy (the phrase quoted was delivered in the 1740s), though he organised it much more successfully than had ever been done before. M. Peters, *The Elder Pitt* (London, Longmans, 1998), pp. 103–8, examines Pitt's claims as a strategist.

6. Robert Harvey, *Clive* (London, Hodder and Stoughton, 1998), p. 346.

7. It was about this campaign that Bernard Shaw offered (in *The Devil's Disciple*) the interchange 'What will history say?' 'History, sir, will tell lies, as usual'; and the reasons for the British defeat seem to have been clouded in misinformation. Piers Mackesy, *The War for America, 1775–1783* (London, Longmans, 1964), pp. 117–18, 130–44.

8. Burke's attitudes to India are discussed in Peter Marshall, 'Burke and Empire', in *Hanoverian Britain and Empire*, ed. S. Taylor et al. (Woodbridge, Boydell Press, 1998), especially pp. 292, 295.

9. Duncan McArthur, 'British North America and the American Revolution', in J. Holland Rose et al., ed., *Cambridge History of the British Empire*, vi (Cambridge, CUP, 1930), p. 197.

10. Geoffrey Blainey, *The Tyranny of Distance* (2nd edn, Melbourne, Macmillan, 1982), pp. 20–34.

11. Peter Fryer, *Staying Power* (London, Pluto, 1984), p. 125. Fryer based his quotations on notes taken by Granville Sharp, who organised Somersett's defence and devoted his life to opposing slavery.

## Notes to Chapter 4: The Only Empire in the World

1. Edmund Burke, *Reflections on the Revolution in France* (New York, Bobbs-Merrill, 1955), p. 258, first published in 1790.

2. Iris Butler, *The Eldest Brother* (London, Hodder and Stoughton, 1973), especially pp. 349–54. P. E. Roberts, *India under Wellesley* (London, Bell, 1929), p. 260; ch. 23 discusses the constitutional position of the company directors, the government's board of control and the governor general, with extensive quotations from the despatches.

3. S. G. Checkland, *The Rise of Industrial Society in Britain* (London, Longmans, 1964); Peter Mathias, *The Transformation of England* (London, Methuen, 1979); F. Crouzet, trans. M. Thom, *Britain Ascendant* (Cambridge, CUP, 1990); Mark Setterfield, *Rapid Growth and Relative Decline* (London, Macmillan, 1997).

4. Brinley Thomas, *Migration and Economic Growth* (2nd edn, Cambridge, CUP, 1973), p. 57.

5. Martin Booth, *Opium* (London, Simon and Schuster, 1996), pp. 9, 51, 110–35.

6. A. H. Imlah, *Economic Elements in the Pax Britannica* (Cambridge, Massachusetts, Harvard University Press, 1958), pp. 70–75, gives a useful estimate of the British balance of payments year by year from 1815 to 1914, with emphasis on the steadily rising total amount of overseas investment. A chart on p. 80 shows the rapid rate of growth of the accumulating balance, 1815–25, and its steady pace in subsequent decades.

7. C. A. Bayly, *Imperial Meridian* (London, Longmans, 1989), in particular pp. 193–96, argues that the British government had a policy of keeping colonies under strict restraint. It seems possible that this was more the result of specific circumstances in several of the colonies which had recently been acquired.

8. 'Cursed be Canaan; a servant of servants shall he be to his brethren.' Genesis, 9, 25. The immediate effect of the text was to give Abraham a claim to the land of Canaan, but later it was assumed that Canaan and his father Ham were black.

9. W. F. Monypenny and G. E. Buckle, *The Life of Benjamin Disraeli* (London, John Murray, 1914), iii, p. 385. Buckle added that Disraeli made this

private comment in 1852 only because he was irritated by the fishing dispute, and pointed to his willingness to explore the idea of colonial representation at Westminster to prove that even then he was a firm believer in imperial unity.

10. J. Kociumbas, *Oxford History of Australia* (Oxford, OUP, 1997), ii, *1770–1860*, ch. 11.

## Notes to Chapter 5: Pause and Expand

1. S. C. Ghosh, *Dalhousie in India, 1848–56* (New Delhi, Munshiram Manoharlal, 1975), pp. 90–92, 108, 124.
2. C. Hibbert, *The Great Mutiny: India 1857* (London, Allen Lane, 1978), pp. 385–86, 390–92.
3. R. Shannon, *Gladstone* (London, Hamish Hamilton, 1982), i, p. 468.
4. Psalm 72; D. G. Creighton, *The Road to Confederation* (Toronto: Macmillan, 1964), p. 423.
5. J. D. Legge, *Britain in Fiji, 1858–1880* (London, Macmillan, 1958), pp. 128–34, 151. W. J. Leyds, *The First Annexation of the Transvaal* (London, Fisher Unwin, 1906), chs 14, 15, 16, discussed the original reasons given by the British for the annexation and argued that there was not much substance in them.
6. J. R. Seeley, *The Expansion of England* (London, Macmillan, 1906), pp. 10, 75. The book was first published in 1883.
7. See ch. 2, 'Greater Britain', in David Nicholls, *The Lost Prime Minister: The Life of Sir Charles Dilke* (London, Hambledon Press, 1995); Richard Symonds, *Oxford and Empire: The Last Lost Cause?* (Oxford, OUP, 1986), p. 25; Joan Abse, *John Ruskin: The Passionate Moralist* (London, Quarter Books, 1980), pp. 224–26.
8. The London Convention, and the earlier Pretoria Convention, are given as appendices I and II in D. M. Schreuder, *Gladstone and Kruger* (London, Routledge Kegan Paul, 1969).
9. Robert Pringle, *Rajahs and Rebels* (Cornell, Cornell University Press, 1970), pp. 97–99. Daniel R. Headrick, *The Tools of Empire* (Oxford, OUP, 1981), deals with the technology behind imperial expansion.
10. This account is largely based on ch. 4 of R. Robinson and J. Gallagher, *Africa and the Victorians* (London, Macmillan, 1961). The wide-ranging influence of this book on writing about the British Empire in the nineteenth century can be seen by looking at volumes 3 and 5 of *The Oxford History of the British Empire* (Oxford, OUP, 1999), and a useful discussion of it can be found in *Imperialism: The Robinson and Gallagher Controversy*, W. R. Louis, ed. (New York, New Viewpoints, 1976).
11. Section 91 of the British North America Act, now the Canada Act, makes this the primary objective of the central or federal government. The phrase is sometimes contrasted with the words in the US constitution about life, liberty and the pursuit of happiness.

12. Joseph Conrad, *Heart of Darkness*, (New York, Knopf, 1971), p. 51, first published in 1902.

13. R. Rotberg, *The Founder: Cecil Rhodes and the Pursuit of Power* (Oxford, OUP, 1988), pp. 339–49. Echoing Francis Bacon, Rhodes warned the Foreign Secretary, Lord Rosebery, 'Never expect a profit from the development of a new country', ibid., p. 585. Investors in the Chartered Company had to wait thirty rather than twenty years for any dividends.

*Notes to Chapter 6: The Too Vast Orb*

1. J. V. Cell, *British Colonial Administration in the Mid-Nineteenth Century* (New Haven, Yale, 1970), ch. 7, 'The Management of Eastern Communications'; Blainey, *The Tyranny of Distance*, pp. 222–26, 265–75.

2. The post-1850 aspects of the table of the British balance of payments, 1815–1914, given by A. H. Imlah in his *Economic Elements in the Pax Britannica* (Cambridge, Massachusetts, Harvard University Press, 1958), pp. 70–75, and a number of other estimates of British overseas investment are discussed in P. J. Cain and A. G. Hopkins, *British Imperialism: Innovation and Expansion, 1688–1914* (London and New York, Longmans, 1993), pp. 170–75. The advantages for the colonies of access to the London money market, and of trustee status, are discussed in Lance E. Davis and Robert A. Huttenback, *Mammon and the Pursuit of Empire* (Cambridge, CUP, 1988), pp. 137–41.

3. Oscar Wilde, *The Importance of Being Earnest*, Act II.

4. Maurice Pope, ed., *Public Servant: The Memoirs of Sir Joseph Pope* (Toronto, OUP, 1960), p. 86.

5. Rudyard Kipling, 'Recessional', published in *The Times*, 17 July 1897.

6. R. Rotberg, *The Founder: Cecil Rhodes and the Pursuit of Power* (Oxford OUP, 1988), pp. 610–12. Rotberg argues that Rhodes used this controversial phrase in order to appeal to Afrikaner voters, but does not explain why he did not simply say 'equal rights for all white men', which would have had a much more direct appeal to them.

7. Paul Kennedy, *The Rise and Fall of the Great Powers* (New York, Random House, 1987), pp. 48, 352–53, 515–21; Matthew Arnold, 'Heine's Grave'.

8. J. A. Hobson, *Imperialism* (London, Allen and Unwin, 1938), first published in 1902; V. I. Lenin, *Imperialism: The Highest Stage of Capitalism* (Moscow, Progress, 1982), first published in 1917.

9. S. Pollard, *Britain's Prime and Britain's Decline* (London, Arnold, 1989), p. 114.

10. Thomas, *Migration and Economic Growth*, p. 57.

11. Winston Churchill, (then under secretary of state for the colonies), speech at Edinburgh, 18 May 1907.

12. The first chapter, 'Indo-British Trade', in Ram Gopal, *British Rule in India* (London, Asia Publishing House, 1963), serves as a fairly concise summing up of the argument that the 'Drain' was unfair to India.

## Notes to Chapter 7: The Two World Wars

1. An account of the steps towards Balfour's letter of 2 November 1917 to Lord Rothschild, usually known as the 'Balfour Declaration', can be found in David Fromkin, *A Peace to End All Peace* (New York, Henry Holt, 1989), p. 297.
2. K. C. Wheare, *The Statute of Westminster and Dominion Status* (5th edn, Oxford, OUP, 1953), p. 28.
3. Wheare, *The Statute of Westminster and Dominion Status*, pp. 315–19, gives the text of the Statute. Clauses 7, 8, 9 and 10 provided that it was not to be applied to Canada, Australia, New Zealand or Newfoundland at that time.
4. P. J. Cain and A. G. Hopkins, *British Imperialism: Crisis and Deconstruction, 1914–1990* (London and New York, Longmans, 1993), pp. 144–45, especially 'Asymmetry in the mutual preferences given, with Britain getting the worst of the deal, was probably essential if the Sterling Area was to work'.
5. Louis, *Imperialism at Bay* (Oxford, Clarendon, 1977), pp. 356–57.
6. Frederick Lugard, *The Dual Mandate in British Tropical Africa* (London, Frank Cass, 1965), p. 617, first published in 1922.
7. J. Brown, *Gandhi* (New Haven, Yale, 1989), pp. 338–40; R. Payne, *Life and Death of Mahatma Gandhi* (New York, Dutton, 1969), p. 493.
8. Winston Churchill, speech of 18 June 1940.
9. Winston Churchill, speech of 10 November 1942.

## Notes to Chapter 8: Towards Decolonialisation

1. John Darwin, *The End of the British Empire: The Historical Debate* (London, Blackwell, 1991), gives a good introduction to the subject examining in turn domestic politics, economic issues, international relations and the rise of colonial nationalism, but concludes (ibid., p. 114) that 'no single cause is sufficient to explain the break-up of the British imperial system'.
2. Kwame Nkrumah, *Neo-Colonialism: The Last Stage of Imperialism* (London, Nelson, 1965), pp. xiii–xiv, summarises the argument.
3. When he was Secretary of State for the Colonies Iain Macleod put it to President Kennedy 'you want us to go as quickly as possible towards independence everywhere else in the world but not on your doorstep in British Guiana'. Robert Shepherd, *Iain Macleod* (London, Hutchinson, 1994), p. 239.
4. George Orwell, who was sometimes ready to stretch a point for the sake of twisting the tails of other people on the left, wrote in a review published in *Horizon* in February 1942: 'We all live by robbing Asiatic coolies, and those of us who are "enlightened" all maintain that these coolies ought to be set free; but our standard of living, and hence our "enlightenment", demands that the robbery shall continue. A humanitarian is always a hypocrite ...'
5. Thomas, *Migration and Economic Growth*, p. 70. British figures were naturally reduced in the 1920s after the establishment of the Irish Free State as a

separate country. About 78,000 people a year emigrated from Britain in the period after 1945, with roughly five-sixths of them going to Commonwealth countries and Australia the single most popular destination. T. E. Smith, *Commonwealth Migration: Flows and Policies* (London, Macmillan, 1981), pp. 93–96.

6. C. Holbrand, *Middle Powers in International Politics* (London, Macmillan, 1984), pp. 57–64.

7. S. Gopal, *Jawarahlal Nehru* (London, Cape, 1975), i, p. 362.

8. David Goldsworthy, *Colonial Issues in British Politics, 1945–1961* (Oxford, OUP, 1971), pp. 29, 31, 34.

9. Trevor Royle, *Winds of Change* (London, John Murray, 1996), pp. 212–21.

10. A. Eden, *Full Circle* (London, Cassell, 1960), p. 426.

11. D. J. Morgan, *The Official History of Colonial Development* (London, Macmillan, 1980), v, pp. 96–102. In the relevant volume of his autobiography, *Riding the Storm* (London, Macmillan, 1971), iv, p. 200, Harold Macmillan alludes obliquely to the Commonwealth survey of January 1957.

12. Macmillan, *Riding the Storm*, pp. 378–79, and *Pointing the Way* (London, Macmillan, 1972), pp. 118–19. Macmillan did not specify when he was given this advice, or name the governor.

## Notes to Chapter 9: After Empire

1. A. Horne, *Harold Macmillan* (London, Macmillan, 1988), ii, p. 195. Chapter 7 of the book is devoted to Macmillan's policy in Africa in 1959 and 1960. While Macmillan wrote about his tour of Africa in chapter 6 of the fifth volume of his memoirs, *Pointing the Way* (London, Macmillan, 1972), he said surprisingly little about Macleod and the decision to end imperial rule; but there was quite a lot that Macmillan was not able to include in his six volumes of memoirs.

2. Robert Shepherd, *Iain Macleod*, chs 8, 9 and 10; John Iliffe, *A Modern History of Tanganyika* (Cambridge, CUP, 1979), pp. 546–47, 566–67.

3. Shepherd, *Iain Macleod*, p. 231.

4. Macleod tried to persuade the governor not to use this phrase, but Sir Patrick said he would resign if he were not allowed to say what he thought. Shepherd, *Iain Macleod*, p. 243.

5. Alan Burns, ed., *History of the British West Indies* (2nd edn, London, Allen and Unwin, 1965), pp. 722–26.

6. B. W. and L. Y. Andaye, *A History of Malaysia* (London, Macmillan, 1982), pp. 270–80.

7. John Salt and Rueben Ford, 'The United Kingdom', in William D. Serow et al., *Handbook on International Migration* (New York, Greenwood, 1990), pp. 328–30; Muhammad Anwar '"New Commonwealth" Migration to the UK', in Robin Cohen, ed., *The Cambridge Survey of World Migration* (Cambridge, CUP, 1995), pp. 274–78.

8. Robert Blake, *A History of Rhodesia* (London, Eyre Methuen, 1977), ch. 28,

discusses the Unilateral Declaration of Independence. Chapter 29 discusses the events of the following dozen years. The acknowledgements suggest that Lord Blake may have been particularly well informed about them

9. Sir William Dale, *The Modern Commonwealth* (London, Butterworth, 1983), p. 68.

10. After the two tense meetings in 1966 the British government had tried to arrange for the next meeting to be held outside London, but the present-day practice of meetings in different countries began with the 1971 meeting in Singapore. Harold Wilson, *The Labour Government, 1964–1970* (London, Weidenfeld and Maxwell Joseph, 1971), pp. 503–4, 590.

11. Edward Heath, *The Course of My Life* (London, Hodder and Stoughton, 1998), pp. 482–83.

12. 'Land of Hope and Glory' (the words are by A. C. Benson and the tune is by Elgar).

13. William Wordsworth, 'National Independence and Liberty'.

# Further Reading

Writing about the British Empire is going to be dominated for some time to come by the five volume *Oxford History of the British Empire*, ed. Roger Louis (Oxford, OUP, 1998–99). Its position as a history for historians is made explicit by the fact that one of its five volumes is entirely devoted to the historiography of the empire, and it does take for granted a considerable knowledge of the facts of imperial development. The old-fashioned eight-volume *Cambridge History of the British Empire*, ed. J. Holland Rose (Cambridge, CUP, 1929–59) is sometimes more useful for readers who want to be able to get a plain statement of the agreed facts of an event. Something of the same division of labour may be found in the history of India: the *New Cambridge History of India*, ed. Gordon Johnson (Cambridge, CUP, 1987–), of which over twenty volumes have appeared, will when complete consist of thirty-two volumes dealing with well-chosen topics picked out of the course of Indian history, since the Mughals, but even so it is not clear that it will provide an integrated account. The old *Cambridge History of India* (6 vols, Cambridge, CUP, 1922–37) laid a solid foundation for the whole of Indian history, but only volumes V and VI, ed. H. H. Dodwell (1929 and 1933), which covered the period from 1497 to 1918, related to the history of the British Empire. But those two volumes contain an outline of what was thought important which may still be a useful preliminary guide.

Some of the needs of readers who want to take a wider view and set the British Empire in the context of European expansion will be met by the ten-volume *Europe in the Age of Expansion* series (Minneapolis, University of Minnesota, 1974–85), ed. Boyd Shaffer. Some volumes in the series, such as W. D. McIntyre's *The Commonwealth of Nations, 1869–1971* (1977), concentrate on a single empire, but most of them take more of a comparative approach. Empires are such large subjects, and by now so much is known about them, that multi–volume histories, inevitably written by several authors, may be the only way to do justice to their diversity, but single volume histories can still be found. David Fieldhouse, *The Colonial Empires* (London, Weidenfeld and Nicolson, 1966), starts late in the eighteenth century and concentrates on economic issues but is very useful. Among the most accessible single volumes on other European empires are C. R. Boxer, *The Dutch Seaborne Empire* (London, Hutchinson, 1965) and *The Portuguese Seaborne Empire* (London, Hutchinson, 1969). Richard Kogan and Geoffrey Parker, eds, *Spain, Europe and the Atlantic World* (Cambridge, CUP, 1995), and three books by J. H. Parry, *The Age of Reconnaissance* (London, Weidenfeld and Nicolson, 1963), *The Spanish Seaborne Empire* (London, Hutchinson, 1966) and *Trade and Dominion* (London, Weidenfeld and Nicolson, 1971), are well worth attention. A one-volume history of the British Empire is a bold undertaking: Lawrence James, *The Rise and Fall of the British Empire* (London, Little, Brown, 1994), and Trevor Lloyd, *The British Empire, 1558–1996* (2nd edn, Oxford, OUP, 1996), have tried covering the full four centuries in a single volume. A natural break in the history of the British Empire can be found at the War of American Independence. Angus Calder, *Revolutionary Empire* (London, Cape, 1981) took the 1780s as the logical end of his story. Three interesting accounts of the last two centuries have treated the years after 1783 as a starting point: Nicholas Mansergh's *The Commonwealth Experience* (London, Weidenfeld and Nicolson, 1969) was written at almost the last moment a writer could feel really cheerful about the Commonwealth; James Morris's *Pax Britannica Trilogy* (3 vols, New York, Harcourt Brace, 1968–78) began with a volume describing imperial scenes at the time of Queen Victoria's Diamond Jubilee, stepped back to a series of evocative sketches of important points in the nineteenth-century expansion of Empire, and then continued the same approach – almost like a travel writer rather than a historian – for a less cheerful account of decolonisation; and the *Cambridge Illustrated History of the British Empire* (Cambridge, CUP, 1996), edited by Peter Marshall, who also wrote almost half of the text, includes altogether more modern and modish doubts about the whole imperial undertaking. The idea that the Empire went through great changes in the late eighteenth century, turning from an Atlantic Ocean community, with a very loose central organisation, into an Indian Ocean organisation much more directly controlled from London owes a good deal to V. T. Harlow, *The Founding of the Second British Empire, 1763–93* (2 vols, London, Longmans, 1952–64). C. A. Bayly, *Imperial Meridian* (London, Longmans, 1989) has more recently continued that approach into the nineteenth century.

The central organisation of the British Empire was always ludicrously small, but efforts were made in the last years of the Empire to rescue some periods of it from obscurity: I. K. Steele, *Politics of Colonial Policy: The Board of Trade in Colonial Administration, 1696–1720* (Oxford, Clarendon Press, 1968), D. M. Young, *The Colonial Office in the Early Nineteenth Century* (London, Longman, 1961), and Robert Kubicek, *The Administration of Imperialism: Joseph Chamberlain at the Colonial Office* (Durham, North Carolina, Duke University Press, 1969) give manageable samples of administrative history.

Bernard Bailyn, *The Peopling of British North America* (New York, Knopf, 1986) is a good introduction to the question of how the British settled in North America. C. M. Andrews, *The Colonial Period of American History* (4 vols, New Haven, Yale University Press, 1934–38) is old, but not yet out of date. I. R. Christie and B. W. Larabee, *Empire and Independence, 1760–1776* (Oxford, Phaidon, 1976) is an interesting piece of Anglo-American cooperation in explaining how the War of Independence happened. Bernard Bailyn, *The Ideological Origins of the American Revolution* (Cambridge, Massachusetts, Harvard University Press, 1967), and John Philip Reid, *Constitutional History of the American Revolution* (Madison, Wisconsin, 1986–1993), take the story further back. Piers Mackesy, *The War for America, 1775–1783* (London, Longmans, 1964) is a good piece of military history.

Alan Burns, *History of the British West Indies* (2nd edn, London, Allen and Unwin, 1965), was written when the region could still be seen as a colony with some prospects of unity, and Carl and Roberta Bridenbaugh, *No Peace Beyond the Line: The English in the Caribbean, 1624–1690* (New York, OUP, 1972) explain how it started in that direction. A. P. Thornton, *West-India Policy under the Restoration* (Oxford, Clarendon Press, 1956) shows the English government wrestling with the fact that it had acquired colonies without expecting to. The region was for almost two centuries obviously shaped by the slave trade, discussed in Hugh Thomas, *The Slave Trade* (London, Picador, 1997) and in Roger Anstey, *The Atlantic Slave Trade and British Abolition, 1760–1810* (London, Macmillan, 1975), and by the local institution of slavery, which can be studied in Richard Dunn, *Sugar and Slaves: The Rise of the Planter Class, 1624–1713* (Chapel Hill, North Carolina, Institute of Early American History and Culture, 1972) and in R. B. Sheridan, *Sugar and Slavery* (Baltimore, Johns Hopkins Press, 1973). For some time Eric Williams, *Capitalism and Slavery* (Chapel Hill, North Carolina, University of North Carolina Press, 1944) won support for the idea that slavery was abandoned only because it was unprofitable; Seymour Drescher, *Econocide: British Slavery in the Era of Abolition* (Pittsburgh, University of Pittsburgh Press, 1977) left matters less simple by showing that the sugar trade was very prosperous when British opinion turned against slavery.

So much British imperial activity was initiated by chartered companies that Sir Percival Griffiths, *A Licence to Trade* (London, E. Benn, 1974) is a useful starting point. W. R. Scott, *Constitution and Finance of English Scottish and Irish Joint-Stock Companies to 1720* (Cambridge, CUP, 1912; reprint 1968), provides a great mass of supporting detail. Two important companies are discussed in K. G. Davies, *The Royal African Company* (London, Longman, 1957) and, for the Hudson's Bay Company, Peter Newman, *Company of Adventurers* and *The Merchant Princes* (Toronto, Viking, 1985 and 1991). The commercial activities of the most important company are analysed in K. N. Chaudhuri, *The English East India Company* (London, Frank Cass, 1963) and *The Trading World of Asia and the English East India Company* (Cambridge, CUP, 1978), and the reasons for its survival in the early years can be found in C. M. Cipolla, *Guns and Sails in Early European Expansion* (London, Collins, 1965). Peter Marshall shows, in *Bengal: The British Bridgehead* (Cambridge, CUP, 1987), how territorial expansion began, and Sir Penderel Moon, *The British Conquest and Dominion of India* (London, Duckworth, 1989) shows how it went on. S. C. Ghosh, *Dalhousie in India, 1848–56* (New Delhi, Munshiram Manoharlal, 1975) gives an account of the work of an extraordinarily ambitious governor-general, and Eric Stokes, *The Peasant Armed* (Cambridge, CUP, 1986) indicates that he had gone too far too fast. C. Hibbert, *The Great Mutiny: India 1857* (London, Allen Lane, 1978) is a more traditional account of the events of 1857, which takes less knowledge for granted.

Several one-volume histories of countries in the Commonwealth appeared around the middle of the twentieth century, though the trend is now towards multi–volume accounts. D. G. Creighton's *Dominion of the North* (Boston, Houghton Mifflin, 1944) was a good example of the genre, though not the work of original scholarship to be seen in his *John A. Macdonald* (2 vols, Toronto, 1952–55). Penguin brought out two very useful short histories: Keith Sinclair, *A History of New Zealand* (Harmondsworth, Penguin, 1959); and Kenneth McNaught, *The Pelican History of Canada* (Harmondsworth, Penguin, 1969). The speed of political change in South Africa can be seen in the effort required to keep T. R. H. Davenport, *A Short*

*History of South Africa* (5th edn, Basingstoke, Macmillan, 2000) up to date. *A New History of Australia*, ed. Frank Crowley (Melbourne, Heinemann, 1974) may be the last one-volume history of Australia. A good deal of popular attention has been attracted by Robert Hughes, *The Fatal Shore* (London, Collins, 1987), about the painful way so many of the early Australians from Britain came to their new country. Geoffrey Blainey, *The Tyranny of Distance* (2nd edn, Melbourne, Macmillan, 1982), about the way Australia's development was affected by the fact that its main market and political ally for 150 years after the first British settlements was so far away, ought to stir historians of other countries to think about the implications of communications. Judith Brown, *Modern India* (Oxford, OUP, 1985), provides a one-volume account of the last two hundred and fifty years of Indian history.

Ronald Hyam, *Britain's Imperial Century, 1815–1914* (2nd edn, Basingstoke, Macmillan, 1993) is an account of the main period of imperial dominance. John Manning Ward, *Colonial Self-Government: The British Experience, 1759–1856* (London and Basingstoke, Macmillan, 1976), explains the constitutional developments that showed British lack of concern about the Empire. C. A. Bodelson, *Studies in Mid-Victorian Imperialism* (reprint, London, Heinemann, 1960, of the 1924 edition) argued that late-Victorian imperial enthusiasm was in part a reaction against mid-Victorian readiness to give colonies up when practicable. P. L. Cottrell and D. H. Aldcroft, eds, *Shipping, Trade and Commerce* (Leicester, Leicester University Press, 1981) looks at some links that made separation improbable. Edward Said, *Orientalism* (New York, Pantheon, 1978), argues that Europeans saw Asia and Africa in terms that made imperial self-assertion natural; this book has made enough impression among students of literature for historians to pay attention to it, often in unfavourable terms. Daniel R. Headrick, *The Tools of Empire* (Oxford, OUP, 1981) deals with some of the technological developments that made European expansion in Africa much easier in the late nineteenth century than previously. The results can be traced in Thomas Pakenham, *The Scramble for Africa* (London, Weidenfeld and Nicolson, 1991); and the involvement of the British government is interpreted in Ronald Robinson and John Gallagher with Alice Denny, *Africa and the Victorians: The Official Mind of Imperialism* (London, Macmillan, 1961). The influence of this book has gone far beyond its immediate concern with imperial activity in Africa; it has encouraged ideas about the influence of people on the periphery of empire and about 'informal empire' that have been applied in many other places, though it should be added that the validity of the idea of 'informal empire' has been challenged, so far as Latin America is concerned, in D. C. M. Platt, *Latin America and British Trade, 1806–1914* (London, A. and C. Black, 1972) and in a volume of essays, D. C. M. Platt, ed., *Business Imperialism, 1840–1930: British Experience in Latin America* (Oxford, Clarendon Press, 1977). A different aspect of European involvement with Africa can be found in Adrian Hastings, *The Church in Africa, 1450–1950* (Oxford, Clarendon Press, 1994). It may be worth mentioning two biographies from the period when historians thought the Empire had been a good thing, John E. Flint, *Sir George Goldie and the Making of Nigeria* (London, OUP, 1960), and Margery Perham, *Lugard* (2 vols, London, Collins, 1956, 1960); and one from a period when they thought it had been a bad thing, R. Rotberg, *The Founder: Cecil Rhodes and the Pursuit of Power* (New York, OUP, 1988).

By the end of the 'Scramble for Africa' empires were coming under the type of attack discussed in A. P. Thornton, *The Imperial Idea and its Enemies* (London, Macmillan, 1959). Britain may have undertaken too much by the end of the nineteenth century, an idea explored in detail in Aaron Friedberg, *The Weary Titan: Britain and the Experience of Relative Decline, 1895–1905* (Princeton, Princeton University Press, 1988), and placed in a much wider perspective in Paul Kennedy, *The Rise and Fall of the Great Powers* (New York, Random House, 1987). One source of strength and of weakness is studied in Kennedy, *The Rise and Fall of British Naval Mastery* (London, Allen Lane, 1976), and the military situation is the background to Donald Gordon, *The Dominion Partnership in Imperial Defence, 1870–1914* (Baltimore, Johns Hopkins, 1965). J. B. Brebner, *North Atlantic Triangle: Canada, the United States and Great Britain* (New Haven, Yale University Press, 1945), points to connections which are not easy to fit into the ordinary run of diplomatic history.

*Fin de siècle* concern about empire and expansion found its most durable theoretical expression in J. A. Hobson, *Imperialism* (London, Allen and Unwin, 1902). Lance E. Davis and Robert A. Huttenback, *Mammon and the Pursuit of Empire* (Cambridge, CUP, 1986), P. J. Cain and A. G. Hopkins, *British Imperialism: Innovation and Expansion, 1688–1914* (London and New York, Longmans, 1993), and their *British Imperialism: Crisis and Deconstruction, 1914–1990* (London and New York, Longman, 1993) contain many ideas that fit into Hobson's idea of the way the Empire worked. A. H. Imlah, *Economic Elements in the Pax Britannica* (Cambridge, Massachusetts,

Harvard University Press, 1958) is full of information on which subsequent historians have built.

Empires overseas were weakened by the First World War. Various sorts of transition can be observed in Lord Beloff, *Imperial Sunset*: 2 vols, *Britain's Liberal Empire, 1897–1921* (London, Methuen, 1969); and *Dreams of Commonwealth, 1921–1947* (Basingstoke, Macmillan, 1989). S. Constantine, ed., *Emigrants and Empire: British Settlement in the Dominions between the Wars* (Manchester, 1990) deals with one aspect of those 'dreams of Commonwealth'. Anthony Clayton, *The British Empire as a Superpower, 1919–39* (Basingstoke, Macmillan, 1986), warns against reading weakness back into the past too readily, and Elizabeth Monroe, *Britain's Moment in the Middle East, 1914–1956* (2nd edn, London, Chatto and Windus, 1981) points out that Britain's involvement in the Arab world became much more noticeable in 1914. W. K. Hancock, *Smuts* (2 vols, Cambridge, CUP, 1962, 1968) is a good account of a career that spanned the whole of the first half of the twentieth century. An equally long career, covering almost exactly the same period, is described in Judith Brown, *Gandhi: Prisoner of Hope* (New Haven, Yale University Press, 1989). The challenge that nationalism would offer to the Empire is foreshadowed in A. Seal, *The Emergence of Indian Nationalism* (Cambridge, CUP, 1968), and the weakening of economic links is described in B. R. Tomlinson, *The Economy of Modern India, 1860–1970* (Cambridge, CUP, 1989).

This led on to Indian independence and partition, which can be studied in Anita Inder Singh, *The Origins of the Partition of India, 1936–47* (New Delhi, OUP, 1987) and Amit Kumar Gupta, ed., *Myth and Reality: The Struggle for Freedom in India, 1945–1947* (New Delhi, Manohar, 1987). There are lives of the opposing political leaders: S. Gopal, *Jawarahlal Nehru*, i (London, Cape, 1975), and Stanley Wolpert, *Jinnah of Pakistan* (New York, OUP, 1984). Writers tried to follow the rapid pace of independence in the 1960s: W. P. Kirkman, *Unscrambling an Empire, 1956–1966* (London, Chatto and Windus, 1966), and Colin Cross, *The Fall of the British Empire* (London, Hodder and Stoughton, 1968), kept up with events while avoiding most of the problems of instant history, and David Goldsworthy, *Colonial Issues in British Politics, 1945–1961* (Oxford, Clarendon Press, 1971) produced a more strictly scholarly account very soon after. John Gallagher offered a very crisp range of thoughts about *The Decline, Revival and Fall of the British Empire* in his Ford Lectures, ed. Anil Seal (Cambridge, CUP, 1982), and J. D. Hargreaves, *Decolonisation in Africa* (London, Longman, 1988) tried to make sense of a confusing situation. John Darwin, *The End of the British Empire: The Historical Debate* (London, Blackwell, 1991), and W. D. McIntyre, *British Decolonization, 1946–1997* (Basingstoke, Macmillan, 1998), offer brief guides to help readers through the debates. Margaret Doxey, *The Commonwealth Secretariat and the Contemporary Commonwealth* (Basingstoke, Macmillan, 1989), is an instructive account of the way the Commonwealth settled down after Empire, though some developments in the 1990s suggest it has rather more life in it than expected.

It used to be fashionable to say that British novelists and other writers paid no attention to the Empire. The rise of the post-colonial school of literary critics (of whom Edward Said with his *Orientalism* is distinctly the most noteworthy) has pushed things a long way in the other direction. Writers have been endowed with colonial links and roots on rather slender evidence.

In reality a few writers, including Kipling, Forster, Conrad and Joyce Cary, had lived for years in one part of the Empire or another, and wrote with some success about the places they knew. Writers in England, from Daniel Defoe onwards, could expect people to have some vague idea of the world beyond Europe. *Robinson Crusoe* was one of the earliest books based on the idea that this outer world was an exciting place to visit; Martin Green, *Dreams of Adventure, Deeds of Empire* (London, Routledge Kegan Paul, 1980) is a stimulating study of this genre, though it leans towards discussing the best authors – more Kipling than Rider Haggard, more Scott than Buchan.

Novels set in Britain could allude to distant and distinct parts of the empire with some confidence that readers would follow the references: Jane Austen's *Mansfield Park*, Wilkie Collins's *Moonstone*, Sir Walter Scott's *Guy Mannering*, William Makepeace Thackeray's *Vanity Fair* and Robert Louis Stevenson's *Kidnapped* all take it for granted that they could refer to India or to West Indian property based on sugar, and expect readers to accept this as something next door to everyday life, without actually setting any scenes in the novels in these distant areas. (Thackeray's *The Virginians* and Stevenson's *The Master of Ballentrae* do visit the colonies, and are thought to be less successful.)

Writers in the colonies (more particularly the English-speaking colonies) were in a more difficult position. Writers in Britain were kept modest by the Greek and Roman authors they were expected to follow, but the classical exemplars were dead; writers in the colonies were kept very humble – in what became called 'the Colonial Cringe' – by the dominance of British literature. One solution was to move to England, as did Aphra Behn, Olive Schreiner and Katherine Mansfield. By the twentieth century it was possible to earn a good living by writing in the colonies, as Mazo de la Roche proved with her series of *Jalna* novels, but this was a long way from being accepted a good writer. In the middle of the century literary critics in the Dominions hoped to find the great Canadian, Australian or South African novel, much as people had hoped to find the great American novel earlier in the century; and books like Hugh MacLennan's *Two Solitudes* (1945) and Alan Paton's *Cry the Beloved Country* (1948) went some way towards meeting this demand.

Literary freedom from imperial rule followed very soon after political freedom. By the end of the century it was possible to claim that 'the Empire writes back' was one important strand in writing in English, though some tensions still remain: when the (almost exclusively British) jury awards the Booker Prize to a writer from outside the British Isles it is likely to be greeted (at least in the recipient's own country) as a judicious recognition of talent, but an award to a British writer is occasionally seen as imperial neglect of vigorous colonial talent. But historians may say that this is just the way the literary world works, and has nothing peculiar to post-colonial relationships about it.

# Index

British South Africa Company ('the
    Chartered Company'), 111, 113
Brooke family, 104
Brown, George, 134
Brunei, 192; sultan of Brunei, 192
Brussels, 196
Brydon, Dr, 89,
Buganda, 112, 189; kabaka of, 112,
    189
Bulgaria, 102
Burgoyne, General John, 43, 51
Burke, Edmund, 32, 55, 63
Burma, 74, 91, 92, 163, 174
Burton, Sir Richard, 100
Butter, 118
Buxar, 43
Byng, Admiral, 41

Cabinet Mission plan for India, 171–72
Cadiz, 5
Cairo, 107, 159
Calais, 5
Calcutta, 21, 51, 54, 55, 91, 136, 138–39
Calvert family, 10
Cambodia, 167
Camden, Lord, 82
Cameroon, Cameroun, 204, 207
Canaan, 77, 213
Canada, up to confederation and the
    creation of the Dominion of Canada,
    29, 44, 51, 58, 59, 60, 70, 71, 73, 78
    79, 81, 84, 97, 98; until Statute of
    Westminster, 99, 108, 109, 118, 119,
    121, 130, 131, 133, 134, 135, 137,
    146, 147, 151, 152, 153; after 1931,
    4, 16, 45, 160, 162, 169, 170, 180,
    194, 196, 203, 207
Canada Company, 8
Canada East, 80, 97, 98
Canada West, 80, 97, 98
Canberra, 122
Candide, 41
Cape Breton Island, 29, 38
Cape Coast Castle, 19

Cape Colony, 69, 77, 81, 100, 104, 107,
    108, 111, 113, 114, 131, 149
Cape of Good Hope 2, 4, 6, 65
Cape Town, 77, 78, 187
Cape York Peninsula, 108
Caribbean, 12, 15, 16, 18, 185, 192, 203
Carleton, Sir Guy, 44, 137
Carolinas, 12, 17, 35, 52, 54
Cartagena, 4
Cawnpore, 94
Ceylon, 65, 69, 174; see also Sri Lanka
Chamberlain, Joseph, 114, 119, 125,
    128, 129, 140, 154
Chamberlain, Neville, 154
Chanak, 151
Charles I, 13
Charles II, 16, 17, 20, 21, 22, 23, 52
Charles II (of Spain) 29
Charles VI (Holy Roman Emperor), 37
Charleston, 17
Charters, for colonies and companies,
    8, 11, 13, 19, 20, 22, 23, 31, 47, 48,
    50, 99, 104, 110, 112, 113
Chartism, 79
Château clique, 79
Cheesemongers, 68
Chelmsford, Lord, 147
Chesapeake Bay, 7, 10, 11, 13, 40, 54
Childs, Sir Josiah, 21, 30, 31
China, 60, 72, 73, 74, 75, 91, 96, 105,
    141, 142, 181, 205, 208
Chinese, 181, 192
Christians, Christianity, 12, 28, 92, 102,
    142, 150, 158, 168, 188, 192
Church of England, Anglican, 8, 10, 12,
    16, 17, 22, 28–29, 34, 53, 134
Churchill, Winston, 165
Civil disobedience, 150, 155, 156, 158
Civil War (American), 96, 98, 105
Civil War (British Isles), 13, 14, 15
Clive, Robert, 39, 42–43, 55, 74, 106, pl. 2
'Closer union', 119, 125
Coal, 71, 72; gas from coal, 72
Cocoa, 141, 180, 200